Find Your Career
With
Springer Publishing Company

WITHDRAWN

101 Careers in Public Health
Beth Seltzer

101 Careers in Counseling
Shannon Hodges

101+ Careers in Gerontology, Second Edition
C. Joanne Grabinski

101 Careers in Social Work, Second Edition
Jessica A. Ritter and Halaevalu F. Ofahengaue Vakalahi

101 Careers in Psychology
Tracey E. Ryan

101 Careers in Education
John S. Carlson and Richard L. Carlson

101 Careers in Healthcare Management
Leonard H. Friedman and Anthony R. Kovner

Careers in Health Information Technology
Brian T. Malec

201 Careers in Nursing
Joyce J. Fitzpatrick and Emerson E. Ea

To learn more and order, visit www.springerpub.com

Careers in Health Information Technology

Brian T. Malec, PhD, presently teaches health information technology (HIT) in the graduate and undergraduate health administration programs at California State University, Northridge (CSUN). In addition, he teaches graduate courses in health care economics, finance, and quantitative decision making. He has served as the program director for the health administration program and is the past chair of the Department of Health Sciences at CSUN. Prior to coming to CSUN in 1990, Dr. Malec was a professor at Governors State University in Illinois, where he taught HIT as well as health care economics.

Dr. Malec has published in the area of HIT since the 1980s and has presented his HIT research at numerous professional conferences, such as the British Computer Society's HC Conferences, World of Health IT, HIMSS Annual Conference, European Health Management Administration (EHMA), and Association of University Programs in Health Administration (AUPHA). Currently he is a member of and contributor to the AUPHA Taskforce on Health Information Management Systems Technology and Analysis (HIMSTA), which is developing curriculum modules on HIT for graduate programs in health administration.

Dr. Malec received his bachelor's degree in education from Northern Illinois University (NIU) and his master's degree in economics, also from NIU. He received his doctorate in economics from Syracuse University's Maxwell School of Citizenship in 1978.

Careers in Health Information Technology

BRIAN T. MALEC, PhD

SPRINGER PUBLISHING COMPANY
NEW YORK

Springer Publishing Company, LLC
11 West 42nd Street
New York, NY 10036
www.springerpub.com

Acquisitions Editor: Sheri W. Sussman
Composition: Amnet

ISBN: 978-0-8261-2993-2
e-book ISBN: 978-0-8261-2994-9

14 15 16 17 / 5 4 3 2 1

The author and the publisher of this Work have made every effort to use sources believed to be reliable to provide information that is accurate and compatible with the standards generally accepted at the time of publication. The author and publisher shall not be liable for any special, consequential, or exemplary damages resulting, in whole or in part, from the readers' use of, or reliance on, the information contained in this book. The publisher has no responsibility for the persistence or accuracy of URLs for external or third-party Internet websites referred to in this publication and does not guarantee that any content on such websites is, or will remain, accurate or appropriate.

Library of Congress Cataloging-in-Publication Data

Malec, Brian T.
  Careers in health information technology / Brian T. Malec, PhD.
    pages cm
  ISBN 978-0-8261-2993-2 (print: alk. paper) — ISBN 978-0-8261-2994-9 (e-book)   1. Medical informatics—Vocational guidance.   2. Medicine—Information technology—Vocational guidance.   I. Title.
  R858.M34 2015
  610.285—dc23

                                                                                        2014016463

Printed in the United States of America by Edwards Brothers.

CONTENTS

CONTRIBUTORS

David E. Garets, FHIMSS, is a semi-retired health care information technology (IT) industry analyst currently engaged as principal at Mountain Summit Advisors, providing mergers and acquisitions, recapitalization/financing, and consulting services to private health care IT firms. He is also a principal at Change Gang, LLC, an advisor and chair of the executive advisory board for SCI Solutions, as well as a senior advisor for Next Wave Health.

Previously, he served as general manager and executive director of the Healthcare IT Suite at the Advisory Board Company, as president and CEO of HIMSS Analytics, as executive vice president (EVP) of the Healthcare Information and Management Systems Society (HIMSS), as EVP at Healthlink, as group vice president at Gartner, Inc., and as an experienced health care chief information officer (CIO).

Mr. Garets served as HIMSS board chair in 2004 and as president of two state HIMSS chapters, Idaho and Washington. He sits on the governing boards of Health Care DataWorks and the PeaceHealth Northwest Network.

He was a charter member of the College of Healthcare Information Management Executives (CHIME) and served on the faculties of the CHIME information management executive courses for 11 years. He is an internationally known author and speaker on health care information strategies, technologies, and change management, and in 2011 was elected to the HIMSS 50-in-50, comprising the 50 most memorable contributors to health care IT in the last 50 years. Mr. Garets is the co-creator of the HIMSS Analytics EMR Adoption Model, the international de facto standard for measuring progress toward a full electronic medical record. He earned a BA in business administration in marketing from Texas Tech University.

John Glaser, PhD, currently serves as chief executive officer of the Health Services Business Unit of Siemens Healthcare, where he is responsible for heading Siemens's global health care IT business.

Prior to joining Siemens, Dr. Glaser was vice president and chief information officer of Partners HealthCare, Inc. Previously, he was vice president of Information Systems at Brigham and Women's Hospital.

Dr. Glaser was the founding chairman of CHIME and is the former chairman of the eHealth Initiative Board and the Board of the National Alliance for Health Information Technology. He is a former senior advisor to the Office of the National Coordinator for Health Information Technology.

He is also past president of HIMSS and is a fellow of HIMSS, CHIME, and the American College of Medical Informatics, where he previously served on the board.

Dr. Glaser has published more than 150 articles and three books on the strategic application of IT in health care. He also gives approximately 100 industry speeches each year.

Dr. Glaser holds a PhD in health care information systems from the University of Minnesota.

David Wyant, PhD, MA, MBA, is an assistant professor of management at Belmont University in Nashville, Tennessee. He holds a PhD in health services research policy and administration from the University of Minnesota, and an MBA in finance and an MA in economics from the Ohio State University. He has taught in health care management programs at several universities since 1995, including Iowa (College of Medicine, College of Public Health), Xavier (College of Social Sciences), Western Kentucky (College of Health and Human Services), and Weber State (College of Health Professions). At Belmont University, he teaches health care financial management, health care information management, and statistics in the Massey College of Business and in the nursing school's doctor of nursing practice program. Prior to academia, Dr. Wyant worked with health care providers and state legislature study commissions, beginning with the Ohio Nursing Home Commission in 1977. His grant awards include funding from the National Institutes of Health to investigate the merging of health care claims data with cancer registry data to study the effectiveness of alternative treatment protocols. His research has been published in leading health care journals, including

Medical Care, Journal of Healthcare Information Management, and *Community Mental Health Journal.* He is active in the Healthcare Financial Management Association, HIMSS, and the Association of University Programs in Health Administration.

FOREWORD

Information technology (IT) and, more recently, "big data" are taking the United States to a new frontier in health care and making clinical advances possible that would not otherwise be available. Careers in health care IT provide some of the most rewarding long-term opportunities that individuals will find, and the breadth of those opportunities offers a future for students and professionals with a wide range of interests, whether they are data analysts, clinicians, project managers, customer service specialists, programmers, and/or those who aspire to management and top leadership positions. Health care IT, including the electronic health record, is one of the leading growth areas of employment in health care.

For decades, providers used IT systems primarily to manage the financial and business dimensions of their organizations. However, in the last decade health care IT has exploded into health care's clinical world. It has been driven by structural, financial, regulatory, and performance demands. At the core of each of these drivers is the mandate to improve the quality of health care delivery—to reduce medical errors and improve patient safety, to drive efficiencies into the system, to expand access to care, and to address the epidemic of chronic disease that consumes a significant portion of health care spending in the United States. IT is the essential tool needed to achieve quality improvement in each of these areas. The almost boundless investments that have been made in health care IT attest to the determination of providers of care to achieve better clinical outcomes for patients and lower the cost of health care.

The explosion of IT in health care has brought with it a corollary expansion in the job market. This is one of the fastest growing job markets in health care, and the expansion is certain to continue because health care providers will continue to invest in, and upgrade, their IT systems for a long time. Career choices in health IT can provide the opportunity for a lifetime of work and job security. However, professions in health IT are about much more than great jobs and job security; they are about impacting the quality of health care that people receive and saving lives—literally!

Employment in a health IT career is ultimately about helping people receive prompt and accurate diagnoses, be healed, and live sustainably healthy lives, as well as prevention of disease and the health of the population. Health care has seriously lagged behind other sectors of the economy in achieving consistently high-quality outcomes. For example, consider the data that tell us how many people have died each year from preventable medical errors. Historically, we did not have the tools to change this pattern of care; we did not have the data to point us to solutions in the prevention of those errors. Blame abounded, but process change did not. Yet, process change is where the real transformation to a safe environment occurs, and to make that happen, data are needed—data that can only be efficiently accessed with a robust IT system. Making this happen requires an equally robust source of skilled IT professionals.

This book is a great resource for those who are thinking about a career in health care information technology. The explanations of the field, and the wide array of job descriptions offered in the chapters that follow, describe the many and varied types of positions that are in demand. For those who are prepared to bring skill, commitment, and dedication to a very rewarding career in which the outcome is measured in healthier lives, the work of Brian T. Malec and his contributing authors provides a solid and informative starting point.

Margaret Schulte, DBA, FACHE, CPHIMS
President and CEO
Commission on Accreditation of Healthcare Management
Education (CAHME)

PREFACE

The growth of the health information technology (HIT) workforce is in direct response to both advances in technology applications that support patient care and national policies that encourage and support advances such as electronic medical records (EMR) and computerized provider order entry. I have always believed in "strategic vision and not technological opportunity" as a driving force for health care providers. But the speed of advancements in technology and the speed of diffusion of those advances make a "chicken and egg" kind of situation for health care providers. The political pressure to move toward a paperless (or at least a paper-light) environment in health care delivery, combined with the availability of new technologies, is forcing providers, vendors, and other concerned groups to rethink their HIT workforce needs. The Health Information Technology for Economic and Clinical Health (HITECH) Act of 2009 provided financial incentives to providers for the adoption of EMR and funds for training a workforce that could help with the selection, implementation, and maintenance of these new systems in medical offices and hospitals. Those education funds helped to focus attention on the need for a variety of educational pathways to expand career choices for individuals. Many private and public organizations have expanded their HIT offerings, resulting in a wide variety of shapes, sizes, and delivery modes.

The reality for the health care delivery side of the industry and the vendor side, which supplies the products and services, is that every job is touched and enhanced by information technology. The present workforce is challenged to meet the growing job demands of employers. In response to the workforce shortages in the marketplace, educational and career development opportunities are expanding and new ones emerging to meet the career path needs of individuals.

The goal of this book is to provide insights into what it means to be an HIT "worker" and how individuals can strategize about their personal career paths. HIT is a blending of the following knowledge and skill domains: computer science, information systems, clinical knowledge/ medical care, and management. HIT jobs represent many variations of these domains, but all jobs will have some of each. The fun part is finding where you fit in this growing and exciting field. Many of the job descriptions in this book came from my students as they were exploring HIT careers. Use the book as a reference and a starting point for your HIT career exploration.[1]

Brian T. Malec, PhD
Professor of Health Administration
Department of Health Sciences
California State University, Northridge

---

[1] Job descriptions in the book are representative of jobs with those particular titles. The same title might be used in different organizations but have different expectations and requirements. The lack of standardization of job titles also means that the same job duties and requirements can have different titles. For some jobs in the book, multiple jobs with the same or almost the same title are presented to give a full exposure to the HIT job market. Information was gathered from current job descriptions in various sectors in the health care industry and then standardized in order to ensure consistency. Professional association websites pointed us to organizations that had job openings and had posted job descriptions.

ACKNOWLEDGMENTS

I would like to acknowledge the many interesting and supportive people who over the years have helped to shape my interest in health information technology (HIT) and its impact on health care delivery. In academia we don't touch patients, dispense medications, or directly support the care delivery process and the management of organizations. But we do teach, and hopefully inspire, those who will do all these things. We may work in our classrooms and engage in research projects, but at the end of the day we do make a difference in patients' lives. My interest in HIT was shaped by Charles Austin and his writing partner Stuart Boxerman as they broke new ground in teaching health administration students about health information systems. As an economist by training, I was always interested in the effective and efficient delivery of health care. I saw how HIT could be the driving force in creating better quality, lower cost, and wider diffusion and access to care for people. As the field of HIT evolved, I met people like Dave Garets and John Glaser, who inspired me to expand my perceptions of health care and the role of HIT. They also made me laugh and enjoy what I was doing as I learned more and more about HIT. In my local community I have been privileged to be a founding member of a southern California organization called CHIEF (California Health Information Executives Forum). It has allowed me, a non-CIO, to join in their meetings and discussions and to learn about the issues and solutions facing CIOs. Rich Rydell, Scott Joslyn, and others helped me to put my academic research into a practical context.

I want to thank my university for awarding me a semester sabbatical so I could devote myself to this interesting and valuable resource for those exploring careers in HIT. Dave Wyant, one of the chapter and interview contributors, wants to thank Dean Pat Raines of the Massey College of Business at Belmont University for providing a research stipend to support his valuable work on the book. In preparing the book I met many interesting HIT professionals who provided great insights in the interviews that we did. That was one of the best parts of this project.

Support from a spouse, family, and friends is also critical anytime one takes on a major project, and I fully appreciate the support and occasional nagging I received to "get the chapter finished."

I ■ INTRODUCTION TO CAREERS IN HEALTH INFORMATION TECHNOLOGY

1 ■ WHAT IS HEALTH INFORMATION TECHNOLOGY?

BRIAN T. MALEC

Broadly defined, health information technology (HIT) is the application of computer and related technologies to the delivery of health care services. Working in a HIT profession requires a combination of skills, knowledge, and experiences that can span aspects of computer science, information systems, clinical knowledge/medical care, and management. The application of these domains, in varying combinations, creates a wide variety of jobs that, as a whole, can be classified as the HIT workforce.

> *I come to work every day knowing that what I do from a desk is helping someone live a better life.*
>
> —*Stacy Cooreman*

Some HIT careers demand the knowledge, skills, and education associated with the field of computer science, while other careers build upon managerial and computer application skills, knowledge, and experiences associated with the fields of information systems and management. Still other careers in HIT build upon clinical and medical professional knowledge and skills such as those needed by physicians, physician assistants, nurses, and many other clinical professionals. There is no single job description for someone who works in the general field of HIT. The goal of this book is to provide realistic examples of current job descriptions across a range of HIT careers and in a variety of organizational settings: hospitals, medical practices, managed care, public health, and the HIT vendor community. Throughout, the book will provide interviews of selected individuals who work in a wide variety of HIT professional careers. The career pathways taken by these interviewees provide real-world examples of how one can progress in the HIT field and achieve personal career satisfaction. Chapter 3 provides additional insights and practical resources for obtaining the educational and professional development necessary for HIT careers.

The demand for a HIT workforce is a direct result of the growth of the U.S. health care industry and the demands placed upon the industry to expand access, reduce the rate of growth of costs, improve quality, and move toward an environment that is electronic and less reliant on paper. Several significant actions by the U.S. government have challenged the health care industry to achieve these goals.

> *There is no need to be famous or in the limelight, just do the right thing and make the right thing easy to do.*
> *—Robert Aboulache*

In 2004 President Bush, through an executive order, created the Office of the National Coordinator for Health Information Technology (ONC). "The objective of the ONC is to support the adoption of HIT by hospitals, medical practices and other medical organizations and to promote the development of technology to achieve the exchange of health information across providers to improve overall healthcare" (www.healthit.gov/newsroom/about-onc).

In 2009, as a part of the American Recovery and Reinvestment Act (ARRA), President Obama signed into law the Health Information Technology for Economic and Clinical Health (HITECH) Act of 2009. Not only did this act affirm the ONC by law, but it also created incentives and support for the adoption and implementation of electronic medical records (EMR). From the standpoint of the HIT workforce, the realization was that the country had a significant shortage of trained and available individuals who could assist with the selection, adoption, and implementation of EMR and also support medical information exchanges. A significant feature of the HITECH Act of 2009 was the funding of educational training programs targeted at creating the workforce necessary to achieve the goals of the ONC and the HITECH Act. The Act created a program to develop curriculum materials that would be given free to community colleges and some 4-year universities. The curriculum that was developed was targeted at HIT careers that are directly related to the goals of exchanging medical information across providers and the adoption of EMR. As of fall 2013, most of these programs are phasing down as the funding runs out. More will be discussed later about these programs and other education pathways necessary to enter or advance in HIT careers.

HIT jobs require a variety of mixtures consisting of the following elements: knowledge of computer systems and software applications;

familiarity with medical processes and terms; analysis of business processes and the information systems that support the process; and management skills and the ability to manage projects. A particular job might be heavily into computer programs while another job might require detailed knowledge of medical coding of diagnosis and treatment. Still other jobs might require the ability to manage a complex project or administrative process and to analyze and diagnose ways to improve the application. To add to the complexity, HIT workers might have identical job titles, such as business analyst, but work in different settings such as hospitals, physician practices, insurance companies, vendor companies—the list can go on. This book has been designed to explore a range of job descriptions and to discuss the "context" of the job related to the actual organizational setting.

The HIT job outlook is very encouraging even if we just look at the overall growth of the health sector and the projected increased demand for medical and other, related services by an aging population. The next 5 to 10 years will also see tremendous activity toward increasing access to health care services and developing paper-light electronic health care records and other areas of technology growth. The Patient Protection and Affordable Care Act of 2010 expands access to many uninsured or underinsured citizens of the United States. What has become known as "Obamacare" and its predecessor in Massachusetts are designed to expand access to health care by requiring individuals to purchase health insurance or take advantage of enlarged state programs for low-income citizens.

The key factor in the current health reform environment is the need for a trained workforce in HIT to staff government and private-sector jobs that enable the health care sector to achieve the political and economic goals. Not surprisingly, HIT-related jobs—across a wide range of organizational settings and with varying mixtures of skills, knowledge, and educational preparation—will be in high demand for many years.

This book is a collaborative undertaking, with chapters devoted to supporting the job exploration of students and mid-career professionals seeking to enter or advance in the HIT career field.

Part I of the book provides a context for HIT careers and strategies for building an effective career pathway. Chapter 2 ("What Is the Field of Health Informatics?") differentiates between the broader field of "health information technology" and the more specific field of "health informatics."

The informaticist is heavily data/information driven to help achieve clinical value from the health information systems. An informaticist can be found in clinical fields such as medicine or nursing, where clinical information helps to drive patient care. An informaticist can also work with medical coded data/information and can provide decision support to medical professionals. The chapter looks at specific skills and knowledge necessary to be successful in this field.

The goal of Chapter 3, "Educational Programs in Health Information Technology," is to explore alternative pathways to HIT careers. Some in-demand careers require an associate's degree, while others may require a master's degree with perhaps a specialized certificate. There are academically based programs in both traditional universities and for-profit universities. Programs that support a pathway to HIT can be online, face to face, or some hybrid format. Some certification programs are provided by professional organizations like American Health Information Management Association (www.AHIMA.org) or Healthcare Information and Management Systems Society (www.himss.org). The professional societies generally require some years of work experience in the field and require an examination in order for one to be "certified." This chapter provides web resources leading to a wide variety of educational opportunities.

The goal of Chapter 4, "Finding a Career in Health Information Technology," is to provide very practical strategies and resources for anyone seeking a career in the broad field of HIT. The chapter serves as a reality check for good strategies for this growing and competitive field. How do you distinguish yourself from others seeking careers in HIT? There are also many websites listed for online resources and specific employers in a variety of sectors in the health care industry. Don't skip this chapter, and keep the references for your future career path as you move up in the HIT field.

Where will the field of HIT be in the next 5 to 10 years? How do you prepare for that future? With the many economic, political, and technical changes impacting health care, where are the new jobs, the ones that don't exist now or are just emerging? Chapter 5, "The Future of HIT Careers," is written by two of the industry's visionaries. The HIT workforce is beginning to see the emergence of careers that are very data driven and heavy in the areas of population management, with titles like knowledge manager or data analytics specialist. The goal of the chapter is to make those planning careers in the field to think about strategies for the future.

Part II of the book provides details about actual HIT careers in various organizational settings. Each HIT job listing has a description that one would find in a search for open positions in HIT. In Chapter 5 there

are examples of websites where one can find HIT jobs in specific organizations. Part II provides examples of a range of job descriptions with a
mixture of entry-level to senior-level positions. Each job description will
provide the following: an overview of what is expected of someone in this
job; the education and work experience necessary to apply; the core competencies and skills required for the job; compensation range; and what
the job market expectations are. In addition, a selection of interviews
with professionals provides insight into the reality of working in this field
and an understanding of the varied career pathways that can help to
build a personal strategy to achieve success in the HIT field.

We hope that this introduction to HIT careers and the resources
that are provided help you to be successful in this high-demand and
growing field.

2 ■ WHAT IS THE FIELD OF HEALTH INFORMATICS?

BRIAN T. MALEC

Health informatics is considered by some as a subset of health information technology (HIT), while others use the two terms interchangeably. In this book, HIT refers to the broad field of the application of information systems and technology to health care. Health informatics can be defined as a more specific blending of patient data, computer science tools and skills, and knowledge of clinical environments. Health informatics has been around for decades as a specialized field, but with the recent focus on electronic medical records and databases, the field has opened up considerably. The role of the informaticist is to manage the information within an organization and provide higher-quality patient care through promoting better management and greater availability of that information to the clinician at the point of care. There is a large-scale view of how data impact hospital strategies and entire health care systems. There are also the more focused areas of informatics that support decision making for the physician, nurse, pharmacy, public health, and medical records (healthinformatics.uic.edu). The implementation of electronic medical record systems across the health care industry has meant a huge growth in the collection and storage of information in data warehouses and the analysis of such data to improve the patient health care experience. The informaticist has become the person responsible for using analytical tools to improve workflow, care processes, and quality patient outcomes. An informaticist will usually, but not always, be a person with some medical training due to the clinical nature of health care data and information. But this person will also have some advanced training, education, or

> There's an old Wayne Gretzky quote that I love. "I skate to where the puck is going to be, not where it has been."
> —Anthony Blash

certification in information technology. An informaticist can be a physician, nurse, pharmacist, physical therapist, radiologist, or a member of one of many other clinical fields. Because of the emphasis on collecting and managing large data and information sources, you can also find informaticists in the field of finance and accounting, medical billing, and insurance. You will find an increasing number of informaticists in the field of public health as the health care system moves toward population management and not just management of the single patient.

The knowledge and skill base of an informaticist can perhaps best be summarized by looking at the accreditation criteria from the Commission on Accreditation of Health Informatics and Information Management (CAHIIM). In Chapter 3 there is an extensive discussion of educational programs that are available from a variety of education and for-profit organizations. CAHIIM accredits both undergraduate and graduate programs in health informatics. A brief look at its criteria will give insights into the knowledge and skill base needed if you aspire to be an informaticist.

In brief, the expected competency areas for a degree in health informatics include:

■ The management of health data and data structures
■ Data analysis using appropriate research methodology and data mining and extraction
■ Health information systems: design, selection, implementation
■ Data security and privacy
■ Information management planning
■ Health care organization and management: leadership, resource management, education, and training[1]

. . .Medical, nursing, or even pharmacy students . . . should consider a clinical rotation through medical informatics.
—Chris Pensinger

When you combine these competency areas with medical training or perhaps a degree in computer science or administration, you encounter a variety of professional descriptions in the health informatics field. The blending of the components of the health informatics field can result

---

[1] www.cahiim.org/accredstnds.html
healthinformatics.uic.edu
www.healthcareitnews.com/news/why-informatics-top-new-career
www.hmi.missouri.edu

in professionals with job titles like nurse informaticist, board-certified physician informaticist, data analyst, clinical informatics analyst, clinical health analyst, chief informaticist, patient care informaticist, and many more.

The following is an interview with a professional who is currently in a health informatics role and is pursuing further educational and career opportunities in nursing health informatics.

RIKA FUKAMACHI
Report Writer Analyst, Hoag Hospital

Describe the sort of work you do. Currently, my role at Hoag Hospital is to design, develop, modify, generate, and test clinical data reports, which in turn support our clinicians' goals of providing high-quality patient care. The hospital staff will present our Reports Team with a business problem where they would need a list of patients or clinicians matching specific criteria. We in turn collaborate with them by exploring their rationale, methodology of how such data are entered, sources where we can collect the data, and options on how they would like the information displayed.

Examples include:

- Downtime reports that clinicians would use to care for their patients in the absence of their electronic health records.
- Ventilated patients reports, which identify all of the patients who are being ventilated and further report on those who have the head of their beds properly elevated, thereby ensuring all clinicians are practicing their care according to hospital guidelines and national standards.
- Patient discharge instructions reports, which allow physicians and nurses to provide patients a paper copy of instructions on how to self-manage their own care once they get home.

Our work is often categorized as operational or project in nature. Operationally, we need to maintain and support the reports that are already being used on a regular basis, and this support may include being on call during nonbusiness hours to fix any reports that break unexpectedly. Project-wise, we participate in many innovations and advances requiring data to be presented in new or different ways.

What is a typical day like at your job? My main goal is to ensure customer satisfaction: Our customers in this case are the clinicians who

(continued)

RIKA FUKAMACHI   (continued)

request new reports and those who currently use our reports. Every morning, we check to ensure that all of the overnight reports were successfully executed. In the case where we find that a particular report has failed, we investigate as to how it happened and how to prevent the failure from happening again. Once we do that, we review our tasks list and re-prioritize as necessary.

Our team's first priority is to resolve any issues that could potentially affect patient safety. If a report that clinicians use to prioritize or manage patient care is pulling incorrect data, this would be considered a patient safety issue. Also of high priority would be those reports that are needed for regulatory purposes and are often subject to auditing and potential fines.

We remain mindful of project timelines and therefore aim to complete our reports within the given deadlines. Once we understand the rationale and the goal of the project, we collect the information required to complete our tasks. Our data collection process includes workflow analysis to allow us to understand where the data are entered and processed so that we may know the exact source for our reports. Once collected, we design and develop the reports per the specifications. There are often many iterations of validation and testing to secure a successful completion.

Lastly, there are many instances where "emergencies" arise and we end up switching gears to address the emergency.

What education or training do you have? Is it typical for your job? I do not have a typical education or training background for my job. I have a blend of formal clinical and technical training. I studied at the University of British Columbia's School of Nursing to attain my Bachelor of Science in Nursing. I then went on to study at the British Columbia Institute of Technology to attain my 2-year diploma in Computer Systems Technology. With the addition of a few Franklin Covey and Global Knowledge courses to improve my leadership skills, this unique combination of skill set and formal knowledge positions me to respond to the clinical, technical, and leadership aspects of my job.

(continued)

RIKA FUKAMACHI   (continued)

What path did you take to get to the job you are in today? I started my career as a registered nurse and almost immediately found myself wanting to improve my patient care and working experience. I began to identify deficiencies that I thought I could help improve on (e.g., double- or triple-documenting the same clinical findings in different places; sitting idly while patient charts were shared and documented on by one clinician at a time; scanning and faxing medication orders to our internal pharmacy department)—all inefficiencies that I began to see could be reduced or resolved through an electronic health record system and better data integration.

I wanted to get to know the minute details of how computers and information systems work and decided to expand my education to a computer science diploma program. This is where I began to learn how to program in C, C++, and Java; query databases in SQL and Oracle; and learn about project management methodologies. These skills in turn helped me get my first nursing informatics job as a clinical trainer/support analyst for Providence Health Care in Canada, an Eclipsys (now known as Allscripts) client site. My next exciting role was becoming an implementation consultant for the vendor Eclipsys. I then moved on to another client site where they hosted a completely different electronic health record called Meditech. Fast forward to another exciting opportunity: my present-day position, which saw me moving from Vancouver, Canada, to sunny California, where I became an application analyst and have since evolved into my current position as a report writer analyst.

Where might you go from here if you wanted to advance your career? I love to continually challenge myself and those around me and have been thinking of following a couple of different paths to get there. I'd like to get my master's in Nursing Informatics to build on the skills and education that I have achieved thus far. Business analysis and Lean Six Sigma is also something I've been interested in to facilitate process improvement and minimize the inefficiencies that inhibit productivity. Improving team morale and fostering self-empowerment is another goal that I'd like to work on by moving on to a management

(continued)

RIKA FUKAMACHI *(continued)*

role. Due to my current role as a report writer, the world of business intelligence is also fascinating to me. Having had two electronic health record systems under my belt, I'd like to learn an additional system such as Epic or McKesson to round out my technical skill set. This would allow me to be a more marketable candidate for hospitals with different electronic health systems.

What is the most challenging part of your job? The most challenging part is the need to complete the full life cycle of a report development in a short period of time. I love gathering requirements and designing the report as requested; however, challenges can arise when assumptions are made that are not fully understood or agreed on by either our own internal IT resources or our clients. Often there is a technical "language barrier," and this is where my clinical background comes in handy. I am able to translate the clinicians' needs into the technical requirements and bridge the understanding gap.

What is the best part? The best part of my job is the challenge—I love writing complex but efficient reports to ensure that our clients get the correct data at the desired time. I also enjoy communicating with our clients to make sure that they are satisfied with the reports and they feel comfortable enough to call me anytime when they come across any problems. I enjoy succeeding in whatever I do and want to make sure that those around me are satisfied with my accomplishments.

What advice would you give to someone contemplating a career like yours? Health care information technology is a field that is growing exponentially, and I feel privileged to be a part of this revolutionary era. A huge advantage that I have is the trifecta of training and experience in clinical, technical, and leadership skills.

My advice is focus first on education in a clinical field where you will end up working directly with patients. Clinical fields include but are not limited to nursing, pharmacy, medicine, respiratory/

(continued)

RIKA FUKAMACHI   (continued)

occupational/physical therapy, and paramedicine. The education you will receive here is priceless as you will be able to understand the physiology of the human body, causes and effects of illnesses, pros and cons of treatment regimens, clinical terminology, and the clinical workflow on a unit. This foundation will provide you the credibility and respect among the clinicians you will serve in the future. Most importantly, this advantage will help you understand why the clinicians, your future clients, would ask for certain configurations or in my case, certain reports.

When you start feeling comfortable working as a clinician, you are ready to move on to the next phase: formal health care IT education. There are many different ways you can achieve this—Clinical Informatics classes, Health IT degree programs, a master's in Health Informatics—or, depending on your level of interest, you can complete a Computer Science degree/diploma.

The reason why I pursued the Computer Science diploma program is because I wanted to get to the bottom of the technical mystery behind how a computer is built, how computer languages communicate electronically, and how databases store and display pertinent information. As many of us will tell you, this was not a necessary step to get into the clinical informatics world, but it substantially improved my odds of understanding complex technical issues and attempts at resolving them.

Opportunities to jump right into this field do exist, but in my experience, they were difficult to come by. If you'd like to try this route, look for consulting positions at electronic health record system vendors where they are willing to take in clinicians and train them on the job.

The quickest way into this field is by getting your Bachelor of Science in Health Informatics or Health Care IT. The reason why I recommend this last is because of the learning curve you would have to struggle through at the beginning of your career.

If you have already been working as a clinician for many years and are looking to switch, the easiest way is to inquire at your hospital about a clinical IT trainer or a "super-user" position. This will allow you to work your way into the IT department and from there, you can look

(continued)

RIKA FUKAMACHI (*continued*)

into joining their support team to help clinicians troubleshoot computer issues. After becoming comfortable in that role, you can move on to helping the team design/configure the system.

RESOURCE

Brown, G., Patrick, T., & Pasupathy, K. (2013). *Health informatics: A systems perspective*. Chicago, IL: Health Administration Press.

3 ■ EDUCATIONAL PROGRAMS IN HEALTH INFORMATION TECHNOLOGY

DAVID WYANT

Requirements for most health information technology (HIT) positions may be met through more than one combination of experience and education. This variety of career paths is partly due to a variety of educational choices. Educational options include professional certifications, certificate programs, undergraduate and graduate degrees, informatics programs for clinicians, and others. This chapter provides a partial list of some of the educational opportunities for a career in HIT.

Before discussing HIT training, we should first note that there are varying uses of the term "credentials." Sometimes "credentials" is only used in connection with a specifically named "credentialing" process that results in the credentials. We use the term more broadly to mean evidence of qualification for a type of work position.

HIT education involves a choice of the type of training and a choice of the source of the training. This chapter is organized by types of training. For training, an individual could target a particular professional association's certification program or a particular academic degree. This still leaves the question of the source of training. For some types of training the sources are clearly defined. For example, some certifications require a degree from a university accredited for the certification. For these we provide websites that list all of the accredited sources for that training. For other types of training the sources are not clearly defined, so we mention a sample of potential sources. Whether or not a source is accredited may influence the availability of federal financial aid, the ability to transfer credits to count toward additional degrees, and

> *Stay current. Health care and technology are both ever-changing industries.*
> —Stacy Cooreman

competitiveness in the job market. For additional detail on sources it is often helpful to look at the websites of professional associations or academic accrediting bodies.

In contrast to many professions, one option is to forgo HIT education and move into a career based on your work experience. For example, an individual who works in patient registration might move into a position with a HIT vendor and demonstrate patient registration software. This employee is valuable to the HIT employer by knowing "the health care side" of HIT. The rapid growth of HIT pulls people into the field who lack HIT training but who have backgrounds as clinicians or other health care workers. Similarly, individuals with IT backgrounds from outside of health care may be drawn into HIT because they know "the IT side." In this manner it is possible for some workers to be hired into HIT positions without HIT-specific training. However, training enhances these individuals' opportunities.

The appendix at the end of this chapter contains websites providing access to the resources discussed in this chapter.

PROFESSIONAL ASSOCIATIONS

Many health care professional associations offer HIT credentials. Requirements for these credentials can include passing exams, work experience, and college degrees. Outside of health care there are also IT professional associations that offer training that may lead to a career in HIT. This section includes a sample of professional associations that train HIT workers.

Healthcare Information and Management Systems Society (HIMSS)

HIMSS offers two levels of certification to individuals who plan to manage in HIT (www.himss.org). These certifications could be viewed as more management oriented and more general than HIT certifications offered by other health profession associations. The Certified Professional in Healthcare Information and Management Systems (CPHIMS) certification demonstrates mastery of a body of knowledge related to the health care information and management systems field. It requires experience in the field and completion of a bachelor's or graduate degree. However, the CPHIMS designation does not require a specific major or accreditation, so many individuals looking to gain credentials in the HIT field will already meet the degree requirement. The Certified Associate in Healthcare Information and Management Systems (CAHIMS) certification demonstrates knowledge of management systems and HIT. It is a relatively new certification designed for individuals who are at the entry level for the field. HIMSS offers training materials for these certifications and a range of other online educational activities, including a complete self-directed introductory online course called the Health Informatics Training System (HITS).

The Association of University Programs in Health Administration (AUPHA), with a grant from HIMSS, developed the Health Information Management Systems Technology and Analysis (HIMSTA) program. This is a free set of educational materials, available from a website, intended for HIT education in graduate health care management programs. It includes 14 modules that each require roughly 10 hours of student engagement. Individuals and faculty may either select part of the materials or use the entire curriculum as a full course.

American Health Information Management Association (AHIMA)

Through the Commission on Certification for Health Informatics and Information Management (CCHIIM), AHIMA offers nine different certifications in medical coding, health information management, and specialties (www.ahima.org/certification).

The medical coding certifications are designed for coding practitioners. These individuals help generate reimbursement for providers by recording onto claims the numeric codes for each diagnosis and procedure in a patient's records. Each certification requires passing an exam and other qualifications that are detailed on the AHIMA website. The Certified Coding Associate (CCA) is an entry-level certification that demonstrates competency in coding in both hospital and physician settings. The Certified Coding Specialist (CCS) shows mastery-level abilities in the hospital setting. The Certified Coding Specialist–Physician-based (CCS–P) shows mastery-level coding expertise in settings such as physician offices, clinics, and group practices.

The health information management credentials Registered Health Information Administrator (RHIA) and Registered Health Information Technician (RHIT) require completion of an academic degree. The RHIT credential requires completion of an associate degree program, which is approved by the Commission on Accreditation for Health

Informatics and Information Management Education (CAHIIM) or foreign equivalent. The RHIA credential requires a bachelor's program approved by CAHIIM or foreign equivalent. Students who are enrolled in their final term of study in CAHIIM-accredited programs for RHIT or RHIA are eligible to take the certification exam.

The specialty certifications include Certified Health Data Analyst (CHDA), Certified in Healthcare Privacy and Security (CHPS), and Clinical Documentation Improvement Practitioner (CDIP). Qualifying to take the exam for each of these credentials requires a particular combination of years of experience and academic degrees.

Another specialty certification, Certified Healthcare Technology Specialist (CHTS), is actually a series of different specialty certifications that each requires passage of an exam. These specialties were converted from a series formerly called HIT Pro, which was established as part of the Health Information Technology for Economic and Clinical Health (HITECH) Act of 2009. That portion of the HITECH Act was designed to fill gaps in the workforce in order to speed the transition to electronic health records (EHR) and improve data exchange. There are six different exams, each covering a HIT workforce role that is important in the development of EHR systems. Specifically, the exams are for:

Look for good mentors and multiple mentors.
—Arvind Kumar

- Clinician/Practitioner Consultant (CHTS-CP)
- Implementation Manager (CHTS-IM)
- Implementation Support Specialist (CHTS-IS)
- Practice Workflow and Information Management Redesign Specialist (CHTS-PW)
- Technical/Software Support Staff (CHTS-TS)
- Trainer (CHTS-TR)

There is no specific education requirement for taking these exams. There are training programs available through some local community colleges. (Check with the community colleges in your area.) Because local labor markets vary, and because the training is very specific, before beginning a particular program it is a good idea to get a sense of the likelihood that these certifications will lead to employment in a particular geographic area.

To find a source of training for certifications that require an accredited degree, the CAHIIM Accredited Program Directory website provides a list of accredited programs. In addition, for those interested in medical coding AHIMA provides a directory to programs affiliated with the Professional Certificate Approval Programs (PCAP). These programs conform to a model curriculum, and recipients of certificates from these programs meet the educational requirements (but not necessarily all requirements) for some CCHIIM coding certifications.

American Medical Informatics Association (AMIA)

AMIA comprises clinicians, researchers, educators, students, and others who work with health information and technology. The AMIA 10 × 10 program has a 10-year goal of training another 10,000 health care professionals in health informatics. This program offers courses in clinical informatics, clinical research informatics, translational bioinformatics, nursing informatics, and public health informatics. Courses are taught by participating universities, which are listed on the AMIA website. AMIA also offers a Clinical Informatics Board Review Course (CIBRC), which assists board-certified physicians with certification in the clinical informatics subspecialty.

CLINICAL CERTIFICATION AND TRAINING

It is possible for individuals with clinical backgrounds to gain additional credentials related to HIT in their professional fields. For example, the American Nurses Association (ANA) offers a certification in nursing informatics. This is offered through the American Nurses Credentialing Center (ANCC). To be eligible, an individual must be a currently licensed registered nurse and must also meet work experience and continuing education requirements. Those who then successfully pass the exam are awarded the credential Registered Nurse–Board Certified (RN–BC). The American Nursing Informatics Association (ANIA) also plays a role in helping nurses transition into informatics; for example, the ANIA website includes a link to a Nursing Informatics Certification Review Series. Nurses interested in HIT training may also want to become familiar with associations that are shaping nursing informatics education and provide information about the field. The Alliance for Nursing Informatics (ANI) links professional societies that have an interest in nursing informatics.

A second group is TIGER, which stands for Technology Informatics Guiding Educational Reform. TIGER is a link between the ANI and major nursing professional groups.

Project Management Institute (PMI)

At the time of the writing of this book, Project Management Professional (PMP) is one of the most sought after HIT employee positions. PMI offers a series of six credentials certifying education, experience, and competency (www.pmi.org). As an example, the PMP certification recognizes competence in directing project teams. It requires professional experience and achievement of education levels that vary depending on the amount of experience. The nature of project management is significantly specialized in health care. Consequently, if a PMP does not have health care experience, education that helps develop an understanding of the health care workplace environment would be helpful in transitioning into health care.

> *If you say you are going to do something . . . do it.*
> —*Tim Moore*

CompTIA

CompTIA is a nonprofit trade association that offers an extensive series of IT certifications. As one example, the CompTIA A+ certification is held by 900,000 technicians and is required by Dell, Intel, and Lenovo for service techs. Most of these certifications are general to IT and are not focused on HIT. However, the CompTIA certifications are sometimes earned in the process of getting a HIT degree. For example, students earn four of the CompTIA certifications in the process of earning a Bachelor of Science in Health Informatics from Western Governors University. Also, there is a CompTIA Healthcare IT Technician exam. For those who are interested in providing future careers for younger students, it is possible to offer CompTIA training through school districts. The Dell Academy Program assists school districts in offering a curriculum which prepares students for the CompTIA A+, Network+, and Server+ certification exams. The Dell Academy Program includes three semester-long courses. In order to prepare teachers, Dell also offers a Train-the-Trainer program.

ACADEMIC PROGRAMS

The traditional division between graduate and undergraduate education with defined majors breaks down in connection with HIT education. For most professions, a particular degree usually leads to a particular type of career. For example, someone who wants to be an economist will probably get an economics degree, and there are clear differences in job expectations for bachelor's, master's, and PhD degrees in economics. But in HIT a particular degree can lead to many different positions, and a particular position may be gained with many different degrees. For this reason, rather than describing particular degrees, this section addresses general considerations in the choice of HIT academic options.

Certificates

The term "certificate" generally describes an academic program shorter than a degree program. For example, a certificate program may consist of only five courses. Certificates may be earned without a degree or in conjunction with associate's, bachelor's, or master's programs. Sometimes the certificate is automatically earned as part of the degree. In other cases, the student chooses electives that result in a certificate along with a degree.

> *The best advice is to do the best you can in whatever you do and to always push yourself to achieve more.*
> —*Randall Barker*

Certificates are offered both by universities and by for-profit corporations. There are both accredited and unaccredited certificates.

Certificate programs can be viewed as a highly focused, and therefore somewhat narrow, training experience. They create a more modular training environment, where individuals can advance in smaller steps. One value to certificates is that they offer someone a chance to make a career change with less transition time. For example, a certificate may be the choice of someone who has an extensive background in either IT or health care and who wants to move into employment in HIT. When considering a certificate, it is important to consider if you will eventually want additional training. Some certificates generate credits that may be transferred to other schools, and the courses may serve as prerequisites for other degrees. Other programs of study are not transferable. Accredited certificates are more likely to have transferable credits. However, not every type of certificate has an accreditation body. There are also some very weak accreditation bodies. If you are considering a particular certificate and expect further education, you might contact universities you are considering attending in the future and ask if they accept course work from that particular certificate program.

Certificates may be geared toward entry-level positions, and they may be designed to enhance advanced training. For example, students who are interested in coding but don't want a full degree might choose a PCAP, discussed previously. At the other end of the spectrum, an individual with a PhD might want to gain additional insight through a highly specialized certificate. For example, the University of Utah offers a five-course graduate-level certificate in Biomedical Informatics.

Associate Degrees

Associate degrees typically require 2 years of course work. Often, the course work includes much of the general requirement courses a student needs in a bachelor's program. For this reason, it is a good idea to check if the course work at a particular associate program would be transferable for credit to other universities.

In HIT the most common type of associate degree program leads to certification as a medical coder. The CAHIIM Accredited Program Directory website has extensive lists of both "distance" and "not distance" accredited associate HIM programs.

Bachelor's Degrees

A student choosing a bachelor's degree and planning a career in HIT is making a significant investment in money and time. Usually the expectation is that the bachelor's will prepare the student not just for an entry-level position, but also for some advancement. To advance in HIT an individual needs to be comfortable with the clinical environment, as well as other areas of health care and IT. The individual also will usually have some management training. There are many ways of blending training in these areas. Someone who has worked in health care might decide to get a management degree and either a major or minor in IT. An individual who has experience in IT outside of health care might decide to get a clinical degree, such as nursing, to add an in-depth understanding of the clinical side of HIT. There are also specific programs for health information management that lead to certifications offered through AHIMA. The choice depends on an individual's background and on the specific

HIT position that the individual might want to pursue. Also, the bachelor's may not be a person's final degree, so combining an undergraduate degree in one area with a master's in another may be an excellent choice (e.g., combining an undergraduate IT degree with a graduate MHA or master's-level HIM degree).

There are many titles for degrees aimed at management in health care, but common titles are health care administration or business administration with a health care track. The Association of University Programs in Health Administration (AUPHA) certifies undergraduate health administration degrees. The AUPHA website includes a database of certified programs. These programs combine courses that apply business principles to health care (e.g., finance, management, law) with health care–specific courses (e.g., medical terminology, quality). A book by Friedman and Kovner (2013), *101 Careers in Healthcare Management*, includes a chapter that discusses choosing between health care management degrees. In comparing health administration degrees, there are differences in focus among programs located in public health departments, health profession departments, and business schools. Part of the difference in the mix is in the emphasis on business principles and health care topics. Another consideration is that health administration programs must have a large number of required courses in order to cover both the major areas of management and the key subjects in health care. Consequently, health administration programs usually have few electives. That makes getting a minor in IT difficult. A business administration degree does not address health care, unless there are electives that cover health care course work. Some business schools do offer tracks in health care.

There are also undergraduate degrees that focus more on the IT side of HIT. A university's management information systems (MIS) program may be located in the business school or in another academic unit. When it is offered as a business degree, this option creates a combination of business skills and applied IT skills. It is also possible to get a degree in computer science. This would likely involve a more in-depth study of the science of computing, including topics such as math, logical reasoning, and modeling, as well as study of topics such as programming and system design.

Another option is a degree in health information management. If such a degree is accredited by CAHIIM, it qualifies the student to sit for the RHIA exam. Therefore, the degree will have prepared someone to be expert in collecting, managing, and analyzing patient health information; to administer information systems; and to use classification systems and medical terminologies. The CAHIIM Accredited Program Directory website lists both "distance" and "not distance" accredited baccalaureate HIM programs.

As stated in Chapter 1, HIT is the integration of several academic disciplines and experiences: computer science, information systems, clinical knowledge/medical care, and management. An individual could focus his or her undergraduate education in a variety of majors such as computer science, or business administration with an emphasis in information systems, or a medical field such as nursing, radiologic technology, or health administration. Building on these undergraduate degrees, one could then layer a certificate or credential in HIT to build an academic portfolio that would lead to a career in the HIT workforce.

Master's Degrees

As is the case for undergraduate programs, a graduate degree in health care IT is likely intended for a career that includes positions in management. Consequently, such a degree will likely have health care, management, and IT components. However, the mix among the three components varies. Students have different backgrounds and different goals, so there is no best choice. A student who wants to focus on management could pursue an MBA with an IT specialization or get a master's in Health Administration (MHA) or the equivalent. Depending on the particular school, these degrees may offer options for including IT in a particular student's curriculum. For example, the MHA program at the University of Missouri offers options both for a MHA/Heath Informatics (MS) dual degree and for a graduate certificate in Informatics in conjunction with an MHA. A list of accredited MHA degrees (and their equivalents) is available at the website of the accrediting body, the Commission on Accreditation of Healthcare Management Education (CAHME). A list of accredited MBA programs is available at the website for the accrediting body, the Association to Advance Collegiate Schools of Business (AACSB).

> *Just because something doesn't do what you planned it to do doesn't mean it's useless.*
> —*Thomas A. Edison*

A master's degree in health information management is a more IT-intensive choice. Titles for master's-level degrees that directly pertain to HIT include Health Information Management, Health Information

Technology, Health Informatics, and Medical Informatics. These degrees focus on the integration of health care information, data management, and support of clinical and administration systems for health care institutions. It is possible to enter some of these programs without a strong HIT background. For example, the College of St. Scholastica offers either a 3-year program for those who do not have their RHIA credential or a 2-year program for those who have their RHIA. For sources of HIM master's training, the CAHIIM accredited program directory lists eight accredited master's degrees. These include five accredited master's (HIM) programs at the College of St. Scholastica (distance), Temple University, University of Maryland University College, University of Pittsburgh, and the University of Tennessee Health Science Center (distance); and three accredited master's (HI) programs at the University of Illinois at Chicago (distance), Marshall University, and Oregon Health & Science University. Besides these accredited degrees, there are a number of other options with varying curricula.

Doctoral Degrees

For many academic and research positions, a doctoral degree is required. Outside of these areas most HIT positions will not require a doctoral degree. A very wide range of doctoral degrees could be applicable to HIT academic and research positions. With the growth in HIT, there is also a growing need for HIT faculty and researchers. See Chapter 11 for job descriptions in the educational and training HIT workforce.

OTHER TYPES OF HIT TRAINING

There is a wide choice of other types of HIT training. Options include both programs offered by for-profit schools and programs offered by IT vendors. For-profit schools offer many of the types of training mentioned earlier, and, depending on the school, may offer other types of training. There are also for-profit organizations whose business includes providing links to different training options—for example, websites that list some of the available online health care degrees.

Some types of training and education from corporations are specific to a particular vendor. For example, the Allscripts Learning Center is a web training site for clients and partners. Other types of training are vendor neutral. As mentioned in Chapter 4, on finding a career, some corporations offer student internships.

As is the case with other types of training, before an individual begins one of these programs, it is a good idea to confirm that the particular option selected will lead to the particular position that the person hopes to have as a career. Also, the individual should consider whether the program is accredited.

APPENDIX
For More Information

- AACSB accredited business schools
  - www.aacsb.net/eweb/DynamicPage.aspx?Site=AACSB& WebKey=ED088FF2-979E-48C6-B104-33768F1DE01D
- AHIMA certification
  - www.ahima.org/certification
- AHIMA CHTS exams
  - www.ahima.org/certification/chts
- AHIMA Approved Coding Certificate Program Directory
  - www.ahima.org/careers/codingprograms.aspx
- Allscripts LearningCenter
  - ceplive.allscripts.com/adfs/ls/?wa=wsignin1.0&wtrealm= https%3a%2f%2falc.allscripts.com%2fALC%2f&wctx=r m%3d0%26id%3dpassive%26ru%3d%252fALC%252f& wct=2013-12-09T04%3a51%3a38Z
- AMIA 10 × 10 courses
  - www.amia.org/education/10x10-courses)
- ANCC Informatics Nursing
  - www.nursecredentialing.org/InformaticsNursing
- American Nursing Informatics Association
  - www.ania.org
- AUPHA Program Directory
  - network.aupha.org/aupha/AUPHANetwork/Directory11/ FindAProgram
- Biomedical Informatics Graduate Certificate Program University of Utah
  - medicine.utah.edu/bmi/academics-education/certificate.php
- CAHIIM Accredited Program Directory
  - www.cahiim.org/accredpgms.asp
- Commission on Accreditation of Healthcare Management Education (CAHME)

- ○ www.cahme.org/dbapp2/program_search.php
- ■ College of St. Scholastica MS Health Information Management
  - ○ www.css.edu/Graduate/Masters-Doctoral-and-Professional-Programs/Areas-of-Study/MS-Health-Information-Management.html
- ■ CompTIA A+
  - ○ certification.comptia.org/getCertified/certifications/a.aspx
- ■ Dell Academy Program
  - ○ www.dell.com/downloads/global/services/tnc_ed_dellacademy.pdf
- ■ Friedman, L. H., & Kovner, A. R. (2013). *101 careers in healthcare management.* New York: Springer Publishing Company.
- ■ HIMSS Health IT Certification
  - ○ www.himss.org/health-it-certification?navItemNumber=17564
- ■ HIMSS Health Informatics Training System (HITS)
  - ○ www.himss.org/health-it-education/online/health-informatics-training-system?navItemNumber=17581
- ■ HIMSS Online
  - ○ www.himss.org/health-it-education/online?navItemNumber=17578
- ■ HIMSS Workforce Survey 2013
  - ○ apps.himss.org/content/files/2013HIMSSWorkforceSurvey.pdf
- ■ HIMSTA Curriculum
  - ○ network.aupha.org/aupha/Resources/HIMSTA
- ■ MU Health Management and Informatics
  - ○ hmi.missouri.edu/prospective/graduate_programs.html#MHA
- ■ Nursing Informatics 101
  - ○ www.himss.org/files/HIMSSorg/handouts/NI101.pdf
- ■ Professional Certificate Approval Program (PCAP)
  - ○ www.ahimafoundation.org/education/pcap.aspx
- ■ Project Management Institute
  - ○ www.pmi.org
- ■ TIGER Initiative
  - ○ www.tigersummit.com/About_Us.html
- ■ Western Governors University Bachelor of Science in Health Informatics
  - ○ www.wgu.edu/online_it_degrees/health_informatics_degree

4 ■ FINDING A CAREER IN HEALTH INFORMATION TECHNOLOGY

BRIAN T. MALEC

The best way to predict the future is to create it.

—Abraham Lincoln

Finding a job and establishing a career is a potentially frustrating process. Assuming that you have made the decision to work in the health care sector and you want to explore health information technology (IIIT), the best advice is to research the types of positions in a variety of areas within health care, such as hospitals, medical groups, managed care, and vendors.

From a practical point of view you need to assess your skills and knowledge of the field of HIT, and gather insight as to areas where you might need further development, such as oral and written communication skills. The majority of HIT positions require a bachelor's degree and some a master's. Associate degrees and high school diplomas can be entry-level criteria in some areas within HIT. To start your career search one of the best places is the Career Center at your community college or university. Attend resumé writing workshops and any other workshops that might help you when looking for a career, any career. Talk to your present and past teachers and check out your fellow alumni either formally through clubs and associations or through personal contacts. HIT is a networking career, and you will need to deliberately develop and maintain networks.

IF YOU ARE STILL IN SCHOOL

If you are still in school and looking to experience the HIT work world, seek volunteer experiences if employment is unavailable. Employers will appreciate your determination and interest in HIT if they can see any related health care experience on your resumé. Many college degree programs require internships, so work with your faculty to have the internship in an IT-related area. Review the job descriptions in Part II of this book to evaluate the educational pathways to HIT jobs and the noncredit certifications that are expected in certain careers in HIT, such as Medical Records Coder. If you have the room in your program, talk to your teachers about extra courses that you might take. A great choice would be communication courses, business writing, and quantitative-related courses such as statistics and Excel-based decision-making courses. These will help you in any career path. Another strategy is to join professional organizations while still a student. There are significant

> *Do whatever you can to get some level of work experience in health care even if it is as a volunteer.*
> —*Mona Karaguozian*

membership discounts for students, and you get access to newsletters, journals, and professional meetings so that you can immerse yourself in the field before leaving the comfort and safety of student life. Some good examples are:

- American College of Healthcare Executives (ACHE)
  www.ache.org/apps/stumem.cfm
- Healthcare Information and Management Systems Society (HIMSS)
  www.himss.org/membership/student?navItemNumber=17904
- American Health Information Management Association (AHIMA)
  www.ahimastore.org/ProductDetailMembership.aspx

Some restrictions apply.
  www.ahima.org/careers

- Career map for AHIMA positions
- Salary survey and other resources
- Medical Group Management Association
  www.mgma.com

In the following you will find links to multiple web resources that will assist you in exploring HIT careers and seeing what jobs are currently in demand. A scavenger hunt through multiple online resources will help to put a perspective on the workforce market and help to develop your 5-year career path.

IF YOU ARE OUT OF SCHOOL AND CURRENTLY WORKING INSIDE OR OUTSIDE OF HEALTH CARE

If you have been exploring advancement in your current health care–related career or if you are working in another industry and want to shift into the health care sector, you have some choices to consider. Just like the current student, you should seek out information and advice from a Career Center and review the job descriptions that you will find in Part II of this book. It is also critical that you look at the professional organizations listed previously. Seek out information, especially in regard to education requirements, credentialing or certification, work experience, and what an employer is looking for in the area of job skills. The interviews and job descriptions in Part II will help you focus your next steps.

An important part of job/career advancement from within a healthcare setting is to talk to people who have "interesting" jobs or jobs that you find challenging or that fit your 5-year career plan. Take the time for informational interviews with chief information officers (CIOs), business analysts, and medical coders, for example. You will find a suggested format for these career exploration interviews in Part II. Use your internal organizational network to ask such individuals if they have just 5 or 10 minutes to talk with you about what they do, how they prepared for their current jobs, and any advice they might have. Make it clear that you are not asking for a job, but just building a portfolio of career options for the future. You would be surprised how interested and encouraging senior managers are when they see initiative and interest from a person who is seeking career change or advancement. And people like to talk about themselves. Perhaps you should discuss your interests with Human Resources. The best source of advice, however, is usually the network that you have formed with your colleagues. When you read the interviews in Part II you will see how these strategies can pay off. Remember, once you are successful in building your career path, pay it forward.

That first job might be as an administrative assistant or working on the help desk, but get "in the door" to learn where you fit best and show the organization what you can deliver.

—Tim Moore

If you are currently in another industry, like banking, manufacturing, aerospace, retail, or one of the service sectors, your strategies for exploring HIT careers will be almost the same. Explore the professional association websites to learn more about IT in the health care sector. If you have an information systems or computer science background, you will find many skills and knowledge areas that are transferable to the health care sector. However, health care is very different from for-profit industries outside the sector. How health care is financed differs greatly from the practice in other industries, and doctors dictate the production process based on medical needs of the patient. If you have other technical skills or management experience from another industry, you might want to consider some additional health care–related education, like a master's in health administration. (See Chapter 3 for information on educational opportunities.) A good starting point to explore the HIT workforce and find what jobs are in demand is to use the resources and web links that are presented in the following.

> *Network. The more people you become acquainted with, the more you can collaborate and stay motivated to think outside the box.*
> *—Stacy Cooreman*

SOME ADDITIONAL REALITY

Employers are sometimes looking for a specific set of skills, experience, and education to fill a very specific job. If you don't match the job description, they won't take a chance with you. On the other hand, some employers are looking for a candidate with positive initiative and enthusiasm, good problem-solving skills, great communication skills (oral and written), comfort with analytics and quantitative skills (Excel), presentation skills, Microsoft Office working knowledge, some knowledge of computer systems, and perhaps database and systems analysis. If you bring a strong package, often the employer will take a chance and will train you to master the job for which you are hired. Not all employers will take this chance, but some will. Understanding the culture of an organization is a key to success whether you are a current employee or new to an organization.

> *As a job seeker, remember this: You only lack experience if they want it done the same old way.*
> *—http://rbrault.blogspot.com*

Career paths are never straight lines. You do not start out as Employee Level 1 and progress through the ranks to Senior VP Level 10. Pathways to the top in HIT careers are twisted and not linear. Many of the interviews you will see in Part II demonstrate this point. A CIO might have started out in a pharmacy, moved to systems analysis, added some education in computer programming, and then earned an MBA, followed by more experience in the IT department, before becoming the CIO. If you have your sights set on a particular position in the future, you should develop a 5-year career strategy and plan to move sideways, vertically, and perhaps backward to gain the experience necessary for a senior position in a health care organization.

> *Do not hesitate to take an entry-level IT job such as help desk or admin assistance.*
> —Carrie Roberts

The next part of this chapter will detail various career sites that you should explore. The web addresses may have changed over time, but the core organizational site should be unchanged. The scavenger hunt will take you in many directions and down some blind alleys, but the adventure will be worth it in the end.

WEB RESOURCES FOR JOB SEARCHES

The HIMSS JobMine website is probably one of the best sources of HIT jobs. Although it is primarily devoted to jobs in the hospital industry, there is a range of opportunities across the United States and to a more limited extent in other sectors of the health care industry. The website is available to browse by job function or by geographic location. The JobMine website is a place to explore a full range of job titles and the educational and work experience requirements. It is easy to set up an account and get alerts and newsletters (jobmine.himss.org/home/home.cfm?site_id=5817).

O*NET OnLine is sponsored by the U.S. Department of Labor and provides an excellent source of information on a full range of jobs across all disciplines. While the website does not list specific job openings, it does provide a wealth of information on what people in these jobs actually do. The website provides the ability to search for occupations in various ways. You can select a keyword, such as "health information technology," and get a wide range of possible job titles. Or you can search by category of jobs, like computer and mathematical. Another search format is by jobs that are related to certain skills or knowledge, such as computers. Regardless of the search format you use, you have to search deeply to find specific job in health care. But when you do find a health-related HIT position, you have a wealth of information on requirements such as knowledge, skills, education, work activities, wages, and related occupations (www.onetonline.org).

JobTarget is a valuable website for job postings across all fields, not just health care. The JobFinder link allows the user to sign in and create a free account. You can surf the job openings for free as well. Keyword searches and specifying a certain geographic location are helpful in narrowing down the range of jobs to ones that you might want to investigate further. Since the site is not specific to health care, there a lot of position openings that are unrelated to jobs in HIT or other health-related occupations (jobtargetjobfinder.com/c2).

There is a specialty website that only has health information management (HIM) jobs and specializes in Coding Consultants, Directors/Managers (HIM), Electronic Health Record (EHR) Specialist, *International Classification of Diseases, 10th revision (ICD-10)* Coders, and other medical coding–related jobs (www.himjobs.com).

A related website that you should research is www.AHIMA.org.

A very popular career site is CareerBuilder.com. While the site covers jobs in many fields, you can drill down to find jobs in HIT. Search for "health care" and then "information technology" (www.careerbuilder.com).

While not a very easy website to navigate for HIT careers, Career Planner does have some very interesting resources. The following address takes you to a great page that describes what a computer systems analyst actually does. While not specific to health care, it does give a generic overview of what someone who has this job title does. Search around and you will find other descriptions of information technology jobs (job-outlook.careerplanner.com/computer-systems-analysts.cfm; if the address is not working, go to the main web page and do a new search).

Healthcare Jobsite is a very useful resource. You can search by keyword, information systems analyst, and by city or zip code. This search takes you to about 20 jobs related to the keyword (www.healthcarejobsite.com/jobs/jobsearch.asp?k=Information%20Systems%20Analyst&l=; if this address is no longer active, you can go to the main web page and start a new search).

One of the growing fields in HIT is that of a project manager. The position can be found in many industries and generally centers on managing, for example, a new IT investment project from start to finish. A project management professional needs to understand all the tasks, resources, and deadlines necessary to complete a project. It requires specialized training to be successful and to become a certified or associate project manager. The Project Management Institute provides the specifics on becoming a professional in this very in-demand specialty (www.pmi.org).

A more generic everyday website might surprise you with the vast amount of information you can obtain. Ehow.com has articles and resources to help you learn about a range of HIT positions. You have to do some searching. The following website demonstrates the type of material that can be found with respect to jobs in HIT. If the site is not open, start a new search (www.ehow.com/search.html?s=healthcare+info rmation+technology&skin=corporate&t=all).

The professional organizations mentioned here also have career and job search advice and resources. For example, the following website will provide you with access to current jobs available in specialized markets like health information management (medical records and coding related; www.ahima.org/careersinhim/default.aspx).

It is also a good idea to search academic programs that have advanced degrees in health informatics or health information management. Chapter 3 is a good source to search for educational programs that are in the field of HIT. One such source is the University of Illinois at Chicago (UIC). This site lists some current job postings: healthinformatics .uic.edu/health-information-management-jobs.

A second UIC site provides you with access to jobs related to Registered Health Information Administrator (RHIA): healthinformatics .uic.edu/rhia-for-hims-health-information-management.

HIT VENDORS

A major growth area in HIT is the vendor and consulting sector. Each year over a thousand HIT vendors attend the Healthcare Information and Management Systems Society (HIMSS) annual conference. Vendors have a workforce that is very different from that of a hospital or other provider organization. Candidates with

MBAs and with sales and marketing backgrounds can find jobs in this sector. Computer programmers and systems implementation trainers are also found in this sector. Often consulting firms are hired by health care organizations to supplement their internal HIT workforce. The website below is the HIMSS Exhibitor's Buyer's Guide, which provides access to vendor websites and other information. If this sector is of interest to you, you will find just about every major HIT vendor and consulting firm listed in the buyer's guide (onlinebuyersguide.himss. org).

> *Do not allow people skills to be an inhibitor; get used to delivering articulate presentations in a business-understandable fashion and to broad audiences at various organizational levels.*
> —*Waleed Bassyoni*

The growth of electronic medical records (EMRs), telemedicine, accountable care organizations (ACOs), and data analytics means that the vendors that supply these products and services will be searching for talent to create, market, install, and maintain their services. The following are some of the major vendors in the HIT space.

AllScripts

AllScripts partners with physician practices and health clinics of all sizes to improve clinical and financial outcomes, leading to the delivery of meaningful value. We offer a variety of ambulatory solutions. We've combined an ambitious but achievable vision with a strong desire to create a company that provides a stimulating, diverse working environment. We're dedicated to promoting work-life flexibility and making sure our employees are satisfied and engaged. We make a point to recognize our employees' accomplishments and encourage collaborative working relationships. If development and career growth are important to you, AllScripts is where you belong. (www3.allscripts.com/en.html)

AllScripts specializes in software solutions in the ambulatory space rather than hospitals. The website below provides an overview of opportunities at this company with interviews with current employees and links to a range of job opportunities. There are a lot of optional links to select carefully to explore the careers available (www3.allscripts.com/en/company/careers/opportunities.html).

Cardinal Health

Cardinal Health is a Fortune 19 company that improves the cost-effectiveness of healthcare. As the business behind healthcare, Cardinal Health helps pharmacies, hospitals and ambulatory care sites focus on patient care while reducing costs, improving efficiency and quality, and increasing profitability. Cardinal Health employs more than 30,000 people worldwide. (www.cardinal.com)

The career page shows recent graduates and has links for college students and existing job openings. Since Cardinal Health is a diverse company, you will find a wide range of job opportunities inside and outside of HIT (www.cardinal.com/us/en/Careers/CollegeStudents/RecentGraduates).

Cerner

Cerner's mission is to contribute to the systemic improvement of health care delivery and the health of communities. We are transforming health care by eliminating error, variance and waste for health care providers and consumers around the world. Our solutions optimize processes for health care organizations ranging from single-doctor practices to entire countries, for the pharmaceutical and medical device industries, and for the field of health care as a whole. Our solutions are licensed by approximately 10,000 facilities worldwide. (www.cerner.com/About_Cerner)

The career page is a very interesting one. You search about categories such as technical roles, provider and clinical roles, and others. Within a category there is a search form that helps you select jobs that are of most interest to you (www.cerner.com/About_Cerner/Careers).

The Cerner career website also has information on special opportunities for student internships. It is worth signing up and exploring (www.cerner.com/About_Cerner/Careers/Student_Development/College_Students).

Epic

Epic makes software for mid-size and large medical groups, hospitals and integrated healthcare organizations—working with customers that include community hospitals, academic facilities, children's organizations, safety net providers and multihospital systems. Our integrated software spans clinical, access and revenue functions and extends into the home. (www.epic.com)

The career website is very interactive, with employee profiles and interesting links to articles about the company (careers.epic.com/epic. php).

MEDITECH

If you haven't looked at us lately, you may be interested to know about our thriving Electronic Health Record. With an EHR, a patient's record follows her electronically. From the physician's office, to the hospital, to her home-based care, and to any other place she receives health services. And, she and her doctors can access all of this information and communicate with a smartphone or computer. This is really happening! Our customer community is very excited. In fact, the hospitals, ambulatory care centers, physicians' offices, long term care and behavioral health facilities, and home care organizations using our EHR around the world love talking about MEDITECH. (www.meditech.com)

The career page takes you to a listing of job opening by category. There is also a link to "See Life at MEDITECH," which is very interesting and helps to give you a sense of the company's culture and work environment (home.meditech.com/en/d/workhere/homepage.htm).

Siemens Healthcare

Siemens Corporation is a U.S. subsidiary of Siemens AG, a global powerhouse in electronics and electrical engineering, operating in the industry, energy, healthcare, and infrastructure & cities sectors. For more than 165 years, Siemens has built a reputation for leading-edge innovation and the quality of its products, services and solutions. (www.usa.siemens.com/en/about_us.htm)

The career page below takes you to a wide range of jobs across the company. First, click on "Search US Jobs." The next screen has a range of menu links such as location, functional area, job type, company, and other options. Select all locations, IT as the functional area, all job types, and start with Siemens Medical Solutions USA as the company (www. usa.siemens.com/en/jobs_careers.htm).

Siemens also has a link to a students page with information about 12-week summer internships and also training and development programs for current employees (www.usa.siemens.com/en/jobs_careers/students.htm).

HEALTH INSURANCE ORGANIZATIONS

For those with an interest in exploring HIT careers in the managed care and insurance industry, the following are a few of the larger companies in this space.

Aetna

> Helping to manage health care, one of the most important things in life. We believe we can help create a better health care system. This belief drives our daily decisions as one of the nation's leading health care benefits companies. We work hard to provide our members with information and resources to help them make informed decisions about their health. (www .aetna.com)

The career page provides information on career types, student programs, and what it is like working at Aetna. Clicking "Student Programs" takes you to links for undergraduate and graduate internships and training programs for recent graduates. Under "Career Types" you can select from a range of categories and then drill down to health informatics and related positions. A feature of the career website is the ability to read employee profiles to learn about people who actually are working in the job positions (www.aetna.com/about-aetna-insurance/aetna-careers/career-types/index.html).

Health Net

> Health Net, Inc. is a publicly traded managed care organization that delivers managed health care services through health plans and government-sponsored managed care plans. Its mission is to help people be healthy, secure and comfortable. Health Net provides and administers health benefits to approximately 5.4 million individuals across the country through group, individual, Medicare (including the Medicare prescription drug benefit commonly referred to as "Part D"), Medicaid, U.S. Department of Defense, including TRICARE, and Veterans Affairs programs. Through its subsidiaries, Health Net also offers behavioral health, substance abuse and employee assistance programs, managed health care products related to prescription drugs, managed health care product coordination for multiregion employers and administrative services for medical groups and self-funded benefits programs. (www. healthnet.com)

The career web page is a place where you can do job searches. The "Job family" for HIT is "Information technology" and from there you can select a location (careersathealthnet.com/searchjobs.asp?id= default).

UnitedHealth Group

We are committed to introducing innovative approaches, products and services that can improve personal health and promote healthier populations in local communities. Our core capabilities in clinical care resources, information and technology uniquely enable us to meet the evolving needs of a changing health care environment as millions more Americans enter a structured system of health benefits and we help build a stronger, higher quality health system that is sustainable for the long term. (www.united-healthgroup.com)

The following is UnitedHealth Group's career page. Search by keyword, geographic location, or job category. By clicking the "Search jobs" button, you will be taken to a listing of current openings. Each has a very brief "quick look" that provides a brief position description (careers. unitedhealthgroup.com).

As with many of the other vendors and managed care organizations, you are also advised to check out the opportunities for students and early career individuals (careers.unitedhealthgroup.com/college/student-programs.aspx).

WellPoint

WellPoint as an organization is highly focused on a commitment to our Purpose to transform health care with trusted and caring solutions. From innovative products that help reduce the ranks of the uninsured and underinsured, to the comprehensive benefits we offer our associates, everything we do is aimed at creating positive outcomes that make a difference in people's lives. As one of the nation's largest publicly traded commercial health benefits companies by membership, we're honored to have the opportunity to impact so many lives. Nearly 36 million members rely on us every day to be leaders, advocates and innovators in the call to improve health, quality of care and value to our members. (www. wellpoint.com)

The WellPoint job search website is set up so that you select a career area, such as information technology, and then select a location, either a state or city. WellPoint has formal internship programs for undergraduates and graduate students. Look on the left side of the page under "Student programs" (www.careersatwellpoint.com/default.aspx).

Your work is going to fill a large part of your life, and the only way to be truly satisfied is to do what you believe is great work. And the only way to do great work is to love what you do.

—Steve Jobs

The challenge for you is to explore your options, your areas of interest, jobs and organizations that might fit you best, and to have fun expanding your knowledge of HIT careers.

5 ■ THE FUTURE OF HIT CAREERS

DAVID E. GARETS AND JOHN GLASER

We don't know what the future holds but that doesn't prevent us from making stuff up and sounding like we do.

—Garets and Glaser

One only has to look at the changes and challenges in the health care industry to determine that the career outlook for health information technology (IIIT) is quite positive. Of course, one may also look at the looming changes and challenges and decide upon a somewhat tamer career—such as joining a crew on the *Deadliest Catch* king-crab–fishing TV series.

> *Employers look for individuals that are energetic, enthusiastic, and tend to be curious—wanting to learn, understand, and make things happen.*
>
> *—Scott Joslyn*

Health care, as a whole, is an industry in a constant state of change, driven by medical breakthroughs, policy and regulatory demands, and technological advances such as the MRI and the electronic health record (EHR). The growing need for information technology in health care is driven by multiple factors: changing payer models, increasing need for documentation, federal regulation, demands for higher quality care, and the growing requirement to manage the care of patients over time and across settings.

The American Recovery and Reinvestment Act of 2009 (ARRA) Health Information Technology for Economic and Clinical Health (HITECH) Act's incentive program for the Meaningful Use of Electronic Health Records created a surge in the demand for HIT resources, one that will continue unabated even if the program officially concludes. Regulation, including reimbursement demands such as the changeover to *International Classification of Diseases, 10th revision (ICD-10)* coding, also requires intensive resources.

The Patient Protection and Affordable Care Act introduces new regulations and new reimbursement models, as well as an increased need for reporting into the health care business office, challenging organizations to be able to measure quality, safety, and performance—all while being able to manage greater numbers of patients.

Overall, however, the largest catalyst for the growth and evolution of HIT job opportunities is the transformation of health care: the exponential growth in clinical knowledge and the change in how we deliver care to a shifting population and how that care is reimbursed. As Todd Park, former chief technology officer of the Department of Health and Human Services, stated when talking about the lofty goals of transforming health care, "You can't make it happen without innovative use of data and IT."[1]

SPECIFIC DRIVERS

Behind this broad transformation of health care there are three specific drivers that will significantly impact the HIT profession (in addition to the traditional driver of the evolution—and at times revolution—of information technology).

Expansion of the reach of the care provider. Traditionally, HIT professionals have been focused on gathering and presenting administrative and clinical data, streamlining core processes such as scheduling, and managing technical infrastructure within the confines of a single organization or defined enterprise. With the demand to manage a patient's health over time and multiple care settings, the HIT professional must manage IT systems and infrastructure that span communities.

Explosion of data. In 2012, approximately, 2.5 exabytes (to put this into scale, it's estimated that 5 exabytes of information would be equal to all of the words ever spoken by mankind)[2] of data are created each day, and the rate is doubling every 40 months.[3] Health care is no exception: It is a treasure trove of data. The volume of clinical data is such that it's virtually impossible for even the most astute clinician to know

---

[1] Miliard, M. (2012, January). The 5-year plan: Where will healthcare be in 2017? *Healthcare IT News.*

[2] *Megabytes, gigabytes, terabytes . . . What are they?* www.whatsabyte.com

[3] McAfee, A., & Brynjolfsson, E. (2012, October). Big data: The management revolution, *Harvard Business Review.*

and manage it all. Being able to leverage clinical evidence will require sophisticated HIT systems that collect, aggregate, and present data in the clinical decision-making process. There are also massive amounts of information collected during the care process for individual patients—information that must be managed and made available across diverse care settings. And such information must be aggregated and analyzed in order to manage the care of populations—an increasing need with the aging population and growth in long-term chronic diseases. Also, it's not just clinical and patient data that are collected. Data are also collected from and about procedures, equipment, physicians, and processes in order to help organizations make decisions about business lines and to improve operations.

Concerted focus on processes. The goal of HIT is to enable the care process—for individual patients, for management of populations with diseases, and for communities—to be more efficient, effective, and safe. With the increased pressures on provider performance, the demands on HIT to truly improve processes will increase. HIT must deliver business value—return on the significant investment—as health care organizations are moving to pay for performance models and are driven to new levels of operational efficiency.

THE EVOLVING INFORMATION TECHNOLOGY PROFESSION

In the future, the most successful health care organizations will be those that optimize the potential of HIT beyond current reimbursement programs, according to health futurist and medical economist Jeffrey Bauer: "Nobody can succeed in the future of healthcare without the best possible IT system." He says that the most successful organizations will be those that moved faster and deeper than required by the ARRA's HITECH program. "By 2017, we will be well down the way to a shift in the clinical paradigm from one-size-fits-all to highly individualized medicine. That can only be done with IT and team-based practice."[4]

Behind the core of the sophisticated HIT systems required for this are people—HIT professionals to design, develop, and manage the systems and the information collected. The U.S. Department of Labor presents a positive outlook for career opportunities in health care, with

---

[4] Miliard, M. (2012, January). The 5-year plan: Where will healthcare be in 2017? *Healthcare IT News.*

one third of the 20 fastest-growing careers occurring in health care. Specifically for HIT, the study projects 21% total job growth through 2020.[5]

> *Personal integrity will show through and you can't hide excellence.*
>
> —*Tim Moore*

For individuals interested in tech fields who also have a desire to give back to their communities, HIT will offer great fulfillment. The composition of HIT roles is also undergoing an evolution, shifting from predominantly a back-office operation mode to one at the forefront of care delivery and medical advances.

HIT PROFESSIONALS WILL BE NEEDED IN SEVERAL EMERGING ROLES

A study completed by the University of California San Diego Extension (UCSD) ranked HIT as number 1 in its list of the top 10 "hot careers" in 2011, citing the need for HIT specialists in the positions of health care integration engineers, health care systems analysts, clinical IT consultants, and technology support specialists in health care organizations.[6] According to the 2013 survey from UCSD, information technology was again ranked high in the top 10 hottest careers.[7]

Core information technology. While health care is behind other industries in technology adoption, it will quickly catch up. Mobility—in the form of smart phones, apps, and devices; cloud-based services; and big data—is becoming a requirement for changing delivery models. In addition to core information technologies, health care will see a growth in IT-based medical devices. Patients will have home-based and wearable devices that measure blood levels and blood pressure and perform EKGs, transmitting information back to the care team. All of this will require sensitive and sophisticated systems to collect, manage, and protect individual information and to trigger appropriate intervention, when indicated.

---

[5] Bureau of Labor Statistics, U.S. Department of Labor. *Occupational outlook handbook, 2012–13 edition.* Medical Records and Health Information Technicians, www.bls.gov/ooh/healthcare/medical-records-and-health-information-technicians.htm

[6] University of California San Diego Extension. (2011). *Hot careers for college graduates 2011: A special report for recent and mid-career college graduates.* San Diego, CA: Author.

[7] University of California San Diego Extension. (2013). *Hot careers for college graduates 2013: A special report for recent and mid-career college graduates.* San Diego, CA: Author.

Connectivity and interoperability. As health care transitions from an acute care–based model to encompass a greater emphasis on ambulatory and home care, accountable care organizations, medical homes, and patient engagement models, HIT will be required for connectivity among geographically and technologically diverse networks. This is more of the traditional HIT role—that of IT managers, help-desk support, and clinical and financial systems implementation and management—but on a deeper and more complex level, requiring secure exchange of information among hospitals, physician practices, long-term care facilities, home health agencies, payers, the government, and the patient.

Process re-engineering. Health care will need IT professionals who can support their clinical and business colleagues to implement, change, and manage clinical processes based on industry best practices, taking clinical knowledge and embedding that knowledge into workflows that orchestrate the processes. Based on clinician definitions, IT managers will help physicians build order sets and rules that govern everything from scheduling of diagnostic testing to housekeeping alerts.

Big data and analytics. Like other industries, health care is joining the "big data" trend, taking advantage of the volumes of data to solve both clinical and business problems. New skills are needed to harness and manage data silos—across multiple providers, payers, and the government. Data scientists are emerging as a "hot" commodity, and there is already a shortage of professionals capable of managing, mining, and converting data into "intelligence." Data mining entails the extraction of specific types of information or patterns from large volumes of structured and unstructured data.

But that's just the first step. The explosion of EHR data and patient-generated data requires specialized skill sets combining IT, statistical, and business and clinical competencies. This gives rise to the demand for data scientists to capitalize on the data collected in health care—to use analytics tools and derive usable information to support clinical operations; to determine the value and profitability of business lines such as cardiology and joint replacement; to report on quality measures and identify areas of risk; and to aggregate data to determine how to best manage specific populations, such as diabetics within an accountable care organization (ACO) or geographic area.

It also gives rise to a new title that may or may not be used in health care organizations depending on political correctness, that of *data garbagolist.* What most first-mover health care organizations trying to set up data warehouses have discovered is that the data they'd been capturing in the source systems, which they thought was complete and comprehensive, is actually riddled with garbage, a condition immortalized in the hackneyed IT explanatory phrase "garbage in, garbage out." These professionals will need clinical and analytical expertise as well as political savvy and muscle to convince users to standardize vocabularies and to be thorough in providing requisite data.

We're also seeing the emergence of a senior executive role with the title of chief knowledge officer, chief transformation officer, or chief strategy officer, a position that is responsible for the conversion of data to information to knowledge. These individuals, in the few health care organizations employing them today, generally report to the CEO. They are responsible for ensuring business intelligence governance, working hand in glove with the CIO, analysts, and informatics professionals to use structured data for predictive and prescriptive modeling to enable the most effective and efficacious management and planning for the health care organization. Their office will be staffed by clinical and financial analysts, predictive and prescriptive data modelers, and data scientists, many of whom will have moved over to the new office from the old one in the IT department.

PREPARING FOR AN HIT CAREER

There are several paths to a career in HIT. Some paths are more appropriate for careers as a data scientist while other paths are more targeted at roles involved in changing clinical processes.

Combining a computer science degree with bioinformatics will become an example route to an HIT career. Hiring managers also look for industry certifications, clinical backgrounds, experience, and aptitude when recruiting new hires. The Commission on Accreditation for Health Informatics and Information Management Education certifies many programs.

CONCLUSION

HIT has traditionally been viewed as a back-office function and a cost center, necessary to conducting the business of health care. However, a combination of factors—increasing cost pressures, consolidation, competition, health care reform, medical advances, and demographics—have thrust HIT into the position of transformer and business enabler, key to helping health care organizations survive.

In addition to mastering current and emerging roles, HIT team members must become more agile in terms of execution and staying technologically current. The changes in health care require that HIT leadership and management become strategic peers to the organization's leadership team. Increasingly, we'll find the CEO and CFO turning to the HIT leadership for direction on how to leverage HIT as a business strategy. Former Aetna Chairman and CEO Ronald Williams wrote that the company transformed itself by using IT as a competitive advantage.[8] To do the same, health care organization leaders must become technology literate and IT leaders must become business savvy.

It's clear that HIT as a strategically executed asset not only can help an organization be competitive and operationally efficient, but can lead the organization to the potential of health care tailored to the unique health care needs of an individual while managing the care of populations.

The reality is that a career in HIT is limitless: HIT will be pivotal in building an effective and cost-sustainable health care system. While predicting the future is challenging, we do know that there will be an increasing obligation of health care organizations to care for the chronically ill and to deliver care that is predictive, personalized, and associated with the best possible outcome—all driven by knowledge and all managed by HIT.

---

[8] www.ronwilliams.net/viewpoint/it-as-strategy

II ■ INTRODUCTION TO JOB DESCRIPTIONS AND INTERVIEWS IN HEALTH INFORMATION TECHNOLOGY

BRIAN T. MALEC

The U.S. workforce market for health information technology (HIT)–related jobs is expected to continue to grow in the coming years according to the Healthcare Information and Management Systems Society (HIMSS) First and Second Workforce Surveys in July 2013 and July 2014. HIMSS interviewed both provider and vendor organizations to determine their past and future hiring trends and barriers to hiring in this field. Of the 200 respondents to the 2014 survey, 85% had hired one or more IT staff members in the past 12 months and 82% reported that they plan on hiring additional staff in the coming 12 months. Health care provider organizations were expecting to increase their HIT staff, but vendors had higher expectations of expanding their workforce. Much of the growth in hiring in both types of organizations is expected to be for seasoned professionals with health care industry experience. Because of the tight workforce marketplace, salaries and benefits are expected to be very competitive.

> *Experience, experience and experience. No job is too small!*
> *—Daniel Nimoy*

The 2013 and 2014 HIMSS Workforce Surveys go on to say that health care providers face barriers in implementing their HIT projects due to staff shortages. Many organizations have been forced to slow down or place on hold a number of IT-related projects. Due to the workforce shortages, a competitive marketplace exists for HIT professionals, resulting in a high demand for their services.

The Workforce Survey indicated other key results:

■ Health care provider organizations are seeking to hire in the areas of clinical applications support and help-desk support positions.

FIGURE II.1 TOP KEY AREAS OF INFORMATION TECHNOLOGY NEEDS
IN HEALTH CARE PROVIDER ORGANIZATIONS—2013 AND 2014

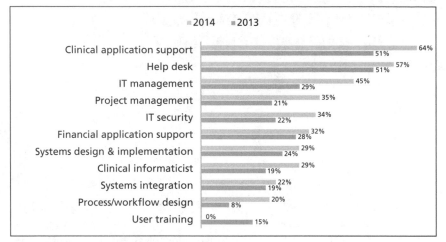

Source: 2014 HIMSS Workforce Survey. Retrieved from www.himssanalytics.org/research/
index.aspx.

- Vendor organizations are expanding in the areas of field staff support and sales and marketing positions.
- A large number of health care provider organizations currently outsource HIT services rather than provide the services with internal staff. In the coming years these organizations see an increase in outsourcing, with growth in project management, clinical applications support, IT security, and other areas.
- Both vendors and health care provider organizations are looking for certifications in certain applicant pools, especially in technical fields like network architecture support and security.

The top key areas in which health care provider organizations hired in the past 12 months are shown in Figure II.1, from the 2014 HIMSS Workforce Survey, and compare the 2013 areas in high demand with the 2014 survey results. In both surveys, clinical application support, help-desk support staff, IT management, project management, and IT security are some of the highest areas in demand.

Figure II.2, also from the 2014 HIMSS Workforce Survey, shows the areas that are more likely to be outsourced instead of staffed with internal hires by health care providers in 2013 and 2014. As indicated, the areas with the highest percentages to be outsourced are project management, clinical application support, IT security, and systems design and implementation.

FIGURE II.2 TOP AREAS OUTSOURCED BY HEALTH CARE PROVIDERS—2013 AND 2014

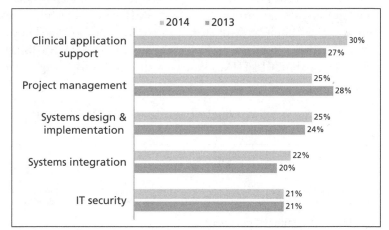

Source: 2014 HIMSS Workforce Survey. Retrieved from www.himssanalytics.org/research/index.aspx.

Outsourcing is an effective means for provider organizations of varying sizes to obtain a workforce when local markets may not have the supply of HIT professionals with appropriate experience and credentials. Consulting firms and vendors are often the source of the outsourcing. Consulting firms have specific product lines that they market—for example, HIT systems selection and implementation, *International Classification of Diseases, 10th revision (ICD-10)* planning and implementation, strategic consulting, health information exchange development, and project management services related to the HIT systems implementation.

Vendor organizations, according to the 2014 survey, anticipate hiring staff in the areas of sales and marketing, implementation support at the client site, product development, finance, and human resources to support the growth of the vendor organizations.

The 2013 survey indicated that both health care providers and vendors are looking for educational preparation and specific certification in key areas. Some of the certification areas they are looking for are security/HIPAA, network/architecture, database administration, project management, and informatics.

Interesting and important points from the two surveys are the methods used by both vendors and health care providers to recruit HIT staff. Figure II.3 shows that networking, job boards, and social media are typical tools used to recruit HIT staff. Vendors use employee referrals as a major tool for recruiting future staff members. This trend by vendors supports the importance of networking and being active in professional associations.

When employers are recruiting new staff, they are heavy users of career websites such as Monster, LinkedIn, and so on. They also advertise in local newspapers and post their jobs on HIMSS JobMine. Figure II.4, from the 2013 HIMSS survey, shows the top five resources

FIGURE II.3   TOP FIVE WIDELY USED SOURCES TO RECRUIT EMPLOYEES—2013 AND 2014

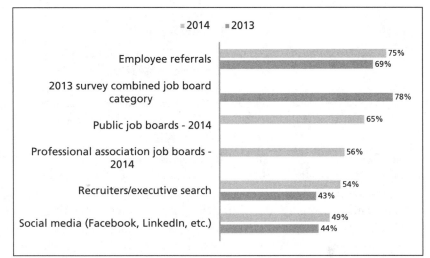

Source: 2014 HIMSS Workforce Survey. Retrieved from www.himssanalytics.org/research/index.aspx.

FIGURE II.4   TOP FIVE SOURCES USED TO RECRUIT STAFF—2013

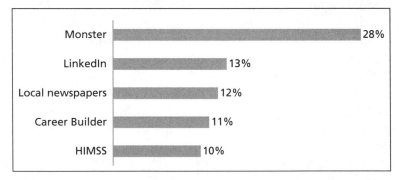

Source: 2013 HIMSS Workforce Survey. Retrieved from www.himssanalytics.org/research/index.aspx.

used to recruit staff. Chapter 4, "Finding a Career in Health Information Technology," discusses the various web resources that employers use and applicants should explore.

STRUCTURE OF PART II

In Part II of this book you will find job descriptions that are generalized to reflect what a person would find when looking for an HIT career path. The job descriptions give a realistic observation of the workforce marketplace and provide practical information on educational and experience requirements for HIT jobs. Each job description has the following standard elements:

- Job title
  - There are few standard job titles, and people doing the same work in different organizations may or may not have the same job title. It is important to look at the descriptions and not just the titles.
  - Employers who really want to hire an excellent candidate will sometimes invent a new job title just so they can attract the best person to come work for them.
- The position description
  - Employers will vary on how much detail is placed in the position description in an open-position posting on a career site. The description should specify the general duties and expectations. Looking at several job descriptions for similar job titles will help in understanding what someone does in the job.
- Educational and experience requirements
  - Most job postings will list specific educational requirements. These can range from a high school diploma to a master's degree and beyond. Some job descriptions state whether they will accept equivalent years of experience.
- Credentials, if any are required
  - HIT jobs can be rather technical and require further education and certification beyond normal degrees. It is important to note the required and recommended credentials that are indicated for a job and plan your strategies accordingly.
- Core competencies and skills
  - Not all job postings are specific as to the set of skills and competencies that are required to perform the job. The

following job descriptions will vary on the depth and mixture of expectations. For some jobs, a very technical set of skills are required, while other employers are looking for a combination of what might be called softer and interpersonal skills. A set of core competencies and skills that are repeatedly posted in job descriptions are:

- ❏ Demonstrated communication skills: oral, written, and presentation
- ❏ Demonstrated problem-solving skills
- ❏ Comfortable with information technology and, in particular, Microsoft Office
- ❏ Meeting deadlines
- ❏ Working independently and in teams

■ Compensation
  ○ Not all job descriptions will list a pay range, and it may be up to you to research a number of positions to find an average salary or hourly rate. Check out the following government website for some average salaries: www.bls.gov/ooh/computer-and-information-technology/home.htm
■ Where in the organization might you find this position?
  ○ Not all HIT jobs are found in the IT department. Some are in specific clinical departments or the business office. In non-hospital settings, an HIT job could be in sales and marketing, implementation and training of systems, or a medical office, and some positions could be "at-home" jobs. It is important to understand the job's place in the organization.
■ Employment outlook
  ○ The information provided in this section of a job description often comes from the U.S. Bureau of Labor Statistics and its projection of the workforce needs in the area of HIT. You are encouraged to browse the following website: www.bls.gov/ooh/computer-and-information-technology/home.htm
■ For more information
  ○ In addition to the government site mentioned, this section of the job description might refer you to professional organizations, specific job listings, or other sources of information to help you learn more about what the people who work in this particular job do.

6 ■ THE HIT JOB ENVIRONMENT IN THE HOSPITAL SECTOR

Health information technology (HIT) jobs in the hospital sector continue to grow at a faster-than-average rate according to the U.S. Bureau of Labor Statistics (BLS). Larger hospitals have a reasonable number of staff in the Information Technology (IT) department. A hospital chain with multiple facilities might have a high degree of centralization of key senior positions like chief information officer (CIO) and chief medical information officer (CMIO). Local facilities may have a number of technical jobs in clinical areas, medical coding and billing, help-desk support positions, and many others to assist with day-to-day operations. It is also not uncommon for hospitals of all sizes to outsource positions to consulting companies.

Moving sideways or even backward might be the best decision to advance in a career path.
—Scott Cebula

Get out of the IT department and into the rest of the hospital to really understand how health care works at the ground level.
—Carrie Roberts

The following are typical HIT jobs found in the hospital sector. Some position descriptions are also common in other sectors of the health care industry, like medical groups and managed care. Where appropriate, the job description will indicate if it is found in these other sectors. This chapter also features interviews with current HIT professionals working in this sector.

POSITION DESCRIPTIONS IN HOSPITAL SETTINGS

1. Help-Desk and Customer Support

As indicated in the introduction to Part II of this book, help-desk and customer-support positions are in high demand and can be interesting entry points for those new to the field. The jobs require great communication skills and an immersion into the clinical and administration applications of an organization. You must be comfortable with technology and have developed people skills that can lead to other positions in the organization. The following are three positions typically found in health care organizations.

2. Help-Desk Staff/Support (Example #1)

POSITION DESCRIPTION   Provide technical assistance to computer systems users, including the use of computer hardware and software, printer installation, word processing, e-mail, and operating systems. Maintain a service perspective including an understanding of relationships, dependencies, and requirements of hardware and software components and the organizations that support them. Answer questions or resolve computer problems for clients in person, via telephone, or from a remote location.

In most cases, the responsibilities of help-desk staff/support include:

- Receive and record technical or application support calls from end users
- Provide investigation, diagnosis, resolution, and recovery for hardware/software problems
- Maintain overall ownership of user's issue and service, ensuring that the user obtains resolution within a reasonable time frame
- Provide enhancement-request feedback to IT regarding technology environment and customer needs through the defined processes
- Ability to work independently and in a team environment
- Ability to communicate well with internal and external contacts
- Provide initial assessment of urgency and business impact on all support calls
- Manage service requests, software installations, new computer setups, upgrades, and so forth.
- Record incident resolutions in the help-desk tool.

EDUCATION AND EXPERIENCE   University degree (BS) or its equivalent in Computer Engineering, Computer Science, or other IT-related disciplines. One to 2 years directly related work experience in a technical help-desk position supporting Windows XP, Microsoft Office 2003 or later (2007 preferred), Internet Explorer, and business applications in a business environment. Knowledge of multiple desktop programs, configuration, and debugging techniques.

CREDENTIALS, LICENSURE, OR CERTIFICATION, IF APPROPRIATE None required.

CORE COMPETENCIES AND SKILLS

- *Interpersonal skills:* Help-desk staff must be patient and sympathetic. They must often help people who are frustrated with the software or hardware they are trying to use.
- *Listening skills:* Support workers must be able to understand the problem that their customers are describing and know when to ask questions to clarify the situation.
- *Problem-solving skills:* Support workers must identify both simple and complex computer problems, analyze them, and provide proper solutions.
- *Speaking skills:* Support workers must describe the solution to a computer problem in a way that a nontechnical person can understand.
- *Writing skills:* Strong writing skills are useful for preparing instructions and e-mail responses for employees and customers.

COMPENSATION Salary ranges from $42,000 per year to a high of $58,000, with an average of $46,260.

WORKPLACE LOCATION Help-desk staff support work in many different industries, including IT, education, finance, health care, and telecommunication.

EMPLOYMENT OUTLOOK Employment of help-desk support is expected to grow 18% from 2010 to 2020, about as fast as the average for all health care occupations. Job prospects should be favorable. Applicants with a bachelor's degree and a strong technical background should have the best job opportunities.

FOR MORE INFORMATION

- www.bls.gov/ooh/computer-and-information-technology/computer-support-specialists.htm

3. Help-Desk and Applications Support Specialist (Example #2)

POSITION DESCRIPTION Under the general direction of the director of training and applications support, the help-desk and applications support specialist will be the primary point of contact for the help-desk hotline. She or he will perform troubleshooting utilizing various techniques for problem resolution, including, but not limited to, screenshots or error messages, attempts to reproduce the reported issue, and use of TeamViewer software to see and resolve reported issues. He or she will triage calls by identifying, classifying, and prioritizing incidents and requests. This person will support multiple applications, including the Electronic Health Record system and the Microsoft Office Suite. This person will provide support for new software launches, including the development of technical training tools and materials.

EDUCATION AND EXPERIENCE   High school diploma or equivalent and 2 to 3 years of relevant experience.

CREDENTIALS, LICENSURE, OR CERTIFICATION, IF APPROPRIATE   None specified.

CORE COMPETENCIES AND SKILLS
- Functions as the customer's single point of contact for problem escalation and resolution as required
- Provides telephone support for Microsoft Office and a range of vendor products specific to a health care organization
- Resolves simple hardware and software problems, including password resets during the initial phone call
- Uses remote desktop software to troubleshoot problems for end users
- Records all incidents utilizing Track-It! software while maintaining accountability and ownership until the problem is resolved
- Interfaces with appropriate technical personnel for customer problems that cannot be resolved quickly on the telephone

COMPENSATION   Salaries for this position are entry level and are competitive with benefits given the region of the country in which the job is located.

WORKPLACE LOCATION   The position is located in the IT department.

EMPLOYMENT OUTLOOK   Along with other, more technical HIT positions, the help-desk and applications support job will continue to be in high demand in the health care industry.

FOR MORE INFORMATION   These positions are very organization specific, and the best resource would be the career websites for local health care organizations. HIMSS JobMine is a good location and provides access to similar positions in a wide variety of states.

4. Customer Service Support Manager (Example #3)

POSITION DESCRIPTION   The customer service support manager is responsible for the daily managing of the service desk team (service analysts) and break/fix team (desktop support) to ensure that the Information Systems (IS) department meets each end-user department's requirements as they relate to the strategic goals and mission of the organization. This person ensures customer-service objectives are achieved by developing and maintaining effective tracking and resolution mechanisms to verify that all areas have full and ongoing support, including creation of benchmarks and monitoring calls.

EDUCATION AND EXPERIENCE   Bachelor's degree in a related field. Master's degree in IT, computer science, or business management desirable. Five to 7 years of experience in an IS management position is desirable.

CREDENTIALS, LICENSURE, OR CERTIFICATION, IF APPROPRIATE   Six Sigma certification, HDI help-desk certification preferred.

CORE COMPETENCIES AND SKILLS
- Responsible for planning and implementation of all activities associated with fulfilling overall service desk and desktop support operations
- Accomplishes customer service and human resource objectives by recruiting, selecting, orienting, training, assigning, scheduling, coaching, counseling, and disciplining employees
- Ensures customer service objectives are achieved by contributing customer service information and recommendations to strategic plans and reviews
- Meets customer service financial objectives by forecasting requirements, preparing an annual budget, scheduling expenditures, analyzing variances, and initiating corrective actions
- Responsible for ensuring that user problems are addressed in a timely fashion through problem recognition, research, isolation and resolution, and follow-up steps

COMPENSATION   The annual salary of computer support specialists ranges from $40,000 to a high of $58,000, with an average of $46,500.

WORKPLACE LOCATION   This position would be found in large health care systems in the IT department. The position oversees the help-desk and other customer-focused IT support activities.

EMPLOYMENT OUTLOOK   Employment of computer support specialists is expected to grow 18% from 2010 to 2020, about as fast as the average for all health care occupations. Job prospects should be favorable. Applicants with a bachelor's degree and a strong technical background should have the best job opportunities.

FOR MORE INFORMATION   These positions are very organization specific, and the best resource would be the career websites for local health care organizations. HIMSS JobMine is a good location and provides access to similar positions in a wide variety of states. Also, consult the website for the Bureau of Labor Statistics:

- www.bls.gov/ooh/computer-and-information-technology/computer-support-specialists.htm

DANIEL NIMOY
Clinical Office Supervisor
The UCLA Health System

Describe the sort of work you do. Currently I am the clinical office supervisor for the UCLA Dermatology Division. I am responsible for managing a staff of 11 full-time-equivalent employees throughout three clinical locations. I do performance reviews, I manage all clinical schedules, and I am the assistant to the department's director on various improvement projects and other department initiatives.

What is a typical day like at your job? This is a really a tough question to answer. Any given day can look totally different from any other day. My primary responsibilities include managing physician complaints, managing the daily clinic throughput and schedules, and managing the daily staffing (including breaks, lunches, and vacation requests). I respond to a large number of e-mails each day, mostly from physicians and staff. My responsibilities also include overseeing cash control and balancing receipts. Because UCLA has a number of VIP clients I often have to coordinate scheduling. And, of course, I often take on special tasks that I am asked to do by the director. Recently, due to the implementation of a new Epic electronic health record (EHR) system, a good majority of my responsibilities have been focused around supporting this transition. Some of the projects I have assisted in include, but are not limited to, the redesign of both clinical and administrative employee positions, assessment of both paper and electronic workflows to determine what should remain on paper and what should be converted to an electronic workflow, assisting physicians with template and smart phrase builds, providing elbow support to both administrative and clinical office staff, and working

(continued)

DANIEL NIMOY   (*continued*)

with physicians to enhance their scheduling templates utilizing a new scheduling system across the board. Many of these projects brought about their very own challenges and obstacles. Dealing with these challenges provided me with an invaluable opportunity and gave me the chance to walk away with some tremendous experience in both IT systems as well as systematic problem-solving skills. Working with my director on these projects, who has a strong IT background, provided me with a strong foundation to build off of as I continually pursue growth within my career.

What education or training do you have? Is it typical for your job? I completed my Master of Science in Health Administration (MSHA) in May 2014. Typically individuals in my position do not possess the same educational and professional training. I have been lucky to get this job while I was still in school, and that is a big advantage as I move forward in my career.

What path did you take to get to the job you are in today? I started as an intern with the UCLA Health System in 2011 (my first semester in graduate school). In late 2011 I was hired as an administrative assistant in a primary care physician office within UCLA. I was promoted to Office Supervisor in late 2012. I have recently been offered a managerial position in the Dermatology Division. However, I have accepted an administrative fellowship with Sharp Healthcare in San Diego and will begin that adventure in July 2014.

Where might you go from here if you wanted to advance your career? In order to advance my career, the new administrative fellowship will help me to explore new management opportunities, perhaps in health information technology or other opportunities.

What is the most challenging part of your job? Because of the nature of working in a busy clinical department, the most challenging part of my job is handling the miscellaneous requests that come in on a daily basis. Whether from physicians or staff, these requests continually keep me on my toes.

(*continued*)

DANIEL NIMOY *(continued)*

What is the best part? The best part of my job would have to be the amount of responsibilities and opportunities I have been provided by both my director and physicians. These opportunities have been one of a kind and have been critical in helping me to get to the point in my career where I am today.

What advice would you give to someone contemplating a career like yours? The biggest piece of advice I can offer to someone contemplating a career like mine would have to be "Experience, Experience, and Experience." Big or small, any experience is truly helpful in promoting both professional and self-development. I have truly learned along the way, there is something to be learned from every situation you are faced with and the responsibilities which are assigned to you. No job is too small! In addition, put yourself out there and promote your abilities. Let senior management and [your] director know what you would like to accomplish and what your goals and aspirations are for your career. Let them know you are open to all possible learning opportunities, both big and small. Last but not least, one of the biggest things I have learned in my young career thus far has been that a "closed mouth never gets fed." Speak up; you may be surprised what opportunities are offered to you and fall your way.

5. Data Analyst

POSITION DESCRIPTION Entry-level position, under close supervision will assist the organization in making strategic decisions by analyzing, manipulating, and tracking internal and external reporting data. This position functions both as analyst and statistical analytics programmer.

Essential functions:

■ Designs and enhances databases
■ Develops reports with accurate, useful information
■ Provides tracking and monitoring tools
■ Designs menu systems that are user friendly working with labor/management

- Participates in the development of outcomes and process measures, to enable population measures, guideline implementation, and data evaluation
- Maintains multifaceted statistical routines using macros, vendor software, and software written by others and self
- Constantly tests and monitors for improper access of data

EDUCATION AND EXPERIENCE   Bachelor of Arts degree in economics, finance, health care administration, public health administration, statistics, mathematics, operations research, or related field required, or equivalent experience.

CREDENTIALS, LICENSURE, OR CERTIFICATION, IF APPROPRIATE   Typically for this practical position there are specific additional credentials or certifications.

CORE COMPETENCIES AND SKILLS
- Microsoft Office skills required
- Work under minimal supervision
- Critical thinking skills, writing skills, communication skills, consulting skills, and ability to apply analytical skills
- Ability to work well with management and colleagues
- Project management experience desirable but not required
- Experience with analytical interpretation and manipulation of large databases
- Analytical consulting experience preferred
- At least 1 year of programming experience in SAS, SQL, VBA, or equivalent analytical programming language

COMPENSATION   Salaries range from $42,500 to $55,000.

WORKPLACE LOCATION   Normally this position can be found in a medical center, hospital, or large medical group.

FOR MORE INFORMATION
- www.onetonline.org
- www.bls.gov/ooh/computer-and-information-technology/home.htm

6. Analytics Manager

POSITION DESCRIPTION   An analytics manager must have experience and background in medicine, actuarial analysis, and finance. The role of an analytics manager is to manage analytics and reporting of financial information. The analytics manager assists in keeping the costs down. She or he helps clients understand treatments, costs, disease processes, payer systems, and health care reform. The position takes the lead to support of quality improvement analytics and reporting. Knowledge of data, definitions, validation, extraction, transformation, and integration required. In addition, the following are other job responsibilities:

- Act as a project team manager
- Report to the health analytics director
- Collaborate with health care managers and other departments to meet the goal
- Review claims data
- Ensure accuracy and integrity of databases
- Monthly accruals
- Be able to communicate and work with employees in a team environment
- Supervise employees and provide leadership
- Be able to work extended hours on occasions when required

EDUCATION AND EXPERIENCE Bachelor of Arts degree in finance, economics, accounting, health care management, or statistics required. Master's degree preferred. Seven to 10 years of analytical experience in a health care setting required.

CREDENTIALS, LICENSURE, OR CERTIFICATION, IF APPROPRIATE Certified health data analyst.

CORE COMPETENCIES AND SKILLS
- Communication skills: written, presentation, and oral skills required
- Interpersonal skills
- Excellent analytical skills
- Understanding of managed care
- Management ability
- Experience with health plans and analytics
- Excellence with Microsoft software and other big data software
- Ability to take general direction and make judgment calls
- Detail oriented
- Innovative thinker
- Cultural competence

COMPENSATION   Salaries range from $90,000 to $100,000.

WORKPLACE LOCATION   Normally this job is located within the IT department of a large organization.

EMPLOYMENT OUTLOOK   According to the U.S. Bureau of Labor Statistics, employment of operation research analysts will increase rapidly and job growth will occur as technology advances. Demand for efficiency in the health care field continues to grow (www.bls.gov/ooh/computer-and-information-technology/home.htm).

FOR MORE INFORMATION
- www.floridatechonline.com/online-degree-resources/health-analytics-director-careers
- jobview.monster.com

7. Information Technology Business Analyst (General Description)

Business analysis is the preparation of enabling change in an organizational context by clarifying the needs and by recommending solutions to stakeholders, which will mean value to them. There are many tasks and techniques available to have a successful outcome. What business analysts do is simple: They manage and they change an organization or business. These tech experts keep all the companies and organizations caught up with the latest technologies and improve efficiency and production, meaning introducing the organizations to better programs and guiding them on how to implement these changes. Their main duty is to make sure that everything related to the projects is or will be achieved and the stakeholders are satisfied. Business analysts lead the organization from the starting line to the finish line; step-by-step leadership is necessary to ensure that the project gets to the desired destination to succeed. These analysts take leadership, define and set goals, form a strategy, identify and resolve issues, and work with all levels of the organization and with stakeholders. The most important fact is that they work with and manage technology. The best qualities for an analyst are being able to make decisions based on what will be most beneficial; therefore, they must have great leadership skills. It is extremely important to know not only basic math but also advanced math, as well as have a great amount of knowledge in using the computer and its software. In addition, it is necessary to know how to manage not only a small team, group, or organization, but also a big one. Finally, an IT business analyst must be able to remain calm and collected in a busy environment. The following two job descriptions are typical of such positions that would be found in a hospital setting.

8. Information Technology Business Analyst (Example #1)

POSITION DESCRIPTION   The Business Solutions Center (BSC) is an IT Business Analysis Center of Excellence. The BSC business analyst has broad responsibility for supporting the strategic objectives of the hospital's business units (e.g., EHR–Revenue Services, Finance, Human Resources, Billing, and other administrative functions). The BSC business analyst works with key customers (both business and technology) and focuses on business analysis activities throughout the solution's life cycle. Typical tasks may include strategic planning, project planning and initiation, process flow analysis, testing, benefits realization calculation, and solution deactivation. The BSC business analyst has a strong understanding of technology and can apply it to a range of small to large complex business operational solutions that enable the organization to achieve its goals.

EDUCATION AND EXPERIENCE   Minimum requirement is a bachelor's degree in information systems or business administration, or equivalent work experience in the IT industry.

CREDENTIALS, LICENSURE, OR CERTIFICATION, IF APPROPRIATE   Preferred/ desired: Certified Business Analyst Professional (CBAP) or Project Management Institute (PMI) certification.

CORE COMPETENCIES AND SKILLS   Strong analytical and product management skills are required, including a thorough understanding of how to interpret customer business needs and translate them into application and operational requirements. This includes technical requirement gathering, specification development, data mapping, systems testing, and/or writing technical user documentation.

- Assist business customers in prioritizing business requests and challenges. High comfort level in developing strategies in partnership with business customers.
- Ability to understand highly complex technology projects and concepts as they relate to high-level business objectives, and

ability to present those concepts to both IT and non-IT audiences in a concise and easily understandable manner.

■ Proven ability to drive complex conceptual and technical discussions and system requirements. This includes the ability to generate innovative ideas to resolve problems.

■ Ability to perform complex analytical research and problem solving for business-critical issues.

■ Proven abilities in problem management, process analysis, and root-cause analysis.

■ Excellent verbal and written communication skills and the ability to interact professionally with a diverse group of executives, managers, and subject-matter experts.

■ Work with minimal guidance; seek guidance only on complex tasks.

■ Ability to handle multiple projects (including a mix of small to complex) at any given time, set priorities, schedule, and meet deadlines.

COMPENSATION   The range of salaries in the job category is from $46,000 to $60,000.

WORKPLACE LOCATION   You can find this job in a variety of health care organizations such as hospitals, large medical groups, and managed care organizations.

EMPLOYMENT OUTLOOK   The U.S. Bureau of Labor Statistics predicts that the field of HIT will continue to expand at an above-average rate between the present and 2020 (www.bls.gov/ooh/computer-and-information-technology/home.htm).

FOR MORE INFORMATION
   ■ jobmine.himss.org/home

9. Lead Business Analyst/Senior Business Analyst (Example #2)

POSITION DESCRIPTION   The business analyst must possess strong analytical skills that can enable him or her to interact with business clients, understand and analyze business processes, develop business cases, and finally meet functional requirements. This person is also responsible for providing client support during systems development and implementation, and development and maintenance of service-level agreements. The person will serve as a primary IT contact with business partners. This entails recognized business knowledge in analyzing and collaborating on new business opportunities and information technology solutions that enable the organization to achieve its goals. Works with other key project team members to define requirements, design the functional solution, identify and resolve project issues, and ensure the IT solutions meet the business needs and requirements.

Professional business analysts are responsible for improving a company's competitiveness and performance across a broad spectrum of criteria.

EDUCATION AND EXPERIENCE   Bachelor's degree in a related field and/or 4 years of equivalent work experience.

CREDENTIALS, LICENSURE, OR CERTIFICATION, IF APPROPRIATE   Proficiency with Microsoft Office (including Word, Excel, and PowerPoint) and Microsoft Visio.

The job requires a minimum of 8 years of experience in documenting functional requirements, analyzing business processes, and developing business cases to support IT solutions. SharePoint experience preferred.

CORE COMPETENCIES AND SKILLS
- Strong analytical skills; experience facilitating meetings with business teams and technical teams both
- Thorough knowledge of policies, practices, and systems
- Regular contributions to the development of new concepts, techniques, and standards
- Frequent contributions to the development of new theories and methods; employment of expertise as a generalist or specialist
- The business analyst must also possess strong interpersonal skills and proven leadership skills in working with diverse and complex projects; solid collaboration, facilitation, and negotiation skills; must be detail oriented and analytical with good organization skills
- Must have the ability to prioritize multiple activities and tasks simultaneously and adapt to a rapidly changing environment; strong problem and issue resolution experience
- Must possess good written and verbal communication skills and be able to communicate effectively with individuals at various levels within the organization

■ Must be highly motivated and be able to work independently with little supervision

COMPENSATION   The average business analyst makes about $62,889. The salary can range from $44,126 to $94,615 according to information found on www.payscale.com. Recent bachelor's graduates will usually start out toward the lower end of the range. The top salaries generally go to business analysts with extensive experience and advanced education.

WORKPLACE LOCATION   Because of the level of responsibilities for the senior or lead business analyst, these positions are generally found in large, complex medical centers.

EMPLOYMENT OUTLOOK   According to U.S. Bureau of Labor Statistics data, employment of management analysts—including business analysts—is expected to soar in coming years. Job growth will occur as industry and government continue to demand the expertise of these professionals to improve performance. With this profession's high earnings potential, competition for jobs should be strong. Business analysts with specialized experience or an advanced degree are likely to enjoy the best career prospects.

FOR MORE INFORMATION
■ www.bls.gov/ooh/computer-and-information-technology/home.htm
■ www.onetonline.org

10. Information Security Analyst (General Description)

As the years go by nothing is as secure as it once used to be. With the dramatic increase in cyber-attacks and hackers, information security analysts are now in great demand. An information security analyst holds the responsibility of protecting all health care organizations' computer networks. These analysts assist in the implementation of new software and ensure conformity to the policies to protect the data of a company. Information security analysts are employed in a wide range of different sectors and departments of the health care industry. A bachelor's degree in computer science or computer engineering is required. The salary of an information security analyst ranges from $77,000 to $84,000. These analysts must be constantly up to date with the newest and latest software so that they can be able to detect any questionable doings and combat attacks on an organization's computer networks. Information security analysts also must obtain systems analysis skills in examining computer network and security features to obtain as much knowledge as possible. Information security analysts must be ready for anything that may occur on or outside the job site and be able to indicate the problems effectively and respond with preventive procedures. These analysts are individuals who are always prepared with plans for emergency use. They must obtain leadership skills if they ever need to train staff members on security procedures. Someone who is an information security analyst has to be honest and loyal at all times to the company he or she is working for. These analysts need to have operational monitoring skills and be alert at all times. They must have social perceptiveness skills and be able to recognize any unusual actions that may be taking place. They are required to keep up with trends and the different tactics used by hackers nowadays in hopes of being able to quickly identify something improper that may possibly be happening. As hackers develop new methods and ways to invade the public's privacy, it's the information security analyst's job to prevent this invasion from occurring. An information security analyst must have a high level of trust and must ensure our health care organizations that the public health is kept secure with the highest level of confidence.

Information security professionals are responsible for keeping all technology in the company secure from cyber-attacks that may try to breach private information or gain control of the internal system. They must be able to evaluate, develop, and implement security standards/procedures. They assist customers in handling security risks to their applications and let them know the appropriate data procedures. They should have strong data analysis skills and be able to utilize Excel, SQL, and MS Access. Information security should have excellent verbal and written skills along with some experience in technology or information systems.

Data security professionals are responsible for the protection of information on various computers. This is a challenging occupation, so they should be able to handle difficult situations and work quickly. They have to be responsible for the physical security of system assets of the business. They should have knowledge in computer software, hardware components, and media devices, and possess basic computer skills. Also, they must have a bachelor's degree along with experience in working as a data security analyst; having a certificate is also a plus. The following three job descriptions are typical of security positions found in hospitals.

11. Information Security Analyst (Example #1)

POSITION DESCRIPTION   The increase in cyber attackers and hackers has led to great demand for information security analysts. Organizations are looking for someone who is honest at all times. The position requires someone who understands firewall systems, prevention systems, data loss prevention, and software development. A successful candidate must be alert and aware of his or her surroundings at all times. Job duties include being able to manage and implement security measures to protect computer systems, data, and information. The position requires someone who would be able to train staff on network and security procedures. Information security analysts work for a variety of different health care organizations.

EDUCATION AND EXPERIENCE   Bachelor's degree in computer science, programming, engineering, or a related field.

Minimum of 3 years of work experience within a related field. A master's in business administration in information systems is preferred. Experience as an information manager or information officer is beneficial.

CREDENTIALS, LICENSURE, OR CERTIFICATION, IF APPROPRIATE   Certification for Information Systems Security Professional or Information Security Manager, Global Information Assurance Certification, or Certified Firewall Analyst status is required. Vendor credentials offered by companies such as Microsoft and Cisco would be an advantage.

CORE COMPETENCIES AND SKILLS
- Systems analysis
- Time management
- Leadership skills
- Operation monitoring
- Communication skills
- Social perceptiveness
- Responsibility
- Reasoning ability

COMPENSATION   Information security analysts earn an annual wage that ranges from $77,000 to $84,000 and can ultimately increase with experience and promotion.

WORKPLACE LOCATION   Information security analysts can be positioned in any organization, in the finance department and information technology.

EMPLOYMENT OUTLOOK According to the BLS, an increase of 22% is set to happen within the years 2010 to 2020 nationwide in this field, which is higher than the health care average of 14%. An employment increase of 65,700 is expected to occur from 2010 to 2020. With the growth of cyber-attacks, information security analysts will be mandated to protect the information technology aspect of health care facilities.

FOR MORE INFORMATION
Job positions:
   ■ www.careerbuilder.com/Jobs/Keyword/Information-Security-Analyst
Education programs in this field:
   ■ www.isc2.org/CISSP/Default.aspx
Professional organization in this field:
   ■ www.sarma.org

12. Information Security Analyst (Example #2)

POSITION DESCRIPTION Completes tasks designed to ensure security of the organization's systems and information assets. Protects against unauthorized access, modification, or destruction of data and information. Works with end users to determine needs of individual departments, implements policies or procedures, and tracks compliance through the organization. Has knowledge of commonly used concepts, practices, and procedures within a particular field. Relies on instructions and preestablished guidelines to perform the functions of the job. Works under immediate supervision. Typically reports to a supervisor or manager.

EDUCATION AND EXPERIENCE Requires a bachelor's degree in a related area with at least 1 to 3 years of experience in the field.

CORE COMPETENCIES AND SKILLS Must have skills in systems administration, network security, problem solving, and be able to understand network protocols, routers, hubs, and switches. Must have good written or oral communication skills.

COMPENSATION Salaries can vary for entry-level positions from $44,000 to a high end with experience to $69,000.

WORKPLACE LOCATION An information security analyst will be working in an administration department in a health care facility.

EMPLOYMENT OUTLOOK   The BLS estimates that the number of working health information technicians will grow 21% from 2010 to 2020. Students pursuing a bachelor's degree may find excellent job prospects as medical or health services managers as well; the number of professionals in that field is expected to increase 22% from 2010 to 2020.

FOR MORE INFORMATION
- www.salary.com
- www.techexams.net
- www.careerbuilder.com
- www.monster.com
- www.indeed.com

13. Data Security (Example #3)

POSITION DESCRIPTION   Data security assists in planning and executing the protection of information available on computers and networks. These professionals ensure that the information available by the company is not misused or illegally transmitted to any unauthorized agencies or persons. Data security must be able to:

- Assist in the operational aspects of the internal data security of the organization
- Install and maintain security software programs
- Train and instruct computer users on the security norms
- Ensure no information is illegally transmitted
- Assist the cyber forensic experts in case of a breach in security
- Assist in educating staff members about security protocols

EDUCATION AND EXPERIENCE   Must have a bachelor's degree in management information systems (MIS). Master's degree is preferred. A minimum of 5 years experience in computer programming or equivalent is recommended. A minimum of 2 years in systems design and a minimum of 2 years of experience in data security systems, including systems programming.

CREDENTIALS, LICENSURE, OR CERTIFICATION, IF APPROPRIATE   No additional credentials or certification is required for this position, but individual employers may have different requirements.

CORE COMPETENCIES AND SKILLS   Have experience with Oracle and MySQL database technologies. Experience in health care or any clinical environment and an understanding of the HIPAA.

COMPENSATION   Salary can range from $89,000 to $115,000.

WORKPLACE LOCATION   A data security professional will be working in an administration department in a health care facility.

EMPLOYMENT OUTLOOK   This field has increased 35% since 2011. Health care, financial services, technology firms, and government are extensively hiring data security professionals to defend their databases.

FOR MORE INFORMATION
- www.techexams.net
- www.careerbuilder.com
- www.monster.com
- www.indeed.com

14. Senior Positions in Information Security

In the field of security and privacy there are senior management positions that oversee the organization's systems for protecting corporate information as well as patient data. The following are two typical senior-level security positions in hospitals.

15. Chief Information Security Officer (Example #1)

POSITION DESCRIPTION   The chief information security officer (CISO) will direct staff in protecting the organization's information assets by identifying, developing, implementing, and managing programs and processes. Aside from assessing and reducing IT risks, the CISO will also be in charge of responding to and managing incidents, training employees about security awareness, and establishing standards and policies regarding IT, as well as other responsibilities.

EDUCATION AND EXPERIENCE   Bachelor's degree is required, preferably in information assurance, technology, risk management, business, or a related field. Master's degree is preferred.

CREDENTIALS, LICENSURE, OR CERTIFICATION, IF APPROPRIATE
Certification—preferably as a certified information systems security professional (CISSP), certified information security manager (CISM), or certified information systems auditor (CISA)—is desired but not required.

CORE COMPETENCIES AND SKILLS   Must have strong interpersonal and communication skills and be able to work with diverse groups of people. Must also be technically astute and knowledgeable. Minimum 1 to 2 years of experience required in management, and at least 5 to 7 years of experience working in IT environments or security-related positions, preferably in health care.

COMPENSATION   Salary is approximately $100,000 to $115,000 per year.

WORKPLACE LOCATION   Normally this job is located within the IT department of a large organization.

EMPLOYMENT OUTLOOK   According to the BLS, the job growth rate for computer and information systems managers will be about 18% from 2010 to 2020.

FOR MORE INFORMATION
   ■ www.bls.gov/ooh/management/computer-and-information-systems-managers.htm
   ■ jobmine.himss.org/home/index.cfm?site_id=5817

16. Chief Information Security Officer (Example #2)

POSITION DESCRIPTION   A CISO is an executive who is responsible for safeguarding data held by a company or organization. Working with business managers, chief executive officers, and IT managers, CISOs observe and monitor the security of websites, applications, computers, and databases. They may establish company-wide security protocols that require user identification and passwords to protect networks from hackers. CISOs must keep current on antivirus software, firewalls, and other security systems. They develop emergency procedures for handling security breaches, manage internal communication regarding systems updates, and provide estimates of budgetary requirements for technical upgrades.

EDUCATION AND EXPERIENCE   To start on the path to becoming a CISO, interested IT professionals could pursue a bachelor's degree in a related field, such as computer science, business administration, or information science and security. Students may take relevant classes, such as programming languages, database management, technical writing, and calculus. In order to hone the business management skills required of this position, candidates would benefit from a master's degree program in business administration (MBA) with a specialization in information security management. Aspiring CISOs enrolled in such an interdisciplinary MBA program can study marketing, accounting, and finance, as well as web analytics and computer systems security.

CREDENTIALS, LICENSURE, OR CERTIFICATION, IF APPROPRIATE The BLS recommends voluntary certification as an additional means of demonstrating technical proficiency. Though not required by all employers, CISOs may obtain product certifications directly from vendors, such as Cisco's certified network associate security designation. Additionally, professional certifications for information security professionals are available through the International Information Systems Security Certification Consortium and the Global Information Assurance Certification.

CORE COMPETENCIES AND SKILLS Many CISOs work their way up from IT positions after acquiring several years of experience in systems security and demonstrating managerial skills. In addition to on-the-job experience, the BLS reports that IT management positions typically require at least a 4-year degree (www.bls.gov).

COMPENSATION The median expected salary for a typical CISO is $166,316.

WORKPLACE LOCATION CISOs may work mainly in hospitals because, with the extensive information they have, they are capable of managing a facility with a high volume of patients. But they can work where they desire, although the probability of being most successful and having a chance of advancement would be in a large facility.

EMPLOYMENT OUTLOOK The Patient Protection and Affordable Care Act has been passed and more people will have access to health care. Health care is expanding and more patients will need to be protected. When entering a health care facility a patient's safety is our number 1 priority. Also, with electronic medical records (EMR) emerging we need to make sure that third parties can't get access to patients' files. Having top security will increase our patients' privacy according to HIPAA laws. Health care is one of the largest employers in the United States, which is another reason to have better security. According to the BLS, employment for chief executives, including CISOs, in health care will grow steadily in coming years. Growth will occur as business technology needs become more complex in a global environment. Competition for these high-level positions will be keen; those with specialized knowledge, experience, and advanced degrees should have the best job prospects.

FOR MORE INFORMATION
- www.onetonline.org
- jobmine.himss.org

17. Clinical Integration Analyst

POSITION DESCRIPTION   A clinical integration analyst will have to collect data and interpret, analyze, test, and validate information based on clinical outcomes. The successful candidate must be able to have a working relationship and work as part of a team with the hospital aspect of the organization along with the technology leaders. The clinical integration analyst candidate must possess project management skills. The analyst must analyze the data and use it in all aspects of the business such as medical cost management, operational reporting, and general financial analysis. The analyst must also have full understanding of IT projects and concepts and must be able to present those concepts to those with IT and non-IT backgrounds.

EDUCATION AND EXPERIENCE   Bachelor's degree or equivalent professional experience required (a master's is preferred). Five years or more in business systems design and analysis in the health care setting is required.

CREDENTIALS, LICENSURE, OR CERTIFICATION, IF APPROPRIATE   If working in the nursing department, must possess a Registered Nurse license.

CORE COMPETENCIES AND SKILLS   The clinical integration analyst must have organizational skills to be able to carry out the project management duties. To work well with the departments involved, the analyst must be able to work as part of a team. Strong analytical skills are required for making difficult financial decisions for the business. Other requirements include software, database, and computer application skills.

COMPENSATION   About $70,000.

WORKPLACE LOCATION   Normally this job is located within the IT department of a large health care organization.

EMPLOYMENT OUTLOOK Employment is expected to grow because the greater reliance on computer systems in organizations throughout the economy will lead to an increase in demand for this occupation.

FOR MORE INFORMATION
- careerassist.ahima.org/jobseeker/search/results
- onchitjobs.himss.org
- jobmine.himss.org/jobseeker/search/results

18. Clinical Systems Analyst

POSITION DESCRIPTION Clinical systems analysts are involved in the installation and development of hospital computer information programs. Their job is to perform systems upgrades and provide systems maintenance whenever necessary. Professionals in this field must have advanced software knowledge and the ability to supervise staff and maintain hospital information confidentiality. Clinical systems analysts may participate in developing policies and creating training tools for hospital information systems users.

EDUCATION AND EXPERIENCE Bachelor's degree from an accredited institution is usually required for a clinical systems analyst. Students should major in areas such as information management, computer science, or health care administration. According to the BLS, you might have a professional advantage in this field by earning a relevant master's degree, such as an MBA with a concentration in management information systems. This could also help you if you already hold a position in the field and wish to advance.

CREDENTIALS, LICENSURE, OR CERTIFICATION, IF APPROPRIATE There is no need for certification; the only requirement is a bachelor's degree in a related field such as computer information or health care information technology.

CORE COMPETENCIES AND SKILLS
- A broad knowledge of hardware, software, and programming
- A creative approach to problem solving
- The ability to gather and interpret information
- Excellent communication skills
- The ability to explain ideas clearly to technical and nontechnical colleagues and clients
- Good negotiating skills

- Good team working skills
- The ability to work under pressure and meet deadlines
- The ability to plan and manage a project
- A sound appreciation of wider business demands
- The ability to work to a budget
- A willingness to keep up to date with developments in technology.

COMPENSATION   The clinical systems analyst's average salary is $60,986 and the median salary is $54,080, with a salary range from $42,224 to $87,500.

WORKPLACE LOCATION   A clinical systems analyst has a great advantage because with the new EHRs and the *International Classification of Diseases, 10th revision (ICD-10)* implementation, he or she can work virtually in any place desired. But, focusing on a specific department, this can range from a hospital to a large medical practice.

EMPLOYMENT OUTLOOK   In 2011, the BLS stated that employment of clinical systems analysts was projected to increase 20% from 2008 to 2018. This is much faster than the national average for all occupations.

FOR MORE INFORMATION
- www.bls.gov/home.htm
- education-portal.com/articles/Clinical_Systems_Analyst_Job_ Description_Duties_and_Requirements.html
- degreedirectory.org/articles/What_Does_a_Systems_Analyst_ Do.html

19. Senior Clinical Informatics Specialist

POSITION DESCRIPTION   The senior clinical informatics specialist (senior CIS) serves as a nursing/clinical informatics expert, supporting all clinical staff roles throughout the care continuum in the specialty of clinical informatics. The senior CIS applies advanced education and experience to effectively address complex clinical-technical challenges in diverse health care delivery environments. The senior CIS plans, coordinates, and monitors the analysis, design, implementation, evaluation, and maintenance of clinical informatics applications and projects within the assigned area. He or she promotes the use of evidence-based clinical practice by establishing and leading clinical informatics councils such as clinical practice transformation and performance improvement councils. The senior CIS advises operational leaders in the selection, implementation, and adoption of clinical technology to support optimal clinical effectiveness and efficiency. The senior CIS coordinates and provides direct support and education to clinicians (physicians, nurses, and other interdisciplinary team members) in their use of health systems technology, including the EHR, and is responsible for ongoing training and competency validation for all clinical information systems as directed. He or she incorporates theories, principles, and concepts from appropriate sciences into informatics practice. (Examples of such theories could include nursing, information, systems, and change theories. Principles and concepts could include project management, implementation methods, organizational culture, and database structures.) The senior CIS integrates ergonomics and human–computer interaction principles into informatics solution design, development, selection, implementation, and evaluation, and systematically determines the social, legal, and ethical impact of an informatics solution within health care. The senior CIS with licensure in a clinical discipline (nursing, respiratory therapy, etc.) brings required comprehensive understanding of that nursing/clinical process and of practice standards, patient flow and operational processes, and clinical informatics systems.

It must be noted that this is a position description for a senior-level clinical informatics specialist and that there are entry-level and junior-level positions with similar responsibilities but less demanding management duties.

Examples of other expectations of a clinical informatics specialist include:

- Develops curriculum for clinical information and communication systems and provides education for current and new customers.
- Coaches, mentors, and provides one-on-one, at-the-elbow support for members of the clinical team in gaining and maintaining competency in use of clinical information and communication systems.
- Provides a learning experience tailored to the learner's individual needs, including, but not limited to, flexibility with time, location, and content.
- Assesses and addresses educational needs related to clinician/ provider use of clinical information systems.
- Leads implementation of procedures and innovative solutions to improve efficient, reliable use of the clinical information systems.

■ Provides recommendations on procedures and innovative solutions to improve efficient, reliable use of the clinical information systems.

EDUCATION AND EXPERIENCE   Bachelor's degree in a clinical discipline or an information technology/informatics, business, management, or related field is required. Bachelor's degree in a clinical discipline such as nursing, medical technology, respiratory therapy, clinical dietetics, rehabilitation therapies, or pharmacy is preferred. Minimum of 5 years of experience in a position that had the same or similar primary duties working with a clinical information system within a health care setting required. Master's degree in education, information technology, business, or health administration, or a clinical discipline such as nursing or other health care field is preferred. Hospital clinical experience or experience working with physicians and other clinical practitioners is required.

CREDENTIALS, LICENSURE, OR CERTIFICATION, IF APPROPRIATE   Informatics certification or credentialing is preferred, and may be equivalent for up to 2 years experience for this position at the hiring manager's discretion.

CORE COMPETENCIES AND SKILLS
■ Demonstrated ability to be self-directed and collaborative, to escalate appropriately, to communicate clearly, and to learn quickly, with strong attention to detail
■ Excellent verbal and written communication skills, both interpersonally and on a technical level
■ Good critical thinking skills used toward analyzing, testing, troubleshooting, and isolating complex problems
■ Education or experience in the area of adult learning and/or informatics
■ Ability to develop and perform competency assessments related to clinician use of information systems, document findings, design and deliver targeted training and remediation as necessary, and evaluate effectiveness of interventions
■ Can synthesize data, information, and knowledge to clarify informatics issues or problems
■ Can analyze multiple approaches/solutions to the informatics issue or problem

- Experience in identifying, analyzing, prioritizing, redesigning, testing, and implementing improvements to existing clinical information systems
- Experience leading root cause analysis efforts related to clinical information systems
- Developed methods, techniques, and evaluation criteria for obtaining clinical information systems performance improvement results
- Demonstrated ability to establish and maintain effective relationships with health care team members
- Demonstrated willingness to respond to and assist clinical customers immediately upon request and follow up on previous interactions to ensure the issue has been resolved

COMPENSATION   This new and evolving informatics position has a salary range from $50,000 for entry level to $115,000 for senior positions depending on the size and location of the health care organization.

WORKPLACE LOCATION   The position would be located in the IT area of a health care facility, but has multiple reporting connections with clinical areas like nursing as well as the chief information officer. The person in the position operates as a member of multiple teams when involved in selection, implementation, and training associated with new and existing health information technology (HIT) clinical systems.

A similar job description could be created for a clinical informaticist, whose clinical domain or base area of expertise is pharmacy, medical, radiology, or other clinical field. Informaticists also work in the field of medical records, and there is a growing interest in public health informatics.

FOR MORE INFORMATION
- jobmine.himss.org
- healthinformaticssalary.org/1/1/salary/Health-Informatics-Salary
- www.salary.com
- healthcareers.about.com/od/nursingcareers/p/Nursing-Informatics-Careers-For-Nurse-Informaticists.htm

CARRIE ROBERTS
Executive Director, Clinical
Information Systems (CIS)
Hoag Hospital

Describe the sort of work you do. I lead the Clinical Information Systems (CSI) and Meaningful Use programs and projects designed to optimize clinical systems, increase safety/quality through IT enablement, and ensure we are using IT systems in a way that is meaningful to our community. These programs include many subprojects such as the rollout of computerized physician order entry and nursing use of bedside bar coding to improve accuracy of medication administration.

I also lead the Clinical Adoption team, which is made up primarily of nurses and other clinicians. This team is responsible for redesigning clinical workflows using Lean methodology and applies technology as appropriate.

Finally, I lead the Training and Client Relations team. This team is accountable for communicating with our business partners throughout Hoag to ensure IT is providing high-quality service to all departments, moving key projects/initiatives forward, and communicating key messages from the IT department.

I am a member of the IT leadership team, so I participate in decision making and IT strategy with my peers. I am a member of the Hoag director team and contribute to overall organizational leadership.

What is a typical day like at your job? *Rounding:* I set aside 90 minutes each day to "round" and speak to my team members and managers. I have five managers reporting to me who each have large teams and major responsibilities. Spending time with them each day allows me to help problem solve and clear issues so they can accomplish their objectives and move things forward. Rounding helps me stay in touch with what is going on in my teams and makes me more accessible to all team members.

(continued)

CARRIE ROBERTS (*continued*)

Meetings: I also spend time in meetings with my peers and other Hoag leaders daily, where we make key decisions and collaborate. I often give presentations related to our programs to groups of up to 150 people, so public speaking is a key component of my role. My teams lead some of our IT governance meetings, so I always participate and contribute.

The rest of my time is spent planning, responding to e-mail, and finishing deliverables like spreadsheets and presentations.

What education or training do you have? Is it typical for your job? I have a BS in Nutrition. I started in health care as a diet technician with the goal of becoming a dietician. There are many different educational backgrounds in IT today. Degrees in IT or Informatics were limited 20 or even 10 years ago. Now you see new hires entering the workforce with more emphasis on IT than before. Many of us in health care IT have some sort of health care background or experience.

What path did you take to get to the job you are in today? Right before I started my required dietician internship I was asked to participate in a project to install Meditech at a local hospital. I was involved for about 6 months and found I really liked the opportunities that existed in IT. I took what felt like a step down and transferred to IT to work on the help desk, where I learned a lot about how hospital departments use IT services. Then the hospital I worked at outsourced their IT department to PerotSystems, who provided IT outsourcing services to many health care clients. I started working for PerotSystems and moved up to manage the help-desk and small application teams. I worked really hard at the beginning of my career and established myself as someone who could execute major tasks. Eventually I became a Client Executive responsible for managing the client relationships for PerotSystems and leading IT departments for local hospitals. The last few Client Executive responsibilities I had were with Tenet facilities that were being sold from Tenet and becoming independent hospitals. I helped them strategize on the applications and technology required to become independent and through PerotSystems could offer a bridge for these organizations to stay on

(*continued*)

91

CARRIE ROBERTS *(continued)*

some Tenet applications so they didn't have to immediately invest the capital required for their own clinical systems.

I started at Hoag Hospital 4 years ago as a director leading client relations and application support teams. I was promoted to executive director and now have more of a strategic project focus.

Where might you go from here if you wanted to advance your career? If I were to move on, one option would be to be a CIO at a health care organization less complex than Hoag.

What is the most challenging part of your job? There are lots of complexities to understand and deal with. Electronic medical record systems are complex, health care today is complex, and medicine is complex. Health care is changing at a rapid pace and keeping current with health care requirements is difficult.

Balance is also a challenge. I need to balance project workload and execution with employee satisfaction. On a personal note, I always do my best to balance my personal life and being a mother of three with my work responsibilities.

What is the best part? Accomplishing milestones and improvements that truly benefit our patients and community. Mentoring people and watching someone on my team really shine and grow in their own career.

What advice would you give to someone contemplating a career like yours? Part of my success has been through communication, specifically the ability to translate complex IT information to clinical and business people in a way that is easy to understand and is not intimidating. Learn to communicate and to really listen to people.

Get out of the IT department and into the rest of the hospital to really understand how health care works at the ground level. Provide great customer service. Always strive to deliver high-quality results within your deadlines. Sounds simple, but so many people struggle in this area.

Finally, do not hesitate to take an entry-level IT job such as help-desk or admin assistance. You can move up quickly if you really work hard.

20. Compliance Analyst

POSITION DESCRIPTION   A compliance analyst is responsible for working independently on assigned compliance work plan initiatives according to established audit techniques and parameters. Compliance analysts generally direct, plan, and monitor programs that their organization has in place to ensure that the practices, procedures, and policies being employed comply with federal, state, and county rules and regulations. Duties include, but are not limited to, performing facility and professional coding, process, and billing reviews and preparing reports for senior management; acting as subject-matter experts for coding and regulatory matters; and responding to all levels of health systems inquiries regarding coding, billing, and regulatory matters.

EDUCATION AND EXPERIENCE   Bachelor's degree in related field or equivalent experience.

CREDENTIALS, LICENSURE, OR CERTIFICATION, IF APPROPRIATE   Must possess and maintain certification as a coding specialist through the American Health Information Management Association or AAPC.

CORE COMPETENCIES AND SKILLS   Advanced experience with and knowledge of instructional notations and conventions of *International Classification of Diseases, 9th Revision, Clinical Modification (ICD-9-CM)*, current procedural terminology, health care common procedure coding system, ambulatory payment classification, and diagnosis-related group classification systems and ability to follow and interpret the detailed guidelines related to their use in assigning single and sequencing multiple diagnosis and procedure codes for appropriate reimbursements and data collection. Comprehensive knowledge of medical terminology with an advanced understanding of disease processes, anatomy, and physiology. Compliance analysts must have excellent research and investigative skills with a high degree of accuracy and attending to detail.

COMPENSATION   Starting salary is around $42,000, but with experience the salary could range in the $70,000s. The median salary is around $58,000.

WORKPLACE LOCATION   Due to the vast increase in government regulations for the health care industry, compliance staffs generally work in larger health care facilities and sometimes in large medical groups and managed care organizations.

EMPLOYMENT OUTLOOK   Career expectations for compliance analysts vary from state to state and employer to employer. Health care is currently offering the most opportunities for a career in this field due to the growth in federal and state regulations.

FOR MORE INFORMATION
- www.ehow.com/about_6327355_compliance-analyst_.html

21. Health Information Data Compliance Manager

POSITION DESCRIPTION   The health information data compliance manager's role includes management of teams, proposals, and procedures. The key member of the staff ensures city, state, and national documentation compliance including storage, safety, coding, and proper interdepartmental flow. The position is expected to be a constant resource to the medical director, group administrators, physicians, and providers. The manager will serve as a mediator on compliance issues and identify resolutions, areas of improvement, and feedback on audit outcomes. Other responsibilities will include recruiting and developing staff for appropriate functional areas, resolve human resource matters, and ensure employee and department safety. Collaboration with national personnel and locations is essential for streamlining future documentation compliance initiatives. The health information data compliance manager should proactively seek to understand and learn regulatory issues and current events, attend industry seminars, complete online training courses, and study appropriate literature.

EDUCATION AND EXPERIENCE
- Bachelor's degree from an accredited institution
  - Health care administration, business, IT, data management degrees preferred
- IT/data management experience ideal
- Proficiency in Microsoft Office, electronic medical record software

CREDENTIALS, LICENSURE, OR CERTIFICATION, IF APPROPRIATE
- Certification in Health Care Compliance is highly desired.
- Certification in one or more of the following: Certified Professional Coder (CPC), Registered Health Information Administrator (RHIA), Registered Health Information Technician (RHIT), Certified Coding Specialist (CCS), and Certified Coding Specialist–Physician (CCS–P).

CORE COMPETENCIES AND SKILLS
- Coding experience and certification required
- Medical facility experience desired
- Supervisor experience including team building, conflict resolution, group interaction, project management, and goal setting
- Experience using EMR systems

COMPENSATION $80,000 to $110,000 per year based on experience and qualifications.

WORKPLACE LOCATION IT department or in central administration.

EMPLOYMENT OUTLOOK A fast-growing area new to health care systems is the area of informatics, which has new career paths opening up due to the adoption of the electronic health record in 2014. This will lead to such positions as health information manager, health information data administrator, and health information data resources administrator. The health care industry is expected to generate 3 million jobs between 2006 and 2016 according to the BLS *Occupational Outlook Handbook 2008–2009*. The expected growth in jobs by 2018 for medical and health services managers is 16%. Jobs in the medical records and HIT sector are expected to grow by 20% by 2018.

FOR MORE INFORMATION
Job positions:
- www.careerbuilder.com/jobseeker/jobs/jobresults.aspx
- jobsearch.monster.com/search

Educational programs in this field:
- www.aupha.org/Careers

Professional organizations in this field:
- www.ahcap.org
- www.aaham.org
- careers.apha.org/post.cfm

22. Health Information Management (General Description)

The field of health information management (HIM) is a fast-growing and high-demand profession that concentrates on patient information and its collection, management, and analysis to support clinical decision making and administration functions such as billing and meeting regulatory requirements. The growth of EMR in both hospital and medical practice settings is driving the job growth in this field. The following two job descriptions are related to management positions that are typically found in hospitals.

23. Health Information Management Director (Example #1)

POSITION DESCRIPTION   The HIM director is responsible for overseeing day-to-day operations of the Health Information Management department and making sure that it abides by the HIM and hospital standards, including the standards set in place by The Joint Commission, California Department of Public Health, and other national and state standards. The HIM director is responsible for developing and assisting with the process of implementation and maintenance of HIM policies, and making sure they correspond with the federal and state standards set in place. The HIM director creates and monitors a process for receiving, documenting, tracking, investigating, and taking necessary action when it comes to all complaints that are filed against the organization's HIM policies and practices.

EDUCATION AND EXPERIENCE   Bachelor's degree in health care or health/business administration or related field. Master's degree in health information management is highly preferred. Minimum of 5 years of experience in a director or managerial role in an acute hospital care setting.

CREDENTIALS, LICENSURE, OR CERTIFICATION, IF APPROPRIATE   Certification as a RHIA, RHIT, or CCS required.

CORE COMPETENCIES AND SKILLS   Must demonstrate effective communication, interpersonal, and organizational skills. Also, must have experience with *ICD-9-CM* and *International Classification of Diseases, 10th Revision, Clinical Modification (ICD-10-CM)* coding. Additionally, must have comprehensive knowledge of the state and federal standards of HIM, including The Joint Commission on Accreditation of Healthcare Organizations (JCAHO) guidelines, the Health Insurance Portability and Accountability Act (HIPAA), and Title 22. Moreover, must be proficient with using Microsoft Office applications, including Word, Excel, PowerPoint, and Outlook.

COMPENSATION   Ranges from $45,000 to $90,000.

WORKPLACE LOCATION   Normally this position is found in a hospital setting in the medical records department.

EMPLOYMENT OUTLOOK   The future employment of HIM professionals is expected to increase by as much as 22% between the years of 2010 and 2020, which is considerably faster than other occupations. Due to the increase in the aging population and implementation of EHR more HIM professionals will be needed. As a matter of fact, according to the U.S. Department of Labor and Statistics, the field of HIT ranks as one of the 20 fastest-growing occupations in the United States.

FOR MORE INFORMATION
   ■ careerassist.ahima.org/jobseeker/search/results
   ■ www.ehow.com/careers/careers
   ■ www.healthcaresource.com

24. Health Information Management Director (Example #2)

POSITION DESCRIPTION   HIM directors have various responsibilities, including leading and directing the HIM services throughout the facility. Some of the duties include building and managing the team in order to support on-site client HIM and coding operations, as well as developing the service delivery strategy. HIM directors must ensure that coding of inpatient and outpatient records is accurately input according to the policies and procedures developed to improve and support the revenue cycle of the organization. The director of HIM provides direction to the hospital and physicians to ensure that coding activities, auditing, and education are being achieved correctly in order to avoid unbilled targets. As a result of the recent regulations presented by the federal government, all health care providers are now required to maintain electronic patient records that are secured. Due to this change, there is now a challenge for the health information managers to keep up with current computer and software programs and with legislative requirements; therefore, there is continuous accountability for an ongoing assessment and for improvement in the coordination of the coding department operations.

EDUCATION AND EXPERIENCE   Most organizations require candidates for the HIM director position to hold at least a bachelor's degree in business or health care administration, finance, information technology, medical records technology, or an equivalent degree. However, there is a preferred qualification for those who hold a master's degree in business administration of a health facility or hospital. In addition, 3 to 5 years of experience as a coding manager or HIM manager are beneficial.

CREDENTIALS, LICENSURE, OR CERTIFICATION, IF APPROPRIATE   RHIA or RHIT certification; must graduate from a Commission on Accreditation for Health Informatics and Information Management (CAHIIM) accredited program in order to take an exam.

In addition, a more advanced certification may include CCS, CCS-P, Certified in Healthcare Privacy and Security (CHPS), or Certified Health Data Analyst (CHDA) designation.

CORE COMPETENCIES AND SKILLS
- Besides experience with EHR and health information systems application, HIM directors must be able to demonstrate themselves as innovative and strategically focused leaders with strong team development and relation-building skills.
- Strong knowledge of HIPAA and JCAHO and other compliance requirements as well as the *ICD-9, ICD-10*, and CPT 4 coding classification systems may also be mandatory for the position depending on the organization.
- Highly skilled judgment will also be in demand when deciding on methods and techniques to solve various problems.
- Professional relationship with the state and national organizations to gain insights on future trends and regulations must be maintained.
- A solid understanding of the regulations and accreditation standards, as well as specific state and federal requirements related to the management of health information, is also a must.

COMPENSATION   According to a survey conducted by AHIMA in the year 2012, the average annual full-time HIM director salary across the national work setting was found to be $58,676, and salaries reached over $105,000.

WORKPLACE LOCATION   Although the name may vary depending on the hospital or organization, departments under the name of Health Information Management or Health Information Technology exist within the facility. HIM directors may be located in this particular department managing and directing the process of the HIM manager and staff operating the systems on the client's health information.

EMPLOYMENT OUTLOOK   According to the most recent BLS report, HIM jobs are projected to grow approximately 21% from 2010 to 2020. In addition, there is a better chance of those certified in a specialty area to benefit in these openings. The adoption of the EHR and the transition from *ICD-9* to *ICD-10* coding are part of the reason for the growth in HIM jobs today. Greater emphasis on reimbursement claims from the aging population and the enhancing technology to process patients are all contributing to increase the national demand for a qualified professional who can fill the HIM positions.

FOR MORE INFORMATION
- www.ahima.org
- careerassist.ahima.org/jobseeker/search/results
- www.ehow.com/careers/careers
- www.healthcaresource.com

25. Chief Technology Officer

POSITION DESCRIPTION   "The chief technology officer's role is to align technology vision with business strategy by integrating company processes with the appropriate technologies. The chief technology officer is also responsible for all aspects of developing, implementing and maintaining technology initiatives within the organization, assuring high performance, consistency, reliability and scalability of all technology offerings. This individual maintains existing enterprise systems, while providing direction in all technology-related issues in support of information operations and core company values."[1]

Duties of a chief technology officer (CTO) include:

- Leads strategic technological planning to achieve business goals by prioritizing technology initiatives and coordinating the evaluation, deployment, and management of current and future technologies.
- Collaborates with the appropriate departments and outside vendors to develop and maintain a technology plan that supports organizational needs.
- Develops/contributes to IT business plans and to staffing, budgeting, and process decisions that support both the long-term and the short-term objectives of the company.
- Develops and communicates business and technology alignment plans to executive team, staff, partners, customers, and stakeholders.

---

[1] www.himss.org/health-it-career-services/healthcare-technology-job-descriptions?navItem Number=17560

- Directs development and execution of an enterprise-wide disaster recovery and business continuity plan.
- Stays abreast of trends and regulations to ensure effectiveness and compliance.
- Provides thought leadership and representation in interoperability work groups, as they relate to the Office of the National Coordinator for Health Information Technology's standards and interoperability framework.
- Analyzes complex business needs presented by the user community and/or clients and recommends technical solutions.

EDUCATION AND EXPERIENCE   CTOs would be required to have a bachelor's degree in computer science and most likely some advanced management experience and/or an MBA or Master of Health Administration (MHA). In addition, most organizations require 10 to 15 years of experience managing or directing technological operations, with a proven ability to lead a progressive IT group to develop and implement IT programs on time and within budget; 10 years of experience working in the health care industry; and up to 10 years of experience in strategic technology planning, execution, and policy development.

CREDENTIALS, LICENSURE, OR CERTIFICATION, IF APPROPRIATE   No specific credential or certificate is required, but many have certification in specific vendor systems like Epic or Cerner. Some CTOs have a credential from HIMSS called Certified Professional in Healthcare Information and Management Systems (CPHIMS).[2]

CORE COMPETENCIES AND SKILLS
- Technical experience with systems networking, databases, web development, and user support
- Exposure to business theory, business processes, management, budgeting, and business office operations
- Excellent understanding of project management principles
- Proven experience in planning, organization, and development
- Superior understanding of the organization's goals and objectives
- Demonstrated ability to apply technology solutions to business problems

---

[2] www.himss.org/health-it-certification/cphims?navItemNumber=13647

- Demonstrated aptitude for learning new technologies and new program development
- In-depth knowledge of applicable laws and regulations as they relate to technology issues
- Extremely organized, highly motivated self-starter with excellent attention to detail
- Exceptional multitasking skills
- Ability to react to change productively
- Proven leadership ability
- Ability to set and manage priorities judiciously
- Excellent written and oral communication skills
- Excellent interpersonal skills
- Strong tactical skills
- Ability to articulate ideas to both technical and non-technical addressees
- Exceptionally self-motivated and directed
- Keen attention to detail
- Superior analytical, evaluative, and problem-solving abilities
- Exceptional service orientation
- Ability to motivate in a team-oriented, collaborative environment

COMPENSATION The range of compensation depends on the size and complexity of the health care organization. It is not uncommon to have salaries in the range of $150,000 to $250,000.

WORKPLACE LOCATION The CTO reports to the CIO and works in the IT department.

EMPLOYMENT OUTLOOK The job market for individuals looking to become a CTO is highly competitive. With consolidation and mergers in the health care industry there will be more system-wide CTOs and perhaps fewer single-hospital CTOs. An individual might envision a career path that evolves from a single hospital to a multihospital system to a very large system.

FOR MORE INFORMATION
- www.himss.org/health-it-career-services/ healthcare-technology-job-descriptions?navItemNumber=17560
- www.himss.org/health-it-certification/ cphims?navItemNumber=13647

TIMOTHY MOORE
Senior Vice President and Chief
Information Officer
Hoag Hospital

Describe the sort of work you do. As the SVP I put on my administrative hat and work with other senior management on strategic and operational issues that impact the hospital and our community. As the CIO I provide technical resources to accomplish the objectives and goals of the hospital's internal business partners. I work to match the demands for resources from areas of business like, for example, our cancer center or our breast center with available resources needed to accomplish their goals. It is always a demand and supply challenge for hospitals to provide the resources for lines of business with the shortage of resources health care organizations face in today's economy. The grounding point for Hoag is what will provide the best outcomes for our community. Return on investment is, of course, a consideration, but the prime motivation is to do what is right for our stakeholders.

What is a typical day like at your job? Each day is different, but there are some consistent patterns over time. I generally put in 10 to 12 hours per day, and that can include Saturday and Sunday if we are engaged in a major new IT implementation. Because my role is to match up the demands for IT resources with the available organizational ability, I am in meetings with our internal lines of business and also with our vendors. There are, of course, the occasional putting out fires, but I have a great staff and colleagues that support me in the process. Once a month I hold a required debriefing session with all of my staff. It is a great opportunity to share my vision and encourage a frank exchange of ideas and develop a sense of achieving common goals for our community.

(continued)

TIMOTHY MOORE *(continued)*

What education or training do you have? Is it typical for your job? When I was an accounting major in college I came to the realization that I was meant to do something else. I changed my major to nursing and it was a great decision. I gained a tremendous understanding of the health care delivery process and the challenges faced by providers. If I had to do it over I would probably seek an MBA or MHA to help provide that understanding of business processes and the health care industry as a whole. My background is neither common nor uncommon for a CIO. To reach my position a person can travel many paths, and it is the combination of experiences and an understanding of the health care industry that can prepare you for a senior position like a CIO. I don't have a computer science education background, but working on the delivery side and on the HIT vendor side of the market I understand how technology can meet the needs of the practitioner and achieve quality care for patients.

What path did you take to get to the job you are in today? I started out as a staff nurse. Because of a family illness, we moved to be close to a children's hospital, and it was here that I had an early opportunity to fill a 6-month position with an international research and development vendor company as a clinical trainer. Associated with my drive and passion to make the training program a success, I was provided numerous opportunities to grow, and often the success was rewarded with a promotion. That helped to set my path because it was fun and challenging and ultimately I learned a lot. Years later, a customer I had worked with called me and asked me to be a regional CIO for a national health care company, Carondelet Health System. A couple of years later I was promoted to the role of VP and Corporate CIO. Ultimately I did not want to move to the Midwest to further advance my career with them, and I accepted a position with a IT vendor, Perot Systems—first as an account chief operating officer, then as the client executive, and ultimately responsible for the largest business unit in the health care section responsible for greater than 80 hospitals and more than 2,000 staff members. I worked for Perot Systems for a number of years, and through my network of

(continued)

TIMOTHY MOORE   *(continued)*

professional connections I was provided an opportunity to move into my present position here at Hoag.

Where might you go from here if you wanted to advance your career? I love my current position and the organization. Hoag is a mid-size health care system of three hospitals, and if I were to advance in my career I might be interested in a larger system or even better expanded responsibility here, such as the chief operating officer. The challenges increase rapidly when one moves to a larger system; however, from past experience, these challenges are also highly rewarding.

What is the most challenging part of your job? Sometimes the job of a CIO is like a circus act. Trying to keep 16 balls in the air at once is typical for this position. There is that feeling late at night or on the weekend, did we do what we needed to do to achieve our business goals for the day?

What is the best part? It is exciting to know and feel that what we do makes a difference in a patient's life and the life of our community. Without that passion this would just be a very busy job, but seeing the difference you make is very rewarding.

What advice would you give to someone contemplating a career like yours? My advice for those seeking a career in HIT and perhaps eventually moving into senior management can be summarized as:

- ■ If you say you're are going to do sometime . . . do it.
- ■ Be sure to understand the business of health care.
- ■ Always seek to excel beyond the expectations of the assignment.
- ■ Technical background is not always required, but communication skills are critical: written, oral, and presentation skills.
- ■ Raise your hand when you can to volunteer for a new assignment and then deliver the task.

(continued)

TIMOTHY MOORE *(continued)*

- Personal integrity will show through and you can't hide excellence.
- Some technical fields require specialized certification, like project management.
- That first job might be as an administrative assistant or working on the help desk, but get "in the door" to learn where you fit best and show the organization what you can deliver. If you can't get a paid position right away, volunteering is a great way to start your career pathway.

26. Electronic Medical Records–Related Jobs

The following two positions are specific to EMR and coding functions and are under the direction of the management positions described previously. EMR positions are also commonly found in medical organizations. See Chapter 8.

27. Electronic Medical Records Application Coordinator (Example #1)

POSITION DESCRIPTION   The application coordinator functions as an expert to configure, build, and install the application. The application coordinator will perform in-depth and precise investigation and documentation of operational specifications and application functionality. Must have in-depth knowledge of the software application as well as understand the policies, procedures, and constraints of the clinical or business operation supported by the application. Must be able to develop and document internal procedures, collect information on and prepare specifications of systems enhancements, analyze functionality of new releases, and test each new release. The application coordinator also assists in the development of user training aids and may train end users in workflow and use of the application. The application coordinator functions as the primary contact to troubleshoot problems and answer questions from end users during stabilization periods.

EDUCATION AND EXPERIENCE   Bachelor's degree preferred, plus 1 to 3 years working experience in the area of EMR implementation.

CREDENTIALS, LICENSURE, OR CERTIFICATION, IF APPROPRIATE   EMR "application" positions usually require a specific credential associated with the HIT vendors, such as Epic certification, Cerner certification, or other vendors' products.

CORE COMPETENCIES AND SKILLS
- Project management skills, including the ability to manage a project plan, lead meetings, prioritize, and resolve conflicts
- Demonstrated knowledge of emergency department workflow and business process flow
- Prior experience with IT systems and systems development projects
- Demonstrated proficiency with information systems technology, including Microsoft Office Suite
- Demonstrated ability to influence and shape consensus, leading group discussions, and presenting in front of groups of clinical and business operation leaders from across the organization
- Ability to identify, research, document, resolve, and/or escalate issues and maintain a complete issues log

COMPENSATION   Salary ranges from $70,000 to $110,000 depending on degrees, certifications, and years of prior experience.

WORKPLACE LOCATION   Generally this position is found in a large medical center.

EMPLOYMENT OUTLOOK   In 2010 there were 179,500 jobs related to EMR. It is projected that by 2020 there will be a 21% increase in the job pool. With the current trends in technology, this is a large increase and a growing field.

FOR MORE INFORMATION
- www.ahima.org

28. Electronic Medical Records Technician (Example #2)

POSITION DESCRIPTION   Responsible for ensuring that all patient records and loose documents are placed and scanned into the electronic or paper patient folder with the highest level of quality possible. The position is to document, test, and support the EMR and picture archiving communication systems (PACS) and related systems, including interfaces with diagnostic equipment and EHR applications. This position supports the day-to-day operations to ensure reliability and stability of the EMR and PACS systems, which consists of many workstations involving thick-and-thin solutions and associated interfaces. Customized software has been developed and will need to be monitored to ensure proper connectivity. A major responsibility of the EMR technician will be to adapt the EMR–PACS to accommodate current and new diagnostic devices, and to ensure staff is instructed on diagnostic equipment usage. The individual will also be responsible for ensuring access to and maintenance of proprietary viewers associated with diagnostic instruments. The EMR technician must demonstrate skills in database and system administration, as well as provide testing, technical documentation, and production support.

EDUCATION AND EXPERIENCE High school graduate or the equivalent (General Educational Development [GED] qualification). Associate's degree in Medical Record Technology or equivalent education. RHIT preferred.

CORE COMPETENCIES AND SKILLS

- This position requires strong independent time management skills, organizational skills, foresight, the ability to sort tasks to prioritize efficiently, and excellent interpersonal skills
- Writing and language skills sufficient to prepare documents ranging from routine business correspondence to detailed technical documents
- Ability to initiate and maintain cooperative relationships with coworkers, managers, supervisors, customers/clients, and members of the public
- Ability to respond to customer service needs and expectations in a supportive and professional manner, with attention to promptness and a focus on solutions to provide excellent customer service
- Ability to prioritize and organize work, determine and meet deadlines, and proactively communicate with others in a clear and concise manner
- Ability to work evenings and weekends as required in support of applications and deadlines. Demonstrated strong testing and debugging skills to ensure proper application
- Knowledge of standard security practices and procedures for authentication, encryption, server configuration, and network configuration

- Demonstrated ability to create technical documentation that is clearly written, well organized, well structured, and accurate
- Demonstrated professional oral and written communication skills
- Knowledge of HIPAA Privacy and Security Standards

CREDENTIALS, LICENSURE, OR CERTIFICATION, IF APPROPRIATE   Advanced Certificate in Computer Science (may be used if BS is not present, but not required).

COMPENSATION   Salary ranges from $59,600 to $85,000 depending on degrees, certifications, and years of prior experience.

WORKPLACE LOCATION   This position of an EMR technician is found in hospitals of all sizes.

EMPLOYMENT OUTLOOK   Employment of medical records and health information technicians is expected to increase by 21% from 2010 to 2020, faster than the average for all occupations. The demand for health services is expected to increase as the population ages. An aging population will need more medical tests, treatments, and procedures. This will also mean more claims for reimbursement from private and public insurance. Additional records, coupled with widespread use of EHR by all types of health care providers, should lead to an increased need for technicians to organize and manage associated information in all areas of the health care industry.

FOR MORE INFORMATION
- http://www.ahima.org

29. Health Level 7 Interface Analyst, Information Technology

POSITION DESCRIPTION   Health Level 7 (HL7) International is an accredited, standards-developing organization dedicated to developing a comprehensive framework for retrieving and exchanging electronic health information in a way that supports effective health care service delivery. Computer systems analysts who specialize in HL7 standards work with hospital and other health care systems to implement systems interfaces and other health care technology solutions. HL7 analysts earn salaries similar to those earned by other computer systems analysts. The interface analyst under general supervision will use structured methodology to independently perform systems integration tasks. These tasks include planning, systems analysis design, interface building, testing, maintenance, support creation, as well as maintenance of interface support documentation and completing special projects work.

EDUCATION AND EXPERIENCE   Knowledge of computer principles at a level normally acquired through completion of a bachelor's degree in computer science, math, or other closely related field in order to be able to perform interface analysis design configuration and testing. Two to 4 years' related work experience in the health care industry and 3 years' experience with HL7 messaging standards. Two to 3 years of work experience preferred.

CREDENTIALS, LICENSURE, OR CERTIFICATION, IF APPROPRIATE   HL7 messaging standards, interface engines, and configuring and troubleshooting interfaces require ConnectR, GE Centricity Business 4.3/5.0, or Allscripts EMR 11.0.

CORE COMPETENCIES AND SKILLS
- Understanding of HL7 interface methodologies
- Knowledge of database management systems (DBMS) and SQL scripting
- Skilled in interface analysis, interoperability setup, and testing of interfaces
- Knowledge of interfacing with various applications, management information systems, data structures, systems analysis and design, and programming languages
- Working knowledge and understanding of EHR, electronic practice management, and health systems workflows
- Ability to work effectively (maintaining accuracy and sensitivity) under tight timelines and schedules
- Ability to sense the importance or impact of issues and situations and take appropriate actions
- Ability to work from an organizational perspective as well as independently and as a contributing team member
- Excellent listening skills and a commitment to communicating in a clear, concise, and timely manner at all times
- Ability to organize time effectively while identifying barriers to progress, proposing solutions, and setting priorities
- Verbal and written communication skills

- Interpersonal/human relations skills
- Ability to maintain confidentiality
- Ability to effectively prioritize and juggle multiple tasks
- Ability to appropriately communicate project status, escalate issues, and effectively coordinate activities with vendors, project leads, systems analysts, and all other technical and operations areas

COMPENSATION   Computer systems analysts, including those who are knowledgeable of HL7 standards and other issues related to health care information technology, earned an average of $81,250 per year in 2010, according to salary and employment data from the BLS. Annual salaries for HL7 interface specialists and other systems analysts ranged from $48,360 to $119,070. The median annual salary for a systems analyst in 2010 was $77,740.

WORKPLACE LOCATION   A HL7 interface analyst position could be either in a consulting firm or in the IT department of a large health care system.

EMPLOYMENT OUTLOOK   Interoperability is the interfacing of multiple HIT vendors to present a single view for the end user. This type of position will be in great demand as the industry moves toward a fully integrated EMR and a paper-light environment.

FOR MORE INFORMATION
- www.advanceweb.com/jobs/healthcare/index.html
- www.ehow.com/info_10007510_salary-hl7-interface-analyst. html#ixzz2k5b6lL9Z

30. Operations Analyst

POSITION DESCRIPTION   Operations analysts gather information by interviewing employees, reading reports, and searching through computer databases. They determine which data are relevant and what methods should be used to analyze them. They then use statistical analysis, simulation, and optimization to develop practical solutions. They advise decision makers on the appropriate courses of action, write memos and reports to document their recommendations, and meet with employees after implementation of a new process to determine its effectiveness. Most analysts work in analytical teams, especially on highly complex problems, and then work with employee teams to assist with implementation of their proposals.

EDUCATION AND EXPERIENCE

Master's degree in business administration, accounting, finance, or economics.

CREDENTIALS, LICENSURE, OR CERTIFICATION, IF APPROPRIATE

- Fluent in project management and related software, including generation of Gantt charts
- Minimum of 1 year experience in contract management
- Experience in biotech/pharma industry
- High degree of computer literacy, including standard office and project management tools

CORE COMPETENCIES AND SKILLS

- Create presentations routinely and on demand
- Able to present to senior management regarding company operations
- Serve as liaison between senior management and operational units as directed
- Strong initiative and ability to manage multiple projects through to on-time completion
- Manage meetings and generate reports
- Excellent written and oral communication skills
- Detail oriented with strong organizational and analytical skills
- Ability to work well with others in fast-paced, dynamic, collaborative environment
- Intuitive and constructive problem-solving abilities in a new and rapidly developing field
- Effective verbal and written communication skills, including presentations, personal organization, business process mapping, managing change in a team environment, and analytical problem solving
- Able to work effectively in a matrix environment and communicate clearly with all levels of the organization
- Excellent understanding of the concepts of clinical research and drug development

COMPENSATION   Operations analysts average $70,500 per year, and salaries can range from $40,500 to over $125,000 depending on the size and location of the health care organization (www.bls.gov).

WORKPLACE LOCATION   Operations analyst positions can be found in health care organization, vendors, and even the biotech industry.

EMPLOYMENT OUTLOOK   The BLS sees jobs for operations analysts increasing by 15% from 2010 to 2020, which is close to the 15% growth predicted for all occupations, but less than the 22% expected for all computer and math occupations. Driving the demand will be the need for companies to develop more efficient operations and lower expenses. The military will be a big employer of analysts. The best jobs will go to analysts who can easily communicate their recommendations to managers and workers outside of operations research. A master's or PhD in the subject will also provide better opportunities.

FOR MORE INFORMATION
   ■ work.chron.com/operations-analyst-job-description-salary-8159. html

31. Systems Analyst (General Description)

Systems analysts must be able to research and report any problems related to computer systems. They must be able to coordinate and problem-solve to ensure that the requirements are met. Systems analysts must have computer skills allowing them to translate their client's request and be able to discuss and develop reports. They should be able to design solutions for the business so that they can work directly with the customers as well as the internal client. They must be able to perform systems testing, understand the requirements that the systems must satisfy, and identify and understand the human impacts of planned systems that will ensure that new technical requirements are properly integrated with existing processes and skill sets.

   Systems analysts should have a college degree (bachelor's) in computer science or information systems. They need to be equipped with necessary computer and mathematical skills while having excellent written and verbal communication abilities. They must be able to attend educational workshops to maintain professional and technical knowledge. Systems analysts are required to have developed intrapersonal skill. This skill is useful in obtaining excellent communication skill, verbal and written. On top of that, it will help prepare them for interviews, observations, questioners, and statistical measurements. There may be times that systems analysts will need to talk to developers and discuss how systems should work and operate to match the user's experiences;

therefore, they must have the ability to work independently and as a member of a team with business process owners and management.

According to the U.S. Department of Labor, employment opportunities for systems analysts are expected to grow 22% from 2010 to 2020, with pay rates averaging $77,740 per year or roughly $37.38 per hour. The following three job descriptions provide an overview of systems analyst positions found in hospitals.

32. Systems Analyst (Example #1)

POSITION DESCRIPTION   Systems analysts provide business applications to support practice management software. They are responsible for providing business and systems analytical support applying to the maintenance and GE Centricity business revenue cycle. They are responsible for leading software implementation projects and must be able to work effectively with IT management and business process owners. They must be able to research problems and plan solutions.

EDUCATION AND EXPERIENCE   Must have a bachelor's degree or 5 years' equivalent work experience or specialized training in IT, computer science, and software engineering. They must have excellent communication skills, both verbal and written, and a background in math, physics, and software engineering.

CORE COMPETENCIES AND SKILLS   Some of the skills and competencies a systems analyst needs are analytical skills, technical skills, management skills, and communication skills. It is recommended that systems analysts have previous experience as well. They must know how to handle software design, software documentation, software testing, software maintenance, software development processes, and software architecture.

COMPENSATION   Depending on experience and degree, compensation ranges from $15.71 to $72.88 per hour.

WORKPLACE LOCATION   Systems analysts are usually located in an IT office or laboratory.

EMPLOYMENT OUTLOOK   Growth is projected at 15%. Demand for this job will increase as organizations continue to adapt to the growing health care industry. Due to higher demand in the future, individuals will have to be more experienced and have a level of skill and expertise with an advanced degree.

FOR MORE INFORMATION

- www.jobtarget.com
- www.monster.com

33. Systems Analyst (Example #2)

POSITION DESCRIPTION   Systems analysts support management software. They will be responsible for providing business and systems application analytical support as it applies to the maintenance and support of GE Centricity business revenue cycle applications, including but not limited to e-commerce, transaction editing system, and paperless collection system. Working knowledge of industry standard and proprietary electronic file formats needed to support business systems and interfaces is required. Also, systems analysts will be responsible for leading software implementation projects. They must be able to work effectively with IT management and business process owners and function as a research and development resource in determining the most efficient means of supporting, maintaining, and utilizing the business applications.

EDUCATION AND EXPERIENCE   A bachelor's degree in a computer or information science field or the equivalent is preferred. Three or more years of experience in systems maintenance support or equivalent information systems experience in a managed care or individual practice association setting, or third-party administrator, health plan, or medical group. Experience in systems design or programming, configuration work, or managing various systems in a multiplatform environment. Experience in voice and data networks, monitoring, and problem resolution/isolation.

CREDENTIALS, LICENSURE, OR CERTIFICATION, IF APPROPRIATE   No specific credentials or certification is required for this position but individual employers will vary as to desirability of additional credentials.

CORE COMPETENCIES AND SKILLS

- Excellent communication skills, both verbal and written
- Ability to work independently and as a member of a team with business process owners and management

■ Physical ability to operate and move computers and other equipment, and to operate and manipulate tools to install and repair equipment
■ Ability to multitask and manage multiple priorities; ability to work under pressure in stressful conditions and under time constraints

COMPENSATION $77,740 per year or $37.38 per hour.

WORKPLACE LOCATION   Systems analysts can be found in a wide variety of organizations and HIT sectors. Generally they will be in the IT department of an integrated delivery system.

EMPLOYMENT OUTLOOK   Employment of systems analysts is expected to grow 22% from 2010 to 2020, faster than the average for all occupations. A greater reliance on computer systems in organizations throughout the economy will lead to an increased demand for this occupation. (U.S. Department of Labor, www.bls.gov/ooh/Computer-and-Information-Technology/Computer-systems-analysts.htm).

FOR MORE INFORMATION
Job information:
■ www.indeed.com/cmp/Murtha-Cullina-LLP/jobs/System-Analyst-b5c1aaa7d32ba39e
Educational program in this field:
■ www.phoenix.edu
Professional organization in this field:
■ www.pmi.org

34. Systems Engineer (Example #3)

POSITION DESCRIPTION   Systems engineering is an interdisciplinary field of engineering that focuses on how to design and manage complex engineering projects over their life cycles. Issues such as reliability, logistics, and coordination of different teams (requirements management), evaluation measurements, and other disciplines become more difficult when dealing with large, complex projects. Systems engineering deals with work processes, optimization methods, and risk management tools in such projects. Systems engineering ensures that all likely aspects of a project or system are considered and integrated into a whole.

EDUCATION AND EXPERIENCE
For most positions you must have a master's degree in computer programming and 5 years' experience minimum. A bachelor's degree along with extensive experience might be considered for some positions.

CREDENTIALS, LICENSURE, OR CERTIFICATION, IF APPROPRIATE   None specified.

CORE COMPETENCIES AND SKILLS   The candidate must have experience working with a variety of software applications; for example:

- Microsoft Windows Server 2008 R2, 2012
- Citrix XenApp 6.5, XenDesktop 7
- Remote Desktop Services (2008 R2, 2012)
- Microsoft Active Directory
- Microsoft Windows 7, 8
- Varied IT environment deployments (clouds, virtual farms, etc.)

COMPENSATION   In this highly technical field the salary can range from $65,000 to $90,000.

WORKPLACE LOCATION   You would find a systems engineer in the IT department of a large health care system.

EMPLOYMENT OUTLOOK   As the health care industry expands there will be a better-than-average growth in and demand for technical expertise to support the growing complexity of the industry.

FOR MORE INFORMATION   For highly technical computer science–related positions, HIMSS JobMine is a good starting point, but individuals should also look into websites for specific health care and vendor organizations. Various educational institutions that specialize in technical fields like systems engineering are also good places to research and look for posted job opportunities. Chapter 3, "Educational Programs in Health Information Technology," can help locate appropriate institutions (e.g., Western Governors University at www.wgu.edu/online_it_degrees/networks_degrees).
Other helpful resources:
- www.ehow.com/about_5601279_system-engineer_.html
- www.ehow.com/facts_5891694_job-description-systems-engineer.html
- en.wikipedia.org/wiki/Systems_engineering

WALEED BASSYONI
Senior Manager
Data Warehouse—Business Intelligence
and Reporting
Hoag Hospital

Describe the sort of work you do. In my systems architect role I am responsible for putting together the layers of IT solution from different vendors. I manage the teams that build and manage the enterprise data warehouse and analytical platform for Hoag. I also manage the data governance initiative and reporting teams. I am responsible for integrating the electronic data warehouse for decision support and analytics. Building dashboards for decision support is a critical part of my job responsibilities.

What is a typical day like at your job? I would have to say that about 40% of my time is working with business partners at Hoag and collaboration on various projects. Another 30% of my time is devoted to resource management, and perhaps 10% is spent on system architecture and working with my teams to find the right vendors to meet our organizational needs. And 20% of my role is administration of the business intelligence (BI) and reporting team in terms of performance reviews, department meetings, and other responsibilities typical of a manager.

What education or training do you have? Is it typical for your job?
- Bachelor of Science in Mechanical Engineering, minor in Computer Science
- Master of Business Administration—IT focus
- Many business intelligence certifications, including CBIP (Certified Business Intelligence Professional) from TDWI (The Data Warehousing Institute), IBM Certified Business Intelligence Consultant, IBM Certified DBA

(*continued*)

WALEED BASSYONI (*continued*)

■ A large body of leadership and people management skills such as facilitative leadership, situational leadership, team building, client relations, and so forth

This is typical as it covers the scientific/technical background needed to get into the field as well as the people and business skills needed to sustain organizational support for the initiatives. Equivalent combinations of education and training can also be sufficient. One thing that is important in this field is to keep learning and taking advantage of advanced certification and participation in professional associations.

What path did you take to get to the job you are in today? Immediately after college I moved into an IT application development role. In this position I acquired working knowledge of the principles of client server applications and database management systems. When a database administrator role became available to support a major project at Kaiser Permanente, I applied and got accepted for the position. Once in the position I sought out industry certifications that support the role and used my own time to learn every facet of what it entails. This allowed me to gain the trust of department leadership and then get promoted into a solution architect role for a larger enterprise data warehouse project. During that 3- to 4-year program, I gained valuable insights into the challenges and techniques necessary to make such an endeavor successful. I also came to appreciate the profound political implications of what it means to break data boundaries between departments that have historically been reluctant to share that data. I also became active with industry institutions related to my profession such TDWI and HDWA, and the peer collaboration allowed me to further accelerate my work and avoid the pitfalls that befell others. Ultimately, in 2011, I joined Hoag as the architect for their DW-BI program and as the project moved into more of the execution phase, I was also asked to run its execution in a management capacity while maintaining the architect role. I had learned through previous projects that rapid value delivery is key, so

(*continued*)

WALEED BASSYONI   (*continued*)

I adopted that agile delivery approach of releasing analytical dashboards. Also I established an ongoing BI value "road-show," which entailed weekly meetings and presentations at client departments. This delighted the business community and resulted in increased demand for the team's services. This year I was promoted to senior manager role and was also asked to lead the reporting team to achieve synergies in end-to-end information delivery.

Where might you go from here if you wanted to advance your career? My future career path would be focused to advance my career as an enterprise analytical leader. Organizations are making business intelligence a high priority and creating executive/officer positions to expand those efforts. I envision my advancement to be in that direction.

What is the most challenging part of your job? Creating the right delivery pace that balances BI value creation with organizational bandwidth and readiness to receive it. It can be challenging when working with areas in the hospital that may be resistant to change. I have learned that someone in the BI field has to be very people oriented and develop public relations skills and be able to build trust across the organization.

What is the best part? Being a significant contributor through data delivery that enables an enterprise success story such as reducing mortality or achieving cost excellence. While perhaps not visible to the community as a whole, I know that what I do makes a difference in people's lives.

What advice would you give to someone contemplating a career like yours?
   ■ Build significant comfort and intellectual curiosity in data management. Master SQL; it's a critical foundation. Set aside at least 7 to 10 hours to work on self-development through consuming BI literature either in the form of printed books or online material.

(*continued*)

WALEED BASSYONI *(continued)*

- Realize and embrace that this career is as much a business relationship management career as it is a technical one and prepare/train accordingly.
- When given the opportunity, seek out and resolve business pain points and appreciate that success in this career will come from many "small wins" before the large ones are possible.
- Do not allow people skills to be an inhibitor. Get used to delivering articulate presentations in a business-understandable fashion to broad audiences at various organizational levels.

35. Health Care Project Manager (General Description)[3]

In any industry, including health care, there is a need for project managers. The project manager may be involved in any aspect of the health care facility's operations, ranging from clinical patient care to technology. The health care project manager often has a unique skill set as well as the ability to interact with all levels of staff and possibly even patients.

Credentials for a health care project manager usually include at least an associate or bachelor's degree. Certifications, such as one specific to project management, may be preferred by the employer. Depending on the seniority of the project manager position, the employer may request that a candidate have a master's degree. The employer may also prefer a degree with a specific emphasis or focus, such as business management or health care administration.

The health care project manager may work in a matrix environment. In a matrix environment the manager may report to one or two supervisors while providing updates and status reports to several other departments. Because the role of a project manager is critical to any project's success, the individual who is in the project management role is likely to interact with a variety of staff. This allows the project manager to have a wide range of exposure leading to potential future career growth.

A key element to ensuring that a program or project is managed successfully is the ability to prioritize. A health care project manager will

---

[3] www.ehow.com/about_6623804_healthcare-project-manager-job-description.html

need to have the ability to balance and coordinate numerous priorities, including competing priorities. Competing priorities occur when there is more than one item or task that needs to be addressed, yet other items or tasks are as equally important. Depending on the structure of the project, the project manager may need to seek input and guidance from a key stakeholder prior to making a final decision. The ability to manage multiple priorities is essential.

Effective communication skills are essential for a project manager. Written, oral, and presentation skills are essential to be successful in this position. The ability to listen and engage a wide variety of professionals in solving problems is a skill that needs to be developed.

Health care project managers need basic computer skills. Proficiency with software applications is another essential skill set. Software programs include word processing, spreadsheets, and presentation programs. The ability to use an electronic mail system, or e-mail, is a basic skill. A project manager needs to be familiar with basic project management software.

> Depending on the company, the project manager may need to have clinical experience. Examples of clinical experience include providing patient care as a nurse, paramedic, or other similar role. Senior-level project management positions may require advanced clinical experience such as a nurse practitioner, physician assistant, or physician. Project management roles that require clinical experience are likely involved in niche markets, such as cardiology or orthopedics.[4]

The following four job descriptions provide a range of opportunities that can typically be found in health care organizations.

36. Information Technology Project Manager (Example #1)

POSITION DESCRIPTION   The IT project manager is responsible for guiding hospital staff with the necessary upgrades and improvements when it comes to having an information technology plan in place. Additionally, the IT project manager will work with clinicians, physicians, and other units within the IT department to make sure that the new or necessary upgrades being made are fulfilling the standards of clinicians and other members of the hospital organization. Also, the IT project manager is in charge of developing training methods, testing, and security plans to meet the business requirements within the hospital.

---

[4] www.ehow.com/about_6623804_healthcare-project-manager-job-description.html

EDUCATION AND EXPERIENCE   Bachelor's degree in a related field or discipline required from an accredited college or university.

CREDENTIALS, LICENSURE, OR CERTIFICATION, IF APPROPRIATE   Project Management Professional (PMP) certification not required, but preferred.

CORE COMPETENCIES AND SKILLS   Three to 5 years of experience in working in an IT project management setting. Additionally, 3 or more years of System Development Life Cycles experience, 3 or more years' experience working with collecting and analyzing data, as well as writing systems requirements. Experience working with test plans and test cases. Must be proficient in using Microsoft Office Suite. Also, preferred qualifications include Perl scripting experience, SQL experience, and health care software development experience.

COMPENSATION   Ranges from $50,000 to $90,000.

WORKPLACE LOCATION   This position is normally found in a large medical center or medical group practice.

EMPLOYMENT OUTLOOK   The future outlook for computer and information technology project managers is expected to increase by as much as 18% between 2010 and 2020, which is about as fast as for other occupations. In fact, there will be a number of occupations created within the field of health care, since the health care industry is a little behind.

FOR MORE INFORMATION
- www.bls.gov/ooh/Management/Computer-and-information-systems-managers.htm#tab-6

37. Project Coordinator/Senior Analyst (Example #2)

POSITION DESCRIPTION   A project coordinator/senior analyst is required to be a professional role model, which includes being a supervisor, a mentor, and a resource for staff to go to when needed. Those filling this position are generally in charge of assigned staff in the IT team and are responsible for evaluation, implementation, training, testing, support, and optimization of assigned computer applications. The management of different tasks is also required and includes the development and expansion of new programs, regular visits to the site in order to ensure that all systems are running smoothly, and to provide help for technical assistance or assessment, analytic deliverables completion, policy analysis and evaluation, provision of support to health IT professionals, and finally, national conference presentations. Project coordinators/senior analysts will also lead members of their staff during the planning, implementation, and closing of projects while adhering to the hospital's technology planning approach. They will also follow established technical, quality, and Lean standards while planning projects. The supervision of other analyst staff that are assigned is also required. A project coordinator/senior analyst will also communicate about the project he or she is working on, coordinate resources, and establish the governance structure of the project.

EDUCATION AND EXPERIENCE   A Bachelor of Arts or Science in Computer Science or a business-related field is required (equivalent experience may be substituted for education). For this position, a minimum of 6 years' experience is required in hospital systems analysis and installations, with an understanding of the functions of the hospital, relationships among departments, and overall organization.

CREDENTIALS, LICENSURE, OR CERTIFICATION, IF APPROPRIATE   There are no certificates, credentials, or licensures required for this position.

CORE COMPETENCIES AND SKILLS
- Experience with specific vendor-based software is usually preferred, such as Meditech Client-Server software or the Kronos HR/Payroll system
- Education in systems concepts and operation.
- Extensive knowledge of and experience with the clinical or financial system. Extensive knowledge of the implementation and support of hospital systems
- Knowledge of database structure, application architecture, and network infrastructure

COMPENSATION   The average salary for a similar position on www.salary.com was between $60,000 and $90,000 per year.

WORKPLACE LOCATION   This position is located in the Information Services department at a hospital.

EMPLOYMENT OUTLOOK   Similar positions, such as a computer systems analyst, are expected to increase between 2010 and 2020 by 22%, which is faster than average as stated on the U.S. Bureau of Labor website.

FOR MORE INFORMATION

- ■ www.indeed.com/q-Project-Coordinator-Senior-Analyst-jobs.html

38. Health Services Information Technology Project Manager (Example #3)

POSITION DESCRIPTION Successful candidates will have to manage and oversee the implementation and integration of assigned projects from inception to user sign-off; serve as liaison among users, designers, technical personnel, and vendors; direct activities of project personnel to ensure the project progresses on schedule and within the prescribed budget; prepare status reports and modify schedules or plans as required; prepare project reports for management, client, or others; establish performance criteria; and maintain a project information database for all projects.

EDUCATION AND EXPERIENCE Bachelor of Arts or Science in Computer Science or a business-related field is preferred (equivalent experience may be substituted for education). Other degrees commonly accepted for project manager position include degrees in accounting, business administration, health services administration, computer science, management information systems, or other closely related fields. For this position, normally a minimum of 6 years' experience is required in hospital systems analysis and installations.

CREDENTIALS, LICENSURE, OR CERTIFICATION, IF APPROPRIATE For more advanced placements, certification by the Project Management Institute (www.pmi.org) is required.

CORE COMPETENCIES AND SKILLS Projects may involve major modifications to existing systems or the implementation of new IT facilities or systems, which include developing and reviewing project proposals or plans to determine time frame, funding requirements, sources and limitations, procedures for accomplishing the project, staffing requirements, and allotment of available resources to various phases of the project.

COMPENSATION The median annual wage of computer and information systems managers was $115,780.

WORKPLACE LOCATION Project managers can be found in a variety of organizations, from hospitals and medical centers to managed care and health technology vendors.

EMPLOYMENT OUTLOOK   Employment in this field is projected to grow 21% from 2010 to 2020, about as fast as the average for all occupations. Growth will be driven by organizations upgrading their IT systems and switching to newer, faster, and more mobile networks.

FOR MORE INFORMATION
- jobmine.himss.org/jobseeker
- www.bls.gov/ooh/Management/Computer-and-information-systems-managers.htm

39. Chief Medical Information Officer

POSITION DESCRIPTION   The chief medical information officer (CMIO) is responsible for supporting the development of clinical information systems that assist clinicians in the delivery of high-quality patient care in an academic setting. The CMIO participates as a member of the Health Care Information Systems Advisory Subcommittee of the Hospital Advisory Committee in representing the needs and requirements of the physician community and serves as an advocate of management in promoting the use of information technology in the clinical setting. The CMIO is an integral member of the Health Care Information Systems (HCIS) department to translate clinician requirements into specifications for new clinical and research systems. The CMIO reports in a matrix structure to the health care chief information officer and the associate dean for clinical affairs.

Typical duties and responsibilities:

- Chairs clinical advisory groups to provide broad-based input into the design of the clinical information system.
- Creates and supervises clinical optimization teams consisting of physicians, nurses, pharmacists and other providers and ancillary staff to review and enhance systems utilization and configuration to improve the efficiency and outcomes of clinical care.
- Leads and facilitates clinician advisory groups in the design of clinical systems to support excellence in patient care, education, and research.
- Engages patient care providers in varying roles, including physicians, pharmacists, nursing practitioners, nursing staff, ancillary department personnel, and medical records professionals to contribute to the development and use of the clinical information system.

- Builds relationships with physicians to gain support of IT initiatives. Is highly responsive to users' needs, including training, to ensure widespread acceptance and provider use of the clinical systems.
- Reviews medical informatics trends, experiences, and approaches; develops technical and application implementation strategies; and assists in the development of strategic plans for clinical information systems.
- Works as a team member of HCIS to design and supervise the implementation of systems supporting patient care, education, and research activities. Advises HCIS division directors on systems configuration and support issues.
- Leads development of clinical "rules" supporting patient care and protocol research as well as the design of clinical systems features supporting protocol management and the use of the system to leverage the clinicians' time and maximize communication with affiliates and referring physicians.
- Serves as a member of the Hospital Information Systems Advisory Subcommittee and Health Information Management Subcommittee.
- Provides clinical leadership in the development and deployment of solutions that cluster information in disease and episodic categories for benchmarking, clinical severity, public reporting, and variance analysis.
- Designs and evaluates collection of data for clinical purposes, including tracking and interpretation of outcomes.
- Assumes a leadership position in reviewing regional and national trends, experiences, and approaches in health information systems to identify best practices that assist in the development of clinical health information strategies. Actively participates in regional and national initiatives relating to health care information technology.
- Works with the leaders of research and education programs to ensure that academic and research needs are taken into account when planning and implementing clinical systems for patient care.
- Facilitates planning and implementation for the integration of clinical and research databases.
- Maintains an active medical practice in the area of specialty and provides patient care in appropriate clinical settings.

EDUCATION AND EXPERIENCE   The successful candidate must have recent medical practice experience in an academic medical center comprising inpatient, outpatient, and procedural experience. Practical experience with electronic health information systems, including configuration, implementation, and support, in an ambulatory or hospital setting, is required. An MD or joint MD–PhD and the appropriate board certification in chosen discipline.

CORE COMPETENCIES AND SKILLS

- Possesses excellent interpersonal skills and can work effectively with diverse personalities. Must be approachable, show respect for others, and be able to present data with effective communication and presentation skills. Must be an effective consensus builder
- Possesses a good grasp of clinical workflow in inpatient, outpatient, and operating room settings, plus an interest in clinical information systems and outcomes measurement
- Must have the ability to develop flexible, transferable models for pathways of care
- Is a strong leader with a mature sense of priorities and solid practical experience who can design and implement systems within the framework of technical boundaries
- Is politically savvy, has a high tolerance for ambiguity, and can work successfully in a matrix management model
- Is a systems thinker with strong organizational skills who can pull all the pieces together and deliver on time and within budget
- Is a strong manager who is adaptable and has a strong collaborative management style
- Is a contemporary clinician who understands major trends in health care and managed care, and is familiar with point-of-care products and medical informatics trends and tools

COMPENSATION   The salary range for a CMIO can range from $175,000 in small hospitals and health care systems up to $350,000 in larger urban areas and larger health care organizations.

WORKPLACE LOCATION   CMIOs are still evolving as a specialty area for physicians. Most CMIOs will continue to work in private practice for 20% to 25% of the time. Generally larger health care organizations will have a defined position of a CMIO, who might report to the chief medical officer or in some cases to the chief information officer.

FOR MORE INFORMATION
- www.amdis.org
- www.payscale.com

40. Information Systems Auditor

POSITION DESCRIPTION   The information systems (IS) internal audit team conducts IS risk-based audits and recommends strategic solutions to the business units within the organization. Auditors work closely with the business unit management. Position expectations can include leading IS risk-based audits; examining and verifying IS processes and procedures from internal organizations in order to determine the reliability and effectiveness of the existing control systems; continuously analyzing business risk profiles and providing assurance that appropriate risk mitigation is practiced; providing management with independent and objective reports, evaluations, appraisals, counsel, and recommendations; and supporting the global IS audit director, company divisions, and subsidiaries in a consulting role by evaluating and recommending improvements to business practices and processes.

EDUCATION AND EXPERIENCE   Bachelor's degree in computer science, management information systems, or related business discipline(s).

CREDENTIALS, LICENSURE, OR CERTIFICATION, IF APPROPRIATE   Certified internal auditor (CIA) or certified information systems auditor (CISA) certification will be considered a plus (certification.about.com/od/certifications/p/CISA.htm).

CORE COMPETENCIES AND SKILLS
- Must demonstrate leadership competencies with the ability to work effectively across all levels and functions within the business
- Strong interpersonal skills with the ability to facilitate diverse groups toward operational efficiencies
- Extensive knowledge of and experience in project management with strong analytical, problem-solving, and organizational skills
- Application development or implementation experience with systems applications products or prescription drug events is preferred
- Effective oral and written communication skills and proven presentation skills
- Proactive and results driven

COMPENSATION   The salary for a certified IS auditor can range from $65,000 to $90,000 depending on work experience, degrees, and current certification.

WORKPLACE LOCATION   Information systems auditors work in many different industries. If employed in the health care sector they would be working in the IS department of a large medical facility or corporate office.

EMPLOYMENT OUTLOOK   Employment is expected to increase 16% between the years 2010 and 2020.

FOR MORE INFORMATION
- jobsearchtech.about.com/od/historyoftechindustry/g/IT_Audit.htm
- www.isaca.org/Certification/CISA-Certified-Information-Systems-Auditor/Pages/default.aspx

41. Director of Clinical Applications

POSITION DESCRIPTION   The director of clinical applications is primarily responsible for planning, coordinating, managing, implementing, and maintaining all patient-centric information systems (e.g., clinical, ancillary, revenue cycle) under the purview of IS and will work closely with those departments that control and maintain their own systems. A significant part of this position is to oversee and manage vendors and IS project managers regarding all aspects of systems acquisition, implementation, and maintenance, as well as end-user leadership to manage resources, timelines, and risk to ensure that operational and strategic goals are defined and met. The director will frequently be involved in the simultaneous management of several large-scale implementations involving multiple project teams.

Summary of responsibilities:

- Working under the direction of the chief information officer (CIO), defining the strategy, plan, and budget for responsible areas/systems.
- Obtaining from relevant authorities any approvals deemed necessary for the implementation of systems solutions within the organization (e.g., Senior Operations Leadership, IT Steering Committee).
- Staying current on all health care industry trends and regulatory requirements in order to anticipate future system needs.

■ Completing assigned work plan tasks within the scheduled time frames.

EDUCATION AND EXPERIENCE Bachelor's degree in nursing, other clinical area, or computer science required. Master's degree preferred. Minimum of 7 years of related technical experience, including 4 years of project management experience, required.

CREDENTIALS, LICENSURE, OR CERTIFICATION, IF APPROPRIATE Project Management certification would be a strong plus.

CORE COMPETENCIES AND SKILLS
■ Demonstrated ability to manage multiple large-scale projects
■ Strong working knowledge of organization-specific vendor products (e.g., Allscripts Sunrise products)
■ Strong working knowledge of clinical and revenue cycle workflows
■ Strong ability to work with clinicians and administration senior leadership
■ Strong working knowledge of pertinent federal and state regulations and initiatives (e.g., health information exchange, HIPAA, meaningful use, physician quality reporting system)
■ Good problem solving, troubleshooting, and analytical skills
■ The ability to communicate with staff at all levels of the practice, as well as with vendors and other outside agents
■ Excellent leadership and teaching abilities

COMPENSATION The salary range for a director of clinical applications is $69,000 to over $100,000. Salaries can vary greatly due to health care organization size, location, candidate experience, and benefits.

WORKPLACE LOCATION This position is typically held in a hospital, multihospital system, or integrated delivery system.

EMPLOYMENT OUTLOOK Clinical directors enjoy a generally positive career outlook. There are expected to be more jobs coming out of the health care field than any other through 2016, according to the BLS Career Guide to Industries (www.bls.gov). Clinical directors' national average salary is $69,000 per year (SimplyHired.com).

FOR MORE INFORMATION

■ www.simplyhired.com/a/jobs/list/q-director+clinical+applications
■ jobmine.himss.org
■ education-portal.com/articles/Clinical_Director_Job_Outlook_
and_Information_About_Starting_a_Career_as_a_Clinical_
Director.html

42. Vice President and Chief Information Officer

POSITION DESCRIPTION[5]   The vice president/chief information officer (VP/CIO) serves as the key executive for the information services
and communications department for the health system. This position
provides leadership, vision, and oversight for information systems and
technology with a focus on service excellence and with overall responsibility for direction, coordination, and management of all IS/IT business
and clinical functions. The VP/CIO builds strong relationships, explains
technology-based business decisions, and fosters consensus at all levels
of the organization to ensure the achievement of objectives. The VP/CIO
will report to the chief operating officer (COO).

As an active and contributing member of senior management, the
VP/CIO will demonstrate the ability to see the big picture in terms of
consequences and scope when planning for the future and responding to
problems in implementing the changes necessary for the future growth
and success of the health system. The VP/CIO promotes a positive organizational culture, is committed to quality services, and represents the
organization in appropriate forums. She or he will remain current with
new technologies, and with national and local issues affecting health care
information technology and their potential influence on the institution.
Particular emphasis will be placed on responsibility for understanding
the impact of advanced information systems technology on patient care.

The VP/CIO will lead, for example, the organization through the
optimization of the EMR and computerized physician order entry systems across the health system. The VP/CIO will evaluate information
systems resources and structure and provide leadership focused on service, accountability, and delivery with a concentration on clinical decision making and process integration.

---

[5]The following job description for a VP and CIO is a quote from a resource that can be found at
www.himss.org. The URL for the website is www.himss.org/health-it-career-services/healthcare-
technologyjob-descriptions?navItemNumber=17560 (click on "Healthcare IT Job Descriptions").
This is an example of the range of resources that are available to research HIT jobs in the hospital
sector. The resource at HIMSS has a number of other complete job descriptions.

The VP/CIO will effect positive change. She or he will be the IT vision leader and will implement business strategies to align the information resources department with organizational goals. A key challenge for the position will be to build strong relationships and alignment with physicians, and explain technology-based business decisions. The incumbent will need to evolve the VP/CIO position and the IT team to meet the challenges of the changing health care environment. The incumbent will need to be extremely adept at moving toward a common goal with various entities across the enterprise. He or she needs to work with physicians and clinicians effectively to implement a paperless environment in a multiple-hospital system.

The VP/CIO is responsible for performing the following duties and responsibilities in a manner consistent with the mission and values of the hospital:

- Provide leadership, support, and direction for information systems through collaboration, education, and relationship building
- Function as a key member of the senior management team and as an advisor and leader to management and physicians on information technology matters
- Encourage and educate leaders regarding how to make technology-based business decisions
- Interact with or present to the board of trustees and other key constituents
- Develop and communicate the IS strategic plan and vision to all levels of the organization
- Ensure IS/IT strategies align with overall organizational mission and vision
- Build strong relationships with physicians and hospital leadership to build trust and support and optimize customer satisfaction at all levels
- Develop and communicate an IS management and governance structure to all levels of the organization
- Develop standards and procedures for selection, implementation, integration, and support of systems
- Monitor the productivity of IS resources and manage those resources in a cost-effective, flexible, and timely manner
- Enhance the utilization of the hospital IS and advanced clinical systems across the health system
- Develop and monitor annual information resources operating and capital budgets to ensure that areas of responsibility have the

necessary funding to carry out established organizational goals and objectives

■ Develop efficient departmental operations and strive to reduce costs whenever possible
■ Stay abreast of current federal and state legislation affecting information technology
■ Develop and implement strategy to ensure compliance with the Patient Protection and Affordable Care Act and to meet meaningful use requirements

EDUCATION AND EXPERIENCE The following are key requirements of the ideal candidate. A bachelor's degree from an accredited college or university is required. A master's degree is strongly preferred. A minimum of 8 years as a successful IT leader at a value-driven community hospital, preferably in a competitive market or other complex health care organization is required. Demonstrated success and expertise in broad IT health care leadership, including past successes with implementing a variety of HIT systems, such as EMR and computerized physician order entry systems.

CORE COMPETENCIES AND SKILLS
■ Executive presence that engenders confidence, enthusiasm, and support in others and a strong passion for quality patient care
■ Excellent communication abilities to articulate the vision and translate complex issues into comprehensible ideas and concepts
■ Strong interpersonal skill to lead and motivate the organization
■ Strategic creativity and the ability to innovate in this complex setting
■ Team building skills that provide leadership and structure to a group of high-performing operational leaders
■ An ability to engage and foster strong relationships with physicians
■ The ability to inspire the quest for excellence
■ Excellent negotiation and vendor management skills
■ Solid knowledge of health care IT strategic planning, technological trends, and systems
■ Experience implementing clinical systems, preferably including EHR and computerized provider order entry
■ Experience with outsourcing or evaluation of outsourcing proposals

COMPENSATION   In large health care organizations this position can command salaries in the range of $150,000 to perhaps $350,000. In smaller hospitals or smaller hospital chains this position would have a salary in the $150,000 to $250,000 range.

FOR MORE INFORMATION
- www.himss.org/health-it-career-services/healthcare-technology-job-descriptions?navItemNumber=17560
- www.cio-chime.org
- jobmine.himss.org

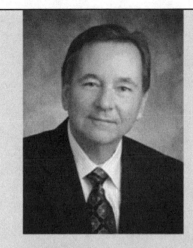

SCOTT JOSLYN
Senior Vice President and CIO
MemorialCare

Describe the sort of work you do. As a senior VP and CIO in a large health care organization I have a range of responsibilities on the senior management team. My job involves:

- Job one is managing a large IT organization supporting an organization that is becoming more vertically integrated while also growing geographically within a region—all against a backdrop of an evolving health care marketplace.
- IT management in our organization has its classic technical elements, but is increasingly about managing the *intersection* between IT and business strategies. It is in many cases working to find opportunity or leverage between the business objectives and the ability of technology to expand and/or accelerate those objectives.
- IT is also expected to identify in some cases and, otherwise in all cases, contribute to the discussion of business strategies, with and without IT components. In my particular case, I am able to bring a clinical, business, and technical background to the conversation.
- Leadership in all its dimensions.
- Creating a common vision within the IT organization that is a reflection of the long-term business vision of the organization, managing the intermediate steps to achieve that vision, and continuing to ensure that basic operations are reliable, technically sound, and cost-effective. *(continued)*

SCOTT JOSLYN   *(continued)*

- Mentoring younger, promising staff members and managers.
- Collaborating with peers across the organization, bringing IT expertise to the table, continuously learning from those peers how their respective functions are evolving, and forecasting their potential IT needs.
- Keeping up with evolving technology that advances more quickly each day, and knowing which of many new things to focus on for early value creating and, occasionally, some potential competitive advantage.

What is a typical day like at your job? There are no typical days, but generally my time is spent in five areas. A quarter of a typical day would be spent in meetings and in collaboration with my senior managers along with teams both inside and outside the IT organization. Another quarter would be devoted to meetings, management, monitoring, and problem solving related to key projects, major deliverables, and basic service delivery. The remaining half would be variously divided among: (1) absorbing information and learning from peers, reading, research, and following current economic trends in the marketplace; (2) planning, writing, and communicating; (3) meeting one-on-one with my direct reports but also key staff members; (4) meeting with key partners and vendors; and (5) pure administration such as budgeting, human resources, and so forth.

What education or training do you have? Is it typical for your job? There is no standard educational or training path for CIOs. Critical thinking skills and an ability to see across disciplines is a skill that comes with experience but can be supported by certain educational experiences. I have a clinical background in pharmacy (PharmD degree) that provides me with an understanding of clinical processes. I later earned an MBA that provided education and insights simply not part of a clinical education. The marketing, economic, operations research, and finance knowledge afforded by an MBA was extremely valuable in preparing for my role as a CIO. The third educational background I have is in data processing and basic computer programming. The

(continued)

SCOTT JOSLYN   *(continued)*

most powerful thing, however, is the resulting synergy that derives from this combined experience, particularly as it spans the conceptual to the operational aspects of the business and the IT function.

What path did you take to get to the job you are in today? I started out in a pharmacy position in a large health care organization followed by a residency in clinical pharmacy. I had an opportunity to join the "data processing" department following the residency, and never looked back. I was involved in programming, systems analysis, and process reengineering (before it was more formally identified). I managed data centers and built the people and, dating myself, the technical infrastructure to support the advance of the personal computer as it made its way into the business. I oversaw clinical information systems, installed our first electronic medical record system, and later became the CIO.

Where might you go from here if you wanted to advance your career? The role of a CIO is still evolving, and I suppose there might be opportunities to broaden my overall scope of management, such as taking on other areas of business, perhaps where IT has become an integral component. I might take on leadership of other functions, but I am more likely to work with young, entrepreneurial companies looking to apply technology to advance the cost, quality, and/or overall value of health care in one way or another.

What is the most challenging part of your job? The pervasiveness of IT across the health care organization creates a lot of pressure to meet the demand for IT services and IT-related projects. Demand invariably exceeds supply. The art today is IT capability deployment for optimal operational, cost, or strategic advantage.

What is the best part? A key factor in finding satisfaction in any job is creating value when delivering a service or project. On time, below budget, and beyond expectations is always nice. I'll take two of those three any day!

(continued)

SCOTT JOSLYN   (*continued*)

What advice would you give to someone contemplating a career like yours? People don't typically start in a career thinking they will become a CIO. You find opportunities along the way and your mentors perhaps steer you in unforeseen directions. Opportunities arise, you take risks on occasion, and you sometimes get lucky. I recommend building strong communication skills, both oral and written business abilities. Develop statistical and data analytic skills and be comfortable with computer technology. That would be useful in most any job. Problem solving and just being a good, innovative thinker will serve one well always. Employers look for individuals who are energetic, enthusiastic, and tend to be curious—wanting to learn, understand, and make things happen.

7 ■ HIT CAREERS IN THE VENDOR SECTOR

The growth in electronic medical records (EMR) and health information exchanges (HIE) and the overall emphasis on improving the delivery of medical services in a quality and cost-effective manner has propelled the vendor marketplace to expand to meet the demand of health care providers. Vendors come in a range of sizes and geographic emphases. Chapter 4 identifies some of the larger vendors in the health care space. There are many small-to-medium HIT vendors that are growing as well with niche markets in specialized areas such as medical groups, operating room information technology (IT) systems, revenue cycle management, security products, voice recognition, telemedicine, and many more. The annual Healthcare Information and Management Systems Society (HIMSS) conference generally has over 1,000 different vendors demonstrating their products and services. Vendors hire both highly technical professionals like programmers, systems developers, systems implementation staff, and marketing and sales staff. Chapter 4 can lead you to vendor websites and job openings. For a comprehensive listing of HIT vendors go to the HIMSS vendor directory at healthcareinformationtechnologydirectory.com.

> *Getting started in a beginning job is often more important than waiting for the perfect job.*
> —*Scott Cebula*

The following job descriptions are typical of HIT positions one would find in the vendor sector of the health care industry. Many of the same job titles can be found in other sectors, but within the vendor sector the positions are focused on developing and marketing products to sell to or consult with their partners in the provider side of the marketplace.

POSITION DESCRIPTIONS IN VENDOR SETTINGS

43. Health Care Information Technology Project Manager

POSITION DESCRIPTION   The health care IT project manager position is for a person with project management experience. The position is designed to support one of the company's customers at its location. The successful candidate will have a proven track record in implementing IT systems in a hospital or clinic setting and delivering a project on time and within budget, and have at least 3 years of experience. Knowledge and experience with electronic health records (EHR) and *International Classification of Diseases, 10th Revision (ICD-10)* is desired. The individual will be expected to lead the planning and implementation of a project; define project tasks and resource requirements; manage the project budget; plan and schedule project timelines; track project deliverables using appropriate tools and software; constantly monitor and report on the progress of projects to stakeholders; implement and manage project changes and interventions to achieve project outputs; and provide project summary evaluations and assessment of the results.

EDUCATION AND EXPERIENCE   A bachelor's degree or equivalent experience is required. Three years of project management work experience is also required.

CREDENTIALS, LICENSURE, OR CERTIFICATION, IF APPROPRIATE   No specific credential required. However, the individual may in the future consider becoming a certified project manager through the Institute of Project Management.

CORE COMPETENCIES AND SKILLS
- Critical thinking and problem-solving skills
- Effective communication skills—written, oral, and presentation
- Effective team building and managing skills
- Ability to negotiate and deal with conflict management
- Ability to be adaptable and to deal with stress
- Proven experience in people management, change management, and strategic planning

COMPENSATION   The range of compensation for a health care IT project manager in a vendor company is between $60,000 and $90,000.

WORKPLACE LOCATION   The position of IT project manager can be found in a wide variety of organizations, including vendors, hospitals, managed care, and large medical groups. This position description is modeled after a typical project manager in an IT vendor environment.

EMPLOYMENT OUTLOOK   Project management positions are growing at an above-average rate in both the vendor and health care delivery sectors. Advanced certification in project management is probably required if one wants to move to higher levels in this field.

FOR MORE INFORMATION   In Chapter 4 there are a number of references to vendor organization's career websites. This job description was modeled after a listing at Siemens Healthcare Systems. One who is interested in the area of project management should investigate the Project Management Institute at www.pmi.org.

44. Project Manager, Information Technology

POSITION DESCRIPTION   IT project managers lead and coordinate technology projects. IT project managers handle a wide range of technology projects and programs, including application development efforts, systems upgrades and installations, technology outsourcing, IT security initiatives, and data center relocations, to name a few. They coordinate resources, establish the project governance structure, and communicate about the project. Other IT project manager responsibilities usually include creating and maintaining project plans, managing the project budget, mitigating project risks, and making sure the project is on track and within budget.

EDUCATION AND EXPERIENCE   The typical educational and experience requirements for IT project managers vary by industry, employer, and project type. While many project managers learn on the job and from continuing education, individuals with an academic background combining course work in project management or IT with business management are well suited for leadership careers in the finance, health care, hospitality, retail, manufacturing, services, government, and education sectors of the economy. A bachelor's or master's in business administration, project management, or information technology is preferred but not required.

CREDENTIALS, LICENSURE, OR CERTIFICATION, IF APPROPRIATE   Employers of IT project managers show a strong preference for individuals with professional credentials, including the Project Management Professional (PMP) and IT Information Library Version 3 (ITILv3) certifications.

CORE COMPETENCIES AND SKILLS   Because there are many different technologies, there are many types of IT project managers who specialize in different technology areas. Research and analysis, resource demand management, budgeting, forecasting, preparing documentation, and project team coordination are some common tasks all IT project managers perform during the delivery of a project. Although the activities of IT project managers vary by project and technology, they are always concerned with achieving project milestones within the constraints of budget, schedule, and resources. Individuals seeking careers in IT project management have specialized knowledge of the best practices for project management and are familiar with various technologies. IT project managers demonstrate leadership and are sensitive to organizational politics. They understand competing priorities, can effectively manage simultaneously occurring tasks, and are adaptable and flexible to the dynamic needs of projects. Their most valuable skill, and one used throughout the entire project management process, is the ability to communicate complex technical information in an easy-to-understand way.

COMPENSATION   The estimated annual compensation for IT project managers is quite lucrative. Salary projections published by the U.S. Department of Labor show that computer and information systems managers, including project managers, in the United States earned annual salaries ranging from $69,900 to $143,590. The estimated median annual income of computer and information systems managers was $113,720. Managers working in the computer systems design and software design industries earn the most and averaged annual mean wages of $130,000 and $136,580, respectively.

WORKPLACE LOCATION   The role of an IT project manager can be found across all sectors of the health care industry and most other industries. The tools and skills associated with this position in the health care sector are unique because of the clinical processes and the complexity of HIT systems. This particular description is typical of a position found in vendors' companies and also large health care providers.

EMPLOYMENT OUTLOOK   Occupational studies published by the U.S. Department of Labor forecast employment of computer and information systems managers, including IT project managers, to grow by 17%, faster than the national average for all health care occupations, through the year 2018. Because of the continued adoption of new and emerging technologies, the job outlook for IT project managers is excellent. Due to the continued industry focus on internal security controls, the job prospects are particularly promising for project managers with IT security expertise.

FOR MORE INFORMATION
- www.pmi.org
- www.andersoneconomicgroup.com
- www.CNNMoney.com

ARVIND P. KUMAR
Senior Vice President for Technology and Alliances
Controlled Risk Insurance Company (CRICO)
Risk Management Foundation of the Harvard Medical Institutions

Describe the sort of work you do. I do strategic thinking and execution involving technology and innovation. For example, I look to apply IT-enabled innovations to solve problems. It really involves collaboration, linkages, sharing of information, sharing of transactions, and bringing in third parties that can add value to our collaboration jointly. It is the classic B2B domain that I work on. Overall, my job requires a significant amount of strategic behavior with rapid operational delivery. I spend more time on strategic context, implications, and planning, knowing that there is an operational component that needs to be resolved by multiple teams, skills, and functions.

CRICO is the Controlled Risk Insurance Company of the Risk Management Foundation of the Harvard Medical Institutions, owned by and serving the Harvard medical community. For more than 30 years, CRICO has provided industry-leading medical professional liability coverage, claims management, and patient safety resources to its members. We serve more than 12,000 physicians, 23 hospitals, and more than 209 other health care organizations. Our mission is to provide superior medical malpractice insurance to our institutions and members and assist them in delivering the safest health care in the world.

Our health care institutions are constantly innovating in our mission of making care safer. The work I do here at CRICO is really aimed at establishing the collaboration and exchange channel, and using technology and business models as an underpinning with the

(*continued*)

ARVIND P. KUMAR *(continued)*

institutions and our covered entities. Sometimes that involves bringing in other vendors or suppliers that may have either intellectual property or software or expertise that will benefit our institutions. I work with the CIOs and clinician leaders who are looking to impact risk mitigation in patient care delivery.

What is a typical day like at your job? Overseeing program management and the multiple ongoing initiatives that are in play with the institutions requires 20% to 30% of my time. There are usually three or four of these initiatives running simultaneously. I have program managers with different levels of expertise. For example, for security innovations we use a consultant and for referral management we have an internal project manager.

I spend another 30% of my time vetting innovations or new models or listening to the institutions and things they may be exploring. In other words, I try to ask myself, "What is the next curve ball that we should expect?" or "What are the next set of tools we should anticipate that could remove the risks that already recognize exist?" This involves me talking to a CIO or a vendor/supplier or an application consultant and creating some level of cross-fertilization.

The remaining 30% of my time is spent internally, most of it in the patient safety area. I look at what our Patient Safety Department is discussing in terms of current risks to our institutions and individual providers. I look at the current patient safety programs they want to put in place and identify the objectives and the planning or product cycle.

What education or training do you have and is that typical for your job? I have an undergraduate degree in mechanical engineering, which really gave me the quantitative and analytical skills necessary for my current job. It was more in the manufacturing space, which is extremely precision oriented. If it's not safe, a manufactured product will not make it to the market. I then completed my master's in industrial engineering, which gave me the process view that I have been able to bring into health care.

(continued)

ARVIND P. KUMAR   (continued)

What path did you take to get to the job you are in today? While my education has been important, I think my involvement in and exposure to health care institutions has been extremely helpful. Early on in my career, I gained consulting exposure—involving multiple clients with a multitude of similar problems, but in different settings. My career is now focused on multiple innovations and fewer institutions. So I kind of flipped the multiple clients—same problem—to multiple innovations, but only involving 10 clients or CRICO shareholders. Having quantitative skills, process skills, and exposure to evolving technology allows you to excel in this setting.

I went right from my graduate program at Northeastern University to Georgetown University Hospital as a management engineer, which was basically process engineering, gathering requirements to build systems, and then testing them. From there I went to a consulting company, Ernst & Young, which gave me the operational consulting experience and exposure to how hospitals operate, both financially and from a labor productivity perspective at a departmental level. Then I joined a strategic consulting group at Mercer Management Consulting that worked with Fortune 100 companies helping the C-suite and boards with validating and modeling disruptive strategies and some operations improvement. Following Mercer, I started my own company, as a subsidiary of a health care software company called IDX. That exposure led me to go and become one of the CIOs at Cincinnati Children's Hospital. From there I made a deep dive into the commercial world, where I started to build new markets and solutions for a consulting firm wrapped around a typical EMR and the health care IT ecosystem. I took a lot of the business international, to places like the UK, Dubai, and southern Europe, and at the same time I was also running the U.S. business. Soon after I was managing a portfolio of about $200 million, half of the health care services business for a $6 billion company. I had become a nomad. I've always needed something that makes me excited to come to work every morning. What excited me there was the number of clients. What excites me here at CRICO is the number of innovations, so I made the shift and that is why I am here.

(continued)

ARVIND P. KUMAR   (continued)

Where might you go from here if you wanted to advance your career? I can see two places. If I choose to go back into the commercial space, I probably could become the CEO of a $50 to $100 million company that's looking to build up its value and either sell or go to an IPO. That is one path I could take even though I'm less inclined, given that the quality of life that it demands is pretty hard. Another path would be to stay within the Harvard family and look for the next opportunity—either run a business unit which is as big as CRICO, or continue to be at CRICO with a larger or growing responsibility. If there is a thirst for driving innovation, I'm here. I don't see any place I need to look out at. I may do more teaching. I may add more board commitments and continue to innovate out of here.

What's the most challenging part of your job? It really is the synchronization of innovation between the institutions and bringing that back to synchronize within CRICO. I think the cultures among our client institutions are different. The paces are different, the needs are different, and so when you have this ultra-disparate equation, it can be challenging to bring it together to get a project up and running. For me, though, that challenge is where the excitement comes from.

What's the best part? The best part of my job is that diversity of innovation and models. While it is challenging, it is also the most exciting part because you get to see so many different views on a particular subject. Getting to see the diversity and figuring out how to thread the different views together is amazing and very exciting. I get to work with the best of the best in the industry and since I'm one of those people who is very curious about how many ways you can solve a problem, I enjoy the process of determining which tool fits a specific environment the best, because there's not one tool or approach that will solve all problems. There are a multitude of tools; even though the problem may feel like it's the same, within an environment it doesn't mean that the same hammer must "nail" it. The pressure may have to be higher or you may need a bigger base, a bigger handle, so innovating around that is amazing to me.

(continued)

147

ARVIND P. KUMAR   (continued)

What advice do you give to someone contemplating a career just like yours? My view is to be well grounded with quantitative skills. Trying to work in the front line early on in your career is very important. Work in actual operations. Work in implementation settings, where projects are being executed. Look for good mentors and multiple mentors. It is important to network. If you're looking to innovate, you have to network and seek ideas and views from others' experiences both formally and informally. And then finally, I think you need to acquire a certain set of sales skills, because you're constantly selling and you're constantly listening. So you need to have that kind of fortitude. I think the rest really involves commitment and hard work. You have to believe in what you do and then you're there.

45. Clinical Applications Project Manager

POSITION DESCRIPTION   The clinical applications project manager is responsible for the execution of the vendor's clinical projects with clients. The position requires the applications of project management skills and tools to facilitate the implementation of complex projects and programs.

EDUCATION AND EXPERIENCE   Bachelor's degree or equivalent experience is required. Health care industry work experience is required. Additional experience in specific vendor applications is desirable.

CREDENTIALS, LICENSURE, OR CERTIFICATION, IF APPROPRIATE   Must be Project Management Professional (PMP) certified, or eligible and willing to become certified.

CORE COMPETENCIES AND SKILLS
- Demonstrate superior customer relationship and communication skills
- Possess excellent diplomacy and negotiation skills
- Have a history of successful use of project management methodologies, best practices, and processes
- Be responsible for ensuring successful execution of the defined project scope

- Create and manage project plans per defined project management methodology
- Manage and track project financials
- Lead project teams
- Provide concise project-related reporting to appropriate audiences
- Possess strong Microsoft Project and Excel skills
- Have a passion for workflow and process improvement
- Have a track record of success in a strong matrix environment

COMPENSATION   According to the Bureau of Labor Statistics website, earnings of medical and health services managers vary by type and size of the facility and by level of responsibility. The range can be from $65,000 to over $105,000 with a median salary of $85,000.

WORKPLACE LOCATION   Project manager in the vendor sector of the health care industry might work in the corporate headquarters of the vendor or could be assigned to a specific client and work on-site.

EMPLOYMENT OUTLOOK   According to the Bureau of Labor Statistics website, employment is projected to grow faster than average. Job opportunities should be good, especially for applicants with work experience in health care and strong business management skills.

FOR MORE INFORMATION
- www.usa.siemens.com/en/jobs_careers/us_jobs.htm
- www.bls.gov/oco/ocos014.htm
- www.indeed.com/jobs?q=Clinical+Applications+Project+Manager&l=

46. Programmer/Analyst

POSITION DESCRIPTION   The role of a programmer/analyst is to work with business process owners to understand the business need and develop technical solutions that integrate existing and future applications into the organization's information systems. The ideal candidate must be proficient with the Microsoft.net framework, for example, and have extensive knowledge of the programming language C++. The individual is also responsible for coordination of the testing that is required before development programs are moved into production. The person must be able to work independently or as part of a team when required. Proven communication and problem-solving skills are critical to successful performance in this role.

EDUCATION AND EXPERIENCE A bachelor's degree in computer science or a related discipline is required. Three to 5 years of experience with C++ is required. The person must understand databases and be fluent in SQL server language. Experience in Microsoft web publishing is a benefit, along with familiarity with SharePoint.

CREDENTIALS, LICENSURE, OR CERTIFICATION, IF APPROPRIATE No specific credentials are required.

CORE COMPETENCIES AND SKILLS
- Excellent oral, written, and interpersonal skills
- Ability to work on multiple tasks and adapt to changing priorities to meet business requirements
- Be able to understand and analyze complete business requirements
- Provide innovative thinking to determine solutions and take appropriate action steps to implement solutions to meet business needs
- Debug software and fix defects uncovered during the testing process
- Learn new technologies as needed to successfully perform duties
- Help define and evolve development standards, guidelines, procedure, process, and metrics

COMPENSATION Based upon education and experience. Estimated to be typically between $60,000 and $90,000.

WORKPLACE LOCATION The position typically is located within the IT department of a vendor organization.

EMPLOYMENT OUTLOOK The overall market for a programmer/analyst is very good and is expected to increase at an above-average rate each year.

FOR MORE INFORMATION This position typically can be found in HIT vendor companies, such as Siemens, Epic, Cerner, McKessen, and many others. See Chapter 4 for various HIT vendor career websites.

47. Health Information Exchange Manager

POSITION DESCRIPTION The health information exchange (HIE) manager's role is to manage the vendor's mobile health information exchange product that is being used to collect, manage, and exchange patient information across providers and health care organizations. The HIE manager interacts with product developers, project management teams, hospital business owners, physician liaisons, and community clinicians to identify clinical business requirements and define product features and capabilities to expand physician alignment with the health care systems markets. The HIE manager is responsible for designing innovative HIE solutions to support clinical workflows and patient engagement over the Nationwide Health Information Network. The HIE manager is expected to remain current with the HIE landscape as the health care industry continues to evolve. The HIE manager will disseminate ideas by conducting webinars, creating fact sheets, and developing other communication materials to educate both internal and external stakeholders.

EDUCATION AND EXPERIENCE A bachelor's degree in an appropriate field is required. An advanced degree in a relevant field is preferred. At least 10 years of experience in health care delivery and/or health care information technology and successful demonstration of core competencies and skills are essential.

CREDENTIALS, LICENSURE, OR CERTIFICATION, IF APPROPRIATE No specific credential or certificate is required.

CORE COMPETENCIES AND SKILLS
- Provide team direction as well as direct knowledge and input into the development of the mobile HIE product
- Understand information exchange solutions inclusive of software applications
- Develop, document, and maintain the roadmap for the HIE product
- Direct and provide deliverable into the cross-functional activities related to training, documentation, tools, sales, marketing implementation, and support
- Plan, create, and deliver webinars on industry trends and health care interoperability
- Organizational and communication skills
- Self-motivated, innovative, and analytical with strong attention to detail and accuracy
- Display a high level of initiative and energy with the ability to work independently, along with demonstrated dependability
- Proactive attitude
- Self-directed with disciplined work ethic

- Demonstrated expertise in the area of HIE, care coordination, and systems workflows
- Demonstrated capability to work in a complex, matrixed organization
- Strong verbal and written communication and presentation skills
- Demonstrated ability to develop team members through mentoring and coaching in complex subjects
- Act as a lead advisor to top management and business partners on advanced clinical and technical matters
- Represent the company as an external contact

COMPENSATION   For a senior position the range can be $100,000 to $150,000.

WORKPLACE LOCATION   In a vendor organization, this position would be found in the IT area with specific responsibility for product development and deployment.

EMPLOYMENT OUTLOOK   The growth of HIE will lead to competition among vendors to develop, market, sell, implement, and maintain HIE solutions. Individuals will need years of experience with a product line to achieve a senior position of this type.

FOR MORE INFORMATION   Chapter 4 lists a number of websites for HIT vendor organizations such as Siemens that have positions in the area of product development and management, and specifically in the area of HIE.

48. Health Information Technology Specialist

POSITION DESCRIPTION   The health information technology (HIT) specialist is to provide support and training to assigned physician practices that have adopted HIT within their facilities. The individual also provides instruction in quality improvement efforts and effective use of data through on-site visits, regional meetings, scheduled conference calls, webinars, and ad hoc requests for additional involvement to assigned practices. The specialist is also expected to recruit physician practices to participate in the HIT adoption and quality improvement implementation. Aside from working with physician practices, the specialist is to work with electronic health record (EHR) vendors to make sure that their products allow practices to effectively utilize care management reporting tools. Working with vendors, the specialist is to attend vendor work group sessions as well as facilitate vendor training and demonstrations on care management reporting. The specialist will also provide input in the design of the clinical software and the reports. Participation in the development of measurement data, presentation feedback, continuous quality improvement tools and techniques, International Organization for Standardization activities, software use, and data interpretation is also required. The specialist will also present project work at professional meetings (including conferences and exhibits) and work closely with external physician consultants, team analysts, and other team members in order to enhance improvement efforts and maintain the knowledge base required to support providers in their improvement efforts. Aside from physician practices and vendors, the specialist is also to partner up with and network with other internal teams to accomplish improvement goals and meet contract deliverables. All in all, the specialist is required to maintain a working knowledge of performance improvement principles and incorporate them into his or her daily function.

EDUCATION AND EXPERIENCE A bachelor's degree in marketing, communications, public health, health care discipline, medical information technology, or equivalent experience is required. A master's degree is preferred. Also, a minimum of 2 years' experience in a health care setting as well as 2 years' experience in HIT applications are required. Educational presentation skills are desired.

CREDENTIALS, LICENSURE, OR CERTIFICATION, IF APPROPRIATE Either a Certified Professional in Electronic Health Records (CPEHR), a Certified Professional in Health Information Technology (CPHIT), or a Certified Professional in Health Information Exchange (CPHIE) designation is required. If one of these certifications is not obtained before hire, it shall be obtained within 1 year of hire.

CORE COMPETENCIES AND SKILLS The HIT specialist must have knowledge of the health care system/environment, Microsoft Excel, Microsoft Word, Microsoft PowerPoint, and medical terminology. The ability to lift boxes weighing 20 to 30 pounds is required as well as the ability to travel.

COMPENSATION The average salary ranges from $50,000 to $75,000.

WORKPLACE LOCATION   The position description is for an information technology specialist in a vendor company.

EMPLOYMENT OUTLOOK   As the vendor marketplace grows due to government regulations and incentives, this type of position is expected to grow at an above-average rate.

FOR MORE INFORMATION
   ■ qsourcecareers.iapplicants.com/ViewJob-360629.html

SCOTT CEBULA
President
Cebula IT Consulting, LLC

Describe the sort of work you do. My firm works with a range of health care organizations including hospitals, medical group practices, and ambulatory care facilities. At any one time there may be six to eight active clients with projects such as

- *ICD-10* planning and implementation
- IT information security
- Project management for various IT installations
- Strategic consulting and advice for organizations
- Health information exchange (HIE) strategy development
- HIE vendor selection and implementation

What is a typical day like at your job? As a small business owner the day-to-day activities vary depending upon client needs and service contract deliverable. Typically Fridays are devoted to running the business and doing status calls on current clients. Running any business requires paperwork and follow-up on existing clients and the market for new clients. I also use Fridays to network with colleagues and take a leading role in local Chief Information Officer (CIO) Forum events. It is critical to stay connected and give back to the profession. Usually Monday through Thursday and usually Saturday I'm in the field delivering services to clients and working with my team. A critical daily activity is project management and making sure we deliver our services as contracted.

(*continued*)

SCOTT CEBULA   *(continued)*

What education or training do you have? Is it typical for your job? My education background may not be typical for my career path. I have an undergraduate in mechanical engineering and a graduate degree in aerospace engineering. I grew up in the microcomputer era and loved programming.

What path did you take to get to the job you are in today? Again, my pathway might be a little different. I started out as a programmer for Fortune 500 companies and moved into health care sort of mid-career. Upon entering health care I was amazed at how behind hospitals were in terms of information technology compared with the Fortune 500 companies I had worked for. A key to my career path was finding a great set of mentors who challenged me and helped me to advance in the health care environment. I became a chief technology officer (CTO) and the interim CIO for a major hospital in the Los Angeles area. Starting my own consulting firm was a great transition and allows me to utilize my technical and past hospital experiences to assist clients with their HIT strategies, building business cases for HIT adoptions and project management activities.

Where might you go from here if you wanted to advance your career? As president of my own company it is a very rewarding position, but one must always be flexible and notice, if not actively seeking, opportunities that might come along. I must realize that my company might expand, perhaps merging with a larger consulting company; or perhaps a past or current client might make an offer I can't refuse. One must always be open to opportunities in the context of family, lifestyle, and the state of the health care economy.

What is the most challenging part of your job? The least energizing parts of the job are the necessary business management activities. I am running a business, and there are contracts and paperwork that must be managed and other basic mechanics of accounting and business management. These activities are required of any entrepreneur, but the reason we are in our chosen careers are the things that inspire us.

(continued)

SCOTT CEBULA   *(continued)*

What is the best part? The things that inspire me are the delivery of quality IT services to clients, networking with colleagues and mentors both upward and downward, and adding value to my profession through my work with the CIO Forum.

What advice would you give to someone contemplating a career like yours? A person needs to have an attitude, enthusiasm, and passion for his or her career. Some practical suggestion might be:

- Have a vision of where you want to be in 5 years.
- Getting started in a beginning job is often more important than waiting for the perfect job.
- Focus on the long term.
- Seek out and develop relationships with mentors and network with colleagues by joining professional associations.
- Be flexible and watch the workforce marketplace to see where the opportunities are developing.
- Moving sideways or even backward might be the best decision to advance in a career path.

49. Network Engineer

POSITION DESCRIPTION   The network engineer is responsible for architecture and the management of critical clinical infrastructure in a wired/wireless environment. He or she provides infrastructure engineering services including storage networking and subsystems such as F5 and Citrix load balancing; Windows/Linux/AIX operating systems; application, system, and network security; VMware server virtualization; and Tier 3 data center operations.

EDUCATION AND EXPERIENCE   Must have a bachelor's degree in a technical discipline. At least 2 years' experience supporting critical infrastructure systems in a 24/7 environment in health care preferred.

CREDENTIALS, LICENSURE, OR CERTIFICATION, IF APPROPRIATE   No specific certificate or credential required. However, the candidate must be knowledgeable of and experienced in many technical engineering and software systems.

CORE COMPETENCIES AND SKILLS   Each network engineer position will be configured differently based on the hardware, HIT vendors, architecture of the organization's infrastructure, and other organization-specific needs. For example:

- Experience supporting Microsoft Active Directory 2008
- Knowledge of VMware and Citrix a plus
- Excellent client relations skills, experience working with end users
- Knowledge of managing/maintaining and troubleshooting LAN/WAN/MAN management and design systems
- Strong knowledge of the OSI model to troubleshoot issues from physical to application layer.

COMPENSATION   The salary for this technical field can range from $55,000 to $90,000 depending on the size of the health care organization and the years of experience and degrees of the applicant.

WORKPLACE LOCATION   Network engineers and network administrators are highly technical positions and require degrees and experience related to complex computer systems. Normally these positions are found in large, complex health care systems and vendor organizations.

EMPLOYMENT OUTLOOK   Demand is strong for individuals with technical skills and experience, but the strongest demand will be for those who have applied those technical skills and knowledge in a health care setting.

FOR MORE INFORMATION   Positions such as network engineer can be found in the HIMSS JobMine as well as on large health care systems websites. Chapter 4 can help direct you to appropriate web resources.

50. Computer and Information Systems Manager

POSITION DESCRIPTION   Medical and health services managers, also called health care executives or health care administrators, plan, direct, and coordinate medical and health services. They might manage an entire facility, specialize in managing a specific clinical area or department, or manage a medical practice for a group of physicians. Duties include

- Review project plans to plan and coordinate project activity.
- Manage backup, security, and user help systems.
- Develop and interpret organizational goals, policies, and procedures.
- Develop computer information resources, providing for data security and control, strategic computing, and disaster recovery.
- Consult with users, management, vendors, and technicians to assess computing needs and system requirements.
- Stay abreast of advances in technology.
- Meet with department heads, managers, supervisors, vendors, and others to solicit cooperation and resolve problems.
- Provide users with technical support for computer problems.
- Recruit, hire, train, and supervise staff, or participate in staffing decisions.
- Evaluate data processing proposals to assess project feasibility and requirements.

EDUCATION AND EXPERIENCE   A 4-year bachelor's degree in computer science is generally required. A master's degree is desirable.

CREDENTIALS, LICENSURE, OR CERTIFICATION, IF APPROPRIATE   A considerable amount of work-related skill, knowledge, or experience is needed for this occupation.

CORE COMPETENCIES AND SKILLS
- Good communication skills, including writing, oral, and presentation skills.
- Using logic and reasoning to identify the strengths and weaknesses of alternative solutions, conclusions, or approaches to problems.
- Identifying complex problems and reviewing related information to develop and evaluate options and implement solutions.
- Determining how a system should work and how changes in conditions, operations, and the environment will affect outcomes.
- Identifying measures or indicators of system performance and the actions needed to improve or correct performance, relative to the goals of the system.
- Managing one's own time and the time of others.

- Conducting tests and inspections of products, services, or processes to evaluate quality or performance.
- Motivating, developing, and directing people as they work, and identifying the best people for the job.

COMPENSATION   The median salary is approximately $118,000.

WORKPLACE LOCATION   Professionals in this field generally work in a variety of industries besides health care. Within health care, a computer information systems manager will work in hospital settings as well as managed care, vendors, and larger medical groups.

EMPLOYMENT OUTLOOK   The U.S. Bureau of Labor Statistics (BLS) estimates that the number of working health information technicians will grow 21% from 2010 to 2020. Students pursuing a bachelor's degree may find excellent job prospects as medical or health services managers as well; the number of professionals in that field is expected to increase 22% from 2010 to 2020.

FOR MORE INFORMATION
- www.onetonline.org/link/details/11-3021.00

51. Health Information Technology Consultant

POSITION DESCRIPTION   Health information technology (HIT) consultants are in charge of supporting, training, and consulting with regard to the computer software programs, multimedia, database systems, and networks for the organization or for individuals running their own health care business. Duties mainly include performing installations, and supporting and updating various systems. The main purpose of HIT consultants in the health care field is to educate others in the medical field on how to use computers effectively and efficiently. The HIT consultant is the link between technology and medical professionals in order to keep the procedures of manipulating the computer system as easy as possible and to respond to any troubleshooting requirement when needed.

EDUCATION AND EXPERIENCE   The education requirements to become a HIT consultant start with obtaining a bachelor's degree in the field of information technology. Accepted degrees include computer science, information technology, and business administration in management information systems. Although the minimum requirement is the bachelor's degree, there is a high recommendation for obtaining a master's or PhD in a field related to computer science in order to stand out among the other competitors who seek employment in the same field. Experience is also a must in order to become a HIT consultant. Many candidates will be required to do on-the-job training that focuses on certain purposes throughout their education program.

CREDENTIALS, LICENSURE, OR CERTIFICATION, IF APPROPRIATE   One of the most basic certifications that can be earned for the position is a Certified Health Informatics System Professional (CHISP) designation, which may be required in most cases in order to become a HIT consultant in an organization. In order to qualify for the CHISP examination, one must have an information technology background or have passed the American Society of Health Informatics Managers training program. There are other certifications that can be obtained, such as the ComTIA Healthcare IT Technician certification and the Certified Healthcare Information Technology certification. The certification requirements will vary among the workplaces, but there is a greater chance of receiving employment if the applicant holds various certifications regarding information technology.

CORE COMPETENCIES AND SKILLS
- Basic business and communication skills. These include professional writing, speaking, presentation, listening, problem-solving, and analyzing skills.
- Knowledge of specific technical, industry, or subject matter will also be required within the firms they work in.
- HIT consultants must also be detailed oriented and be able to effectively time manage their schedules.

COMPENSATION   Although the range may vary, there is a recent report that estimates that the median HIT consultant salary hits somewhere around $77,000 annually. This number can vary due to the workplace, location, and personal work experience.

WORKPLACE LOCATION   The workplace location for HIT consultants may depend on where they are hired, but it is noted that most consultants will be required to travel to different clients.

EMPLOYMENT OUTLOOK   Experts report that there is a need for over 50,000 HIT experts nationally, with a 50% growth occurring every year. However, many organizations strongly demand IT experts who are well educated, hold multiple certifications, and have the necessary skills to make a good fit with the company.

FOR MORE INFORMATION
- www.hitconsultant.net
- healthcareittoday.com
- aidhit.org/cpages/become-a-consultant

52. Product Specialist

POSITION DESCRIPTION   The product specialist will become the expert for showing the company's software solutions in action to clients. In this role, the key contributions will be:

- Travel to client sites and provide product demonstrations for a variety of the company's software products.
- Act as internal "product expert" for the sales department.
- Represent the company at trade association meetings to demonstrate and promote products.
- Responsible for actively keeping up with and educating self regarding ongoing changes and trends in the health care industry that may affect the positioning of the company's solutions.
- Actively participate in development of and in driving new messaging, "scripting," and talking points for product demonstrations, presentations, value propositions, and so on.

EDUCATION AND EXPERIENCE   Bachelor's degree in business administration, health administration, or equivalent experience. Three to 5 years of experience delivering medical product demonstrations. Sales or customer support experience preferred.

CREDENTIALS, LICENSURE, OR CERTIFICATION, IF APPROPRIATE   Depends on the specific organizational requirement.

CORE COMPETENCIES AND SKILLS
- Demonstrated sales/marketing/business development skills and knowledge
- Excellent communication and presentation skills
- Outstanding verbal and written communication skills
- Available for significant overnight travel (50%–75%)
- Ability to work from a home office

COMPENSATION   Positions like this can either be 100% salary or a combination of salary and incentive bonuses. A typical salary range could be between $65,000 and $125,000 depending on the size of the vendor organization.

WORKPLACE LOCATION   Positions like this one can be found in most HIT vendor companies in the sales or marketing department.

EMPLOYMENT OUTLOOK   The outlook for vendor-based product specialists is highly dependent on the growth of the overall HIT sector. As hospitals and other providers move toward more electronic medical records and other IT solutions, vendor companies will be expanding their workforce in the areas of sales and marketing.

FOR MORE INFORMATION
- www.bls.gov
- www.jobmine.himss.org

53. Business Analyst

POSITION DESCRIPTION   The business analyst position is designed for an entry-level junior professional. The vendor expects the individual to work in a manner that benefits the projects and, ultimately, return of investment on projects is attained. The business analyst works with the project manager, client providers, and support staff to clearly define, at project onset, the benefits of a project. The business analyst collects baseline information and evaluates at project completion whether goals were attained. The business analyst facilitates the implementation and measures the success of process changes. The business analyst will prepare reports throughout the benefits process on specific projects and on the sum of all projects. The business analyst will support the development of repeatable processes and templates to make the benefits assessment process scalable.

EDUCATION AND EXPERIENCE   A bachelor's degree is required. Fields such as business administration, information systems, or health administration are preferred.

CORE COMPETENCIES AND SKILLS
- Possess decision-making skills as well as the ability to deal with ambiguity

- Strong analytic, data analysis, and problem-solving abilities
- Demonstrated ability to work on multiple projects simultaneously and prioritize work to meet adapting deadlines and attention to detail
- Excellent computer skills, including Microsoft Office Suite
- Strong verbal and written communication skills
- Ability to work overtime and irregular hours when needed
- This position requires a critical thinker, self-starter, and innovative associate who identifies opportunities for process improvements, provides analysis, proposes change strategies, and communicates proposed strategies

COMPENSATION   This entry-level position can have a salary range of $50,000 to perhaps $75,000 depending on the combination of educational achievements and the size and location of the vendor.

WORKPLACE LOCATION   A business analyst in the vendor health care sector is likely to work in the corporate headquarters of the organization.

EMPLOYMENT OUTLOOK   The employment outlook for the vendor sector is strong. All large HIT vendor organizations are working to develop their HIT products and services in response to demands by providers to meet the federal government incentives and market demand.

FOR MORE INFORMATION
- www.cerner.com/About_Cerner/Careers

54. Information Security/eDiscovery Specialist

POSITION DESCRIPTION   Under the supervision of the chief informatics officer (CIO), the individual's primary role is to create the standards for HIPAA/protected health information (PHI) and eDiscovery policy and procedures for an organization. This person will assist the organization with understanding, applying, and implementing HIPAA/PHI and eDiscovery privacy and security standards and integrating them with other patient privacy and security regulations to meet federal and state regulations and The Joint Commission standards. The specialist will provide to the CIO analytical support and documentation related to the latest changes to HIPAA/PHI as they relate to eDiscovery, and must research and stay current on all federal and state regulations on patient privacy and security standards as they relate to health care. The specialist must understand and implement the Core Measures for Meaningful Use for stages 1 and 2 as they relate to protected health information created or maintained by the certified electronic health record technology through the implementation of appropriate technical capabilities such as audit log, integrity, authentication, general encryption, and encryption when exchanging electronic health information. The information security/eDiscovery specialist will also function as the IS security officer. The position will carry out security measures to protect an organization's computer network and systems.

EDUCATION AND EXPERIENCE   A bachelor's degree, 2 years of experience working directly in an Information Services department, and previous experience with HIPAA/PHI compliance programs, policies, procedures, risk assessments, and audits are required.

CREDENTIALS, LICENSURE, OR CERTIFICATION, IF APPROPRIATE   Not applicable to this position.

CORE COMPETENCIES AND SKILLS
- Must have knowledge of HIPAA/PHI and the HITECH Act.
- Must be able to apply logic to the analysis, development, and implementation of complex workflow and information system solutions and be able to successfully implement these solutions in the assigned area.
- Organizational and multitasking skills are essential for working in a complex and varied work environment.
- Ability to work with multiple implementations in great detail, deal with interruptions, coordinate and negotiate different expectations and commitments among multiple hospital departments and physicians.
- Conflict management skills are necessary to resolve conflicts within and among departments and disciplines throughout the organization and with physicians.
- Change management skills are necessary to lead implementations that will result in significant changes to the workflow process for associates, physicians, and physicians' office staffs throughout the organization.
- Knowledge of operations and regulatory requirements pertaining to assigned areas of responsibility. Proficiency in use of project management, word processing, flowcharting, database, and electronic mail software applications. Ability to learn in a short

period of time and an ability to comprehend and utilize technical skills for database management.
■ Analytical and grammatical skills are necessary to communicate effectively verbally and in writing. Must comply with HIPAA regulations and company confidentiality policies and procedures.

COMPENSATION   According to indeed.com, the average Information Security/eDiscovery Specialist can earn $107,000 a year.

WORKPLACE LOCATION   This position in the vendor health care sector is likely to work in the corporate headquarters of the organization.

EMPLOYMENT OUTLOOK   According to the Bureau of Labor Statistics website, employment is expected to grow much faster than average, and job prospects should be excellent.

FOR MORE INFORMATION
■ www.bls.gov/ooh/computer-and-information-technology/information-security-analysts.htm
■ www.indeed.com/salary?q1=Information+Security+Ediscovery+Specialist&l1=

MONA KARAGUOZIAN
Business Development Consultant
and Executive Assistant to CEO
Aligned Telehealth, Inc.

Describe the sort of work you do. Aligned is a Behavioral Health Hospitalist and Telemedicine company that provides health care services to various types of facilities both on the ground and via telemedicine. We provide inpatient behavioral health services as well as 24/7 telepsychiatry coverage for hospital emergency departments. The shortage of behavioral health (BH) services in rural areas and certain other communities demonstrates a need to provide access to populations who otherwise would have to travel many miles to see a professional. The work I do consists of business development, looking for strategic alliances, assisting the CEO with day-to-day operational needs, and recruiting health care providers for the company. This includes working on preparing marketing materials and reaching out to potential clients in regard to our services and also building our national network of providers.

What is a typical day like at your job? The best part of my job is that there is no typical day. Every day is different, but mostly it consists of finding ways to promote the company and its services to potential clients and working with the executive office on key projects and business development. I create a list of potential clients, reach out to them via phone, e-mail, or mail and perform a needs analysis to determine what type of services they are looking for or may need. My day also consists of recruiting providers for our national network, which includes marketing our opportunities and interviewing potential providers that are interested and drafting their contractual agreements.

(continued)

167

MONA KARAGUOZIAN   (*continued*)

What education or training do you have? Is it typical for your job? I have a Master of Science in Health Administration from California State University, Northridge. I am not sure if it is typical to have this particular degree for my current position, but I have noticed that at other companies and facilities, people who work in business development tend to have graduate degrees in health administration or business administration.

What path did you take to get to the job you are in today? I didn't have much experience in the health care industry when I decided to pursue Health Administration. In fact, I was planning on going to law school after graduating with a master's degree. I decided to delay that career goal because I gained a real interest in the health care industry on the management side. Upon graduating, I started applying for jobs in the industry. I was unsuccessful with my search through online applications due to the economic status and lack of available positions in 2009. Through networking, I was able to arrange an interview with my current employer. I was fascinated with this novel concept of telemedicine in the health care industry. I accepted the offer because of my interest and also because I thought it would be a good place to get the kind of experience I was looking for and needed.

Where might you go from here if you wanted to advance your career? I definitely plan to grow within the company I work in right now. At my current position I have exposure to operations and management activities and am able to learn and have the kind of experience that I may not receive at another company. Down the line I hope and strive to move up the ranks toward an executive-level position.

What is the most challenging part of your job? Multitasking projects is always a challenge, but nonetheless a challenge I enjoy taking on. The most challenging aspect of my job is when I am speaking to leads or potential clients or providers who are not familiar with the concept of telemedicine and show a little resistance due to the fact that they have no experience with it.

(*continued*)

MONA KARAGUOZIAN   (*continued*)

What is the best part? On the same note, it is also great speaking with people who are unfamiliar with the concept of telemedicine but are eager to understand and embrace it and have the desire to keep up with advances in technology. However, the best part is going to work every day and knowing that the impact of this technology and medium with which the health care services are being provided results in an increase to access to health care, quality improvement and cost efficiencies, and innovative ways of delivering health care services. I feel great to be a part of the growth of telemedicine.

What advice would you give to someone contemplating a career like yours? I definitely recommend pursuing a career in health care that involves technology. It is a cliché to say, "It is the wave of the future," but clichés ring true for a reason. My advice to others is to do whatever you can to get some level of work experience in health care even if it is as a volunteer. Employers are impressed by the demonstrated desire to be in health care that comes from both the educational achievements as well as work experience. We are going to see much more of telemedicine in the near future. We do not realize that a great part of the United States is rural and vast, and that there is a huge shortage of health care professionals. Telemedicine bridges that gap in health care by providing much-needed services to those areas. It is critical, I believe, for those who want get into the telemedicine side of health care to use their networks to obtain connections in this growing field.

8 ■ HIT CAREERS IN THE PHYSICIAN PRACTICE AND MEDICAL GROUP SECTORS

Legislative and economic pressures on physicians are the driving forces pushing technological change into physician practices and larger medical groups. The Health Information Technology for Economic and Clinical Health (HITECH) Act of 2009 created both expectations toward the adoption of electronic medical records (EMR) and financial incentives to encourage the adoption. The barrier to adoption by physicians is a real limitation on achieving a paper-light medical office environment that perhaps facilitates the exchange of appropriate medical information between providers and health care facilities. Even with government incentives for achieving what is called meaningful use of EMR, small physician practices are still limited in achieving success. Physicians in small practices, with perhaps fewer than five doctors, face a lot of challenges when it comes to health information technology (HIT) and EMR selection, implementation, and maintenance. These smaller offices sometimes join a medical service organization (MSO), which can act as a group cooperative in a number of areas like finance and technology.

> *Be flexible and watch the workforce to see where the opportunties are developing.*
> *—Scott Cebula*

Some of the barriers faced by smaller physician practices include manpower issues and the lack of staff that can do the technical work of redesigning the workflow to facilitate the use of new technology. These small practices often turn to vendors or consultants to provide the technical expertise.

Larger medical groups are much better positioned to engage in the selection, implementation, and continued maintenance of an HIT system like EMR. But they also have staff limitations, challenges with the financial burden of expensive systems, and a lack of integration across clinical and financial systems.

Some of the following job descriptions of HIT positions in medical practices (starting on p. 175) come from the Medical Group Management Association (MGMA) and represent typical jobs one would find in this environment. It is common for different organizations to use either similar titles but different job responsibilities or same responsibilities with different titles. It is therefore important for a job seeker to review multiple job descriptions to be clear on what is expected in a particular job category.

CHRIS PENSINGER
Medical Director of Informatics, Fairview Medical Group
Chair, Ambulatory Informatics and Decision Support Committees, Fairview Health Services

Describe the sort of work you do. As the medical director of informatics, it is my role to provide leadership and coordination to the Electronic Health Record (EHR) implementation at Fairview Health Services. In 2009, we chose Epic as our system-wide EHR vendor and we just finished the installation of their EHR systems in our six hospitals and all ambulatory facilities. I am also chair of the Inpatient Clinical Decision Support Committee and in that role I work with our providers to optimize the EHR to better serve the clinical needs of our physicians and maximize the Epic EHR system's capabilities. For example, we create targeted clinical order sets or guidelines and thus reduce unnecessary alerts. On the implementation side I work with teams to support physicians as they adopt the EHR. Often it is managing change, and there are always eager early adopters and those that need more hand holding.

What is a typical day like at your job? There a few "typical" days because of the dynamics of the health informatics field and the challenges of moving a large system toward maximizing the benefits of an EHR. I am 75% in my role as director of medical informatics and 25% still practicing in either the hospital or an ambulatory setting. Outside of my clinical responsibilities, I am 50% attending or running meetings and 50% working and delivering products on various projects. Some of those projects might be helping clinicians with both technical and adaptive changes or providing input to the chief medical information officer (CMIO).

What education or training do you have? Is it typical for your job? I studied to be a family practice physician and started practicing in the early

(continued)

CHRIS PENSINGER *(continued)*

1990s. It was great timing for me because early electronic health records were beginning to penetrate the market and I was intrigued by the technology. I went back to pursue a master's in health informatics (MHI) at the University of Minnesota, where I did my medical training—a great program which really helped to set my future career path. I also have several certifications related to Epic software. I think the MHI or some advanced degree like an MBA or MHA will become more expected in the future in order to be successful in this profession.

What path did you take to get to the job you are in today? I began practicing and admitting to Fairview Health System in the early '90s. I was involved in our first installation of the Epic ambulatory system in 1998 and I guess I was hooked into my future career path. In 2008 I began my current position. A formal education path will probably become more typical in the future as the demand for medical informaticists is increasing and more people in the medical community see the future of this field.

Where might you go from here if you wanted to advance your career? I have a great, challenging job that is both creative and innovative, and the rewards of interacting with colleagues to improve the care of patients are wonderful. The CMIO position can be further removed from direct patient care, more administrative and strategically focused. I enjoy the balance between patient care and applying my technologic skills to provide for more efficient care.

What is the most challenging part of your job? Because of the complexity of EHR systems there are always multiple projects and deadlines all going on at the same time. Time management is a critical skill in informatics. If you don't become a master at it, you quickly become overwhelmed. An informaticist can start the day with a set calendar with readily identifiable tasks, but then an e-mail or call comes in and now your day is hijacked resolving something that you didn't expect. My job requires considerable patience and people skills, including the ability to act as an icon of serenity so that our mutual end goals can be reached. This can be quite challenging some days.

(continued)

CHRIS PENSINGER   *(continued)*

What is the best part? I enjoy when a plan comes together and we see results that impact people's lives, the care they received, and the cost savings the organization achieved. When providers are more efficient and productive and patients are better it is a good day. I also like it when the phone is quiet and no one has called to complain. No one calls when things are going right.

What advice would you give to someone contemplating a career like yours? Medical, nursing, or even pharmacy students should consider a clinical rotation through medical informatics. They should consider an advanced education that complements their interest in informatics. In today's labor market, new MDs or nurse informaticists need to be flexible in terms of where they work and its geographical location. Some areas of the country are well established in terms of EHRs and those jobs might be harder to find. Other areas might have a shortage of those trained in informatics.

POSITION DESCRIPTIONS IN MEDICAL GROUP
AND PHYSICIAN PRACTICE SETTINGS

55. Registered Health Information Technician and Registered Health Information Administrator (General Descriptions)

Registered health information technicians (RHITs) and registered health information administrators (RHIAs) are certified medical coders. RHIAs and RHITs are responsible for organizing and managing health information data by ensuring its quality, accuracy, accessibility, and security in both paper and electronic systems. Technicians document patients' health information, including medical history, symptoms, examination and test results, treatments, and other information about health care provider services. They use various classification systems to code and categorize patient information for insurance reimbursement purposes, for databases and registries, and to maintain patients' medical and treatment histories.

Medical coders' duties vary with the size of the facility in which they work. They typically perform a variety of duties that may include managing other health care information professionals and preparing budgets; using computer applications to assemble and analyze patient data for the purpose of improving patient care or controlling costs; reviewing patient records for timeliness, completeness, accuracy, and appropriateness of health data; organizing and maintaining data for clinical databases and registries; tracking patient outcomes for quality assessment; using classification software to assign clinical codes for reimbursement and data analysis; electronically recording data for collection, storage, analysis, retrieval, and reporting; protecting patients' health information for confidentiality, authorized access for treatment, and data security; reviewing patient information for pre-existing conditions and patient records for medical personnel; and working as a liaison between the health clinician and billing offices.

These positions can be found in both medical groups and hospitals because both have responsibilities for medical coding and billing. The following six job descriptions show the range of responsibilities associated with similar titles. The first two job descriptions are for early careers while the last two demonstrate more senior management or director positions in health information management (HIM).

56. Registered Health Information Technician

POSITION DESCRIPTION   Medical coders are specially trained health care professionals that are responsible for managing patient data so that other health care professionals can utilize it. They help maintain patient medical records in hospitals, doctors' offices, and other health care facilities.

EDUCATION AND EXPERIENCE   Minimum requirements include an associate's degree in HIT. A degree from a 4-year university program in HIT or business administration is preferred.

CREDENTIALS, LICENSURE, OR CERTIFICATION, IF APPROPRIATE   Those wishing to work as medical coders can become certified through several organizations. Some organizations base certification on passing an exam. Others require graduation from an accredited program. Once certified, technicians typically must renew their certification regularly and take continuing education courses. The majority of employers prefer to hire medical records and health information technicians who have professional certification.

CORE COMPETENCIES AND SKILLS

- Proficient in medical coding
- Strong computer background
- Strong communication skills
- Strong clinical, administrative, and management background
- Understand and follow medical records and diagnoses, and then decide how best to code them in a patient's medical records
- Pay attention to details to ensure accurate recording and coding of patient information
- Discuss patient information, discrepancies, and data requirements with other professionals such as physicians and finance personnel
- Be familiar with, or be able to learn, electronic health record (EHR) computer software, follow EHR security and privacy practices, and analyze electronic data
- Use coding and classification software and the EHR system that the health care organization or physician practice has adopted

COMPENSATION   The salary for this and similar positions in HIM can range from $37,000 to $75,000 for lower-level HIM positions and up to $96,000 for manager positions, depending on level of experience and the size and location of the organization.

WORKPLACE LOCATION   Medical coders may work at hospitals, private physician practices, clinics, behavioral health establishments, insurance companies, or government agencies. Though the duties required for each of these positions are typically the same, the workplace location may vary depending on the specific duties. Technicians typically work at desks or in offices in the IT or administration department.

EMPLOYMENT OUTLOOK   RHIT or RHIA employment is expected to increase by 21% from 2010 to 2020, faster than the average for all health care occupations. The demand for health services is expected to increase as the population ages. Additional records, coupled with widespread use of EHR by all types of health care providers, should lead to an increased need for medical coders to organize and manage the associated information in all areas of the health care industry.

FOR MORE INFORMATION
Job positions:
- www.careerbuilder.com/Jobs/Keyword/Rhit

Educational programs in this field:

- www.allhealthcaredegrees.com/him_rhit.htm#
  Provides a list of various institutions and online programs offered throughout the country.
  Professional organization in this field:
- www.pahcs.org
- U.S. Department of Labor, Bureau of Labor Statistics. (n.d.). *Occupational outlook handbook, 2012–13 edition: Medical records and health information technicians.* Retrieved from www.bls.gov/ooh/Healthcare/Medical-records-and-health-information-technicians.htm

57. Registered Health Information Administrator

POSITION DESCRIPTION   Working as a critical link among care providers, payers, and patients, the RHIA is an expert in managing patient health information and medical records, administering computer information systems, collecting and analyzing patient data, and using classification systems and medical terminologies. RHIAs possess comprehensive knowledge of medical, administrative, ethical, and legal requirements and standards related to health care delivery and the privacy of protected patient information. They are often upper-level management who manage people and operational units, participate in administrative committees, and prepare budgets. RHIA professionals are required to have strong communication skills, a sharp eye for detail, knowledge of computer systems, and management skills. Strong organization skills and the ability to plan projects are important traits. A bachelor's degree or higher is highly preferred for RHIA positions.

EDUCATION AND EXPERIENCE   The majority of employers are looking for the following designations: RHIA, RHIT, Certified Coding Specialist (CCS), Certified Coding Specialist–Physician-based (CCS-P), and Certified Professional Coder (CPC). Employers are seeking professionals who carry one or more of these certifications along with an average minimum of 2 years' experience coding patient records in a hospital HIM department.

The employee must have a thorough knowledge of medical terminology, anatomy, and physiology to understand diagnoses and to ensure proper billing. The separation between the RHIT and RHIA positions is that the RHIA is usually associated with a bachelor's-level HIM program accredited by the Commission on Accreditation for Health Informatics and Information Management Education (CAHIIM). RHIAs are usually in management positions.

COMPENSATION The salary for this and similar positions in HIM can range from $47,000 to $75,000 for lower-level HIM positions and up to $96,000 for manager positions, depending on level of experience and the size and location of the organization.

WORKPLACE LOCATION Job opportunities exist in various settings throughout the health care industry. These settings include hospitals, multispecialty clinics and physician practices, long-term care, mental health, and other ambulatory care settings. The profession has seen significant expansion in non–patient care settings, with careers in managed care and insurance companies, software vendors, consulting services, government agencies, education, and pharmaceutical companies.

EMPLOYMENT OUTLOOK Medical and health services management is expected to grow faster than the average for all occupations. Employment in HIT is expected to grow by 21% between 2010 and 2020, according to the U.S. Bureau of Labor Statistics. Health care reimbursement will be centered on patient care and satisfaction. HIT will play a crucial part by helping maintain EMR that will allow reduction of unwarranted testing, allow faster access to results, and lead to increased patient satisfaction. As a result, according to the Patient Protection and Affordable Care Act, more HIT professionals will be needed over the coming years.

FOR MORE INFORMATION
- www.ehow.com/facts_5873604_job-medical-coding-_amp_-billing_.html#ixzz2NXzQg85E
- jobsearch.monster.com/search/Registered-Health-Information-Technician-__28RHIT__29_5?

58. Coding Review Manager/Coder Trainer Auditor

POSITION DESCRIPTION A coder trainer auditor is actively involved in mentoring and training for all functions and services related to hospital medical coding, medical documentation, physician queries, abstracting, and data collection. The successful candidate must possess a proficient understanding of the Inpatient and Outpatient Prospective Payment Systems (IPPS/OPPS), Medical Severity Diagnosis-Related Groups (MS-DRG), National Correct Coding Initiative Edits (NCCI), the *International Classification of Diseases, 9th Revision, Clinical Modification (ICD-9-CM)* and *International Classification of Diseases, 10th Revision, Clinical Modification (ICD-10-CM)* Official Guidelines for Coding and Reporting, and Coding Clinic. Additional responsibilities include being able to work in a labor-management partnership environment, and working with coding supervisors and the HIM director to develop, implement, evaluate, and improve coders participating in the HIM department on-the-job training (OJT) program. Duties will include:

- Coordinates, monitors, and audits all lines of hospital business for coding, to include all outpatient, inpatient, and ambulatory surgery cases.
- Monitors the accuracy and quality of coding assignments and Present on Admission (POA) indicators, and conducts internal coding audits.
- Responsible for being the regional coding contact person for the HIM department to work with Clinical Documentation Specialists to support education and coding requirements.
- Develops reports of audit results to regional and facility staff and senior management. Provides oversight and training for "coding compliance software" to the coding staff.
- Runs audit selection lists and reports, as well as providing education, feedback, and guidance based upon data mining activities and processes.
- May provide insight into planning, directing, and monitoring of Charge Capture Initiatives for Facility and Professional Charges as well as inpatient medical records including Centers for Medicare and Medicaid Services (CMS), Fiscal Intermediary, Commercial and Self-Funded billing guidelines retrieval, assembly, delivery, abstracting/analyzing, coding, completion, transcriptions, release of information, and vital statistics registration.
- May provide oversight of the accuracy of data for Office of Statewide Health Planning and Development reporting.
- Collaborates with the HIM director/manager on matters relating to coding accuracy and coding functions to ensure that timely and accurate completion of work is consistent with regulatory agency requirements.
- Prepares statistical and or annual coding accuracy reports as requested. Ensures compliance with federal, state, and local regulations.

- May assist in regional and facility budgets as requested, and identifies and recommends opportunities to decrease costs and improve service.
- Functions as a liaison for other departments regarding coding questions/issues. Implements changes resulting from internal or external audits, which impact collection and reporting of medical records.
- Participates in regional HIM staff meeting and process-improvement initiatives.

EDUCATION AND EXPERIENCE   Associate's degree required, but bachelor's degree preferred.

CREDENTIALS, LICENSURE, OR CERTIFICATION, IF APPROPRIATE   Certified Coding Specialist (CCS). May also possess RHIT or RHIA or RHIA/RHIT credentials.

CORE COMPETENCIES AND SKILLS   Minimum of 4 years of Acute Care: Inpatient, Outpatient, MS-DRG, hierarchical condition categories, and ambulatory payment classification (APC) coding required. Coding Review Manager also requires 4 or more years of supervisory experience in a Medical Records department. In-depth understanding of all state/federal regulations and CMRI, National Committee for Quality Assurance (NCQA), JCAHO, and CMS regulations. Demonstrated strong interpersonal communication skills. Ability to develop and provide high-quality in-services and seminars on coding and coding-related topics. Working knowledge of state/federal, CMRI, NCQA, JCAHO, and CMS regulations.

COMPENSATION   The salary for this and similar positions in HIM can range from $37,000 to $75,000 for lower-level HIM positions and up to $96,000 for manager positions, depending on level of experience and the size and location of the organization.

WORKPLACE LOCATION   You can find this job in a variety of health care organizations such as hospitals, medical coding outsourcing firms, and larger medical groups and managed service organization (MSOs).

EMPLOYMENT OUTLOOK   Employment is expected to grow by 20% from 2010 to 2020 (www.bls.gov/ooh/computer-and-information-technology/home.htm).

FOR MORE INFORMATION

- healthcareconsultantsinc.applicantstack.com/x/detail/a2hzi7fmhxdr

59. Director of Health Information Management for Coding Operations

POSITION DESCRIPTION A director of HIM for coding operations should have extensive coding and supervision experience. Under the direction of the chief financial officer, the director plans, organizes, directs, and supervises the medical records or medical coding operations of the HIM division of the medical center; develops, recommends, implements, evaluates, and monitors goals, objectives, policies, and procedures related to health information; provides staff support to higher-level management; and selects, trains, and supervises subordinate professional, technical, and clerical staff.

The director of HIM for coding operations has the primary responsibility of overseeing the coding staff and *ICD-9* and *-10* and CPT coding functions. Coded data generated by coding operations is utilized for mandated reporting, quality measurement, compliance, reimbursement, and other purposes. The timeliness, completeness, and accuracy of coding data generated and reported is increasingly important to operations. Job duties include:

- Organize, supervise, and monitor the activities of assigned HIM section
- Develop, recommend, implement, evaluate, and monitor goals, objectives, policies, procedures, and priorities for the assigned unit
- Prepare cost estimates and justifications for budget recommendations; monitor and control expenditures to ensure accomplishment of objectives within an approved budget
- Direct coding functions of hospital-based, professional fee, and charge capture coders to ensure accurate provider documentation and coding for appropriate, compliant, and optimal reporting and reimbursement purposes
- Develop and maintain coding guidelines consistent with professional standards, legal/regulatory standards, and medical center goals related to coding and billing

EDUCATION AND EXPERIENCE Any combination of education and experience that would qualify a person for the job. Education equivalent to a bachelor's degree from an accredited college or university with a major in business, health information systems, nursing, or a related field. Three years of experience in health care or health information management, including at least 2 years of experience supervising staff and operations of a medical coding or medical records unit.

CORE COMPETENCIES AND SKILLS In-depth experience with medical records coding. At least 2 years of supervisory experience within an inpatient hospital setting and/or outpatient clinical setting. Experience as a coding supervisor for a physician or medical group practice. Knowledge of *ICD-9* and *-10* and CPT coding and of MS-DRG and APC payment systems. Knowledge of coding software, including groupers, compliance tools, editors, optimizers, and encoders. Ability to understand third-party billing guidelines and regulations.

CREDENTIALS, LICENSURE, OR CERTIFICATION, IF APPROPRIATE Must be certified as a RHIA and/or RHIT, preferably with Certified Coding Specialist (CCS) or Certified Professional Coder (CPC) status. Certification must be issued by the American Health Information Management Association (AHIMA).

COMPENSATION The salary for this and similar positions can range from $37,000 to $75,000 for lower-level HIM positions and up to $96,000 for manager positions, depending on level of experience and the size and location of the organization.

WORKPLACE LOCATION HIM/coding department in a large medical center.

EMPLOYMENT OUTLOOK According to the Bureau of Labor Statistics (BLS), employment of medical records and health information technicians is expected to increase by 21% from 2010 to 2020, faster than the average for all other occupations.

FOR MORE INFORMATION
- www.ahima.org/careers
- www.bls.gov/ooh/computer-and-information-technology/home.htm

60. RHIT and RHIA Medical Coder Positions Found Primarily in Medical Groups

The following three job descriptions are similar to the RHIT and RHIA position descriptions previously, but these are primarily found in medical group practices and have a specific focus on the activities in a physician organization.

61. Health Information Coder 2, HIM

POSITION DESCRIPTION   The health information/medical (HIM) records department is a support service of the medical group; its primary purpose is to contribute to the quality of patient care through the development and maintenance of a comprehensive, centralized medical record system.

The health information coder 2 is a middle-level coder. Patient records are coded and abstracted according to medical center policies and procedures, with a focus on a range of hospital charts, with minimal review of coding for quality. The coding and abstracting must comply with the official guidelines for coding and reporting, practice standards, and code of ethics for health insurance management systems (HIMS) coders.

EDUCATION AND EXPERIENCE   High school diploma or equivalent is required.

CREDENTIALS, LICENSURE, OR CERTIFICATION, IF APPROPRIATE   A certificate as a registered health information technician or administrator is required. At least 2 years of experience doing coding and abstracting in an acute health care facility is required.

CORE COMPETENCIES AND SKILLS
- Must code all records with 95% accuracy
- Basic computer skills, including Windows, Word, and Excel, and proven excellent communication and cooperative skills
- Ability to analyze information, make decisions, and exercise independent judgment
- Ability to follow written directions, prioritize work, and manage time effectively
- Ability to meet deadlines and perform well under pressure

Preferred qualifications include:

- Knowledge of medical terminology, medical abbreviations, disease processes, anatomy, and physiology

■ Knowledge of the *ICD-9-CM, ICD-10-CM, ICD-10-PCS,* and CPT classification systems
■ Knowledge of HIMS database systems and procedures

COMPENSATION   The salary for this and similar positions in HIM can range from $37,000 to $75,000 for lower-level HIM positions and up to $96,000 for manager positions, depending on level of experience and the size and location of the organization.

WORKPLACE LOCATION   This type of position is usually found in a large medical group. Sometimes a coder can be a work-at-home position.

EMPLOYMENT OUTLOOK   The BLS estimates that the number of working health information technicians will grow 21% from 2010 to 2020. Students pursuing a bachelor's degree may find excellent job prospects as medical or health services managers as well; the number of professionals in that field is expected to increase 22% from 2010 to 2020.

FOR MORE INFORMATION   A good source of information on medical coder positions is the Healthcare Information and Management Systems Society (HIMSS) JobMine site (jobmine.himss.org/home). Also check out AHIMA (www.ahima.com). See other references in Chapter 4 on finding jobs in the HIT marketplace.

62. Medical and Health Services Manager

POSITION DESCRIPTION   Some of the duties and responsibilities of medical and health services managers are to find ways to improve the quality and efficiency of the health care services they provide, create work schedules, and manage the finances of the facility. Another responsibility is to keep up to date with all current regulations and laws in order to make sure that the facility stays in compliance. Other duties are to keep organized records of all the services the facility provides to its patients, communicate with the various department heads and medical staff, and represent the facility in governing board meetings as well as investor meetings.

EDUCATION AND EXPERIENCE   Bachelor's degree or master's degree in health services administration, long-term care administration, public administration, public health, or business administration. (Management- or director-level positions often require a master's degree.)

CREDENTIALS, LICENSURE, OR CERTIFICATION, IF APPROPRIATE   A passing score on the licensing exam and completion of a state-approved training program are required.

CORE COMPETENCIES AND SKILLS
- Analytical and communication skills
- Detail oriented
- Interpersonal skills
- Problem-solving skills
- Technical skills

COMPENSATION   Salaries can range from $55,000 to a high of $84,270 per year.

WORKPLACE LOCATION   Hospitals, physicians' offices, nursing care facilities, home health care services, and outpatient care centers.

EMPLOYMENT OUTLOOK   The BLS estimates that the number of working health information technicians will grow 21% from 2010 to 2020. Students pursuing a bachelor's degree may find excellent job prospects as medical or health services managers as well; the number of professionals in that field is expected to increase 22% from 2010 to 2020.

FOR MORE INFORMATION   A good source of information is HIMSS (jobmine. himss.org/home). Also check out AHIMA (www.ahima.com) and the Professional Association of Health Care Office Management (www. pahcom.com). See other references in Chapter 4 on finding jobs in the HIT marketplace.

63. Medical Coder or Technician

POSITION DESCRIPTION   A medical coder or technician will be responsible for the assignment of *ICD-9-CM/-10-CM* diagnostic and procedure codes and abstracting of multiple-hospital patient encounters. Medical records and health information technicians organize and manage health information data by ensuring its quality, accuracy, accessibility, and security in both paper and electronic systems. The individual in this position ensures optimal reimbursement for multiple hospitals' inpatient Medicare cases under the DRG system. He or she assigns appropriate CPT codes whenever necessary. He or she collects, compiles, and records medical record data and analyzes and corrects semi-annual indices. The position can, in some institutions, be a remote, home-based position.

EDUCATION AND EXPERIENCE Associate's degree or equivalent. Additional minimum requirements: 3 to 5 years of experience with *ICD-9-CM/-10-CM* and CPT-4 coding; knowledge of coding systems in an acute care hospital; 3 to 5 years of experience in coding facility inpatient, outpatient, and emergency department services.

CREDENTIALS, LICENSURE, OR CERTIFICATION, IF APPROPRIATE Must possess and maintain one of the following current certifications:
- CCS
- RHIA
- CPC
- RHIT

CORE COMPETENCIES AND SKILLS
- Ability to use information within a medical record to determine correct codes
- Ability to critically think and interpret complex medical documented information to achieve correct code assignment
- Strong working knowledge of *ICD-9-CM/-10-CM*, CPT-4, MS-DRG, and APC
- Knowledge of anatomy, physiology, and medical terminology
- The ability to use and understand the 3M encoder and various abstracting systems
- Must have a working knowledge of Microsoft Office Suite
- Effective communication, both verbal and written
- Analytical skills: Must be able to understand and follow medical records and diagnoses, and then decide how best to code them in a patient's medical records
- Detail oriented: Must pay attention to details to be accurate when recording and coding patient information
- Interpersonal skills: Need to be able to discuss patient information, discrepancies, and data requirements with other professionals such as physicians and finance personnel
- Technical skills: Must be able to use coding and classification software and the EHR system that their health care organization or physician practice has adopted

COMPENSATION   The salary for this and similar positions in HIM can range from $30,000 to $55,000, depending on level of experience and the size and location of the organization.

WORKPLACE LOCATION   The position of a medical coder is usually found in the Medical Records department in a large medical group. It is also common for a position like a medical coder to be a home-based position. For those with good organizational skills, a home-based position can be very productive.

EMPLOYMENT OUTLOOK   The BLS estimates that the number of working health information technicians will grow 21% from 2010 to 2020. Students pursuing a bachelor's degree may find excellent job prospects as medical or health services managers as well; the number of professionals in that field is expected to increase 22% from 2010 to 2020.

FOR MORE INFORMATION   A good source of information on the medical coder position is HIMSS JobMine (jobmine.himss.org/home). Also, check out the AHIMA website (www.ahima.com). See other references in Chapter 4 on finding jobs in HIT.

64. Physician Coding Compliance Educator

POSITION DESCRIPTION   The physician coding compliance educator performs quarterly audits of encounter documentation and provides education and training on medical services documentation to physicians and non-physician providers in a large multispecialty medical group practice. Preparation will require conducting audits of medical documentation and the analysis of coding patterns to determine the need for focused training. The goal is to ensure compliant coding. Success is dependent upon the ability to accurately code, audit, and educate to achieve anticipated results within the allotted time frame. The position reviews the work of staff coding employees and ensures compliance with appropriate standards for quality assurance. The position also tracks all work in progress to make necessary adjustments to meet quarterly deadlines for physician audits.

EDUCATION AND EXPERIENCE   Bachelor's degree in health administration, business, or related field is preferred. Minimum 5 to 7 years' experience. Extensive experience with evaluation and management (E/M) chart auditing applying CMS 1997 documentation guidelines.

CREDENTIALS, LICENSURE, OR CERTIFICATION, IF APPROPRIATE CCS-P or CPC required; *ICD-10* certified and proficient a plus.

CORE COMPETENCIES AND SKILLS
- Setting priorities and meeting goals
- Conducting quality audits of staff coders
- Excellent demeanor for education of providers in medical services documentation
- Auditing medical documentation to determine coding and billing adequacy
- Compiling trend reports and identifying opportunities for focused training
- Third-party medical insurance billing
- Strong background in 1997 Evaluation and Management (E/M) Documentation Guidelines
- Understanding of medical coding and billing compliance concepts
- Proficiency in Microsoft Excel, Word, and PowerPoint (proficiency in Access is a plus)
- Strong analytical, problem-solving skills
- Self-starter capable of working with minimal supervision
- Understanding of medical group operations
- Excellent customer service and communication skills
- Expert proficiency in presentation applications
- Delivery of complex material to large groups

COMPENSATION Because of the technical nature surrounding physician coding issues, this is a more advanced position than a medical coder. The salary range of $45,000 to $90,000 will vary by the size and location of the medical group.

WORKPLACE LOCATION This position would be in the HIM department of a larger medical group organization.

EMPLOYMENT OUTLOOK The HITECH Act of 2009 created expectations for medical groups and hospitals to implement EMR with the goal of achieving meaningful and demonstrable outcomes. The employment outlook is very good into the foreseeable future.

FOR MORE INFORMATION

- www.bls.gov
- www.mgma.com
- http://jobmine.himss.org

65. Information Systems Auditor—Certified

POSITION DESCRIPTION   The information systems internal audit team conducts information systems (IS) risk-based audits and recommends strategic solutions to the business units within the organization. The team works closely with the business management unit. Examples of position expectations can include:

- Lead IS risk-based audits
- Examine and verify IS processes and procedures from internal organizations in order to determine the reliability and effectiveness of the existing control systems
- Continuously analyze business risk profiles and provide assurance that appropriate risk mitigation is taken
- Provide management with independent and objective reports, evaluations, appraisals, counsel, and recommendations
- Support the Global IS audit director, company divisions, and subsidiaries in a consulting role by evaluating and recommending improvements to business practices and processes.

EDUCATION AND EXPERIENCE   Bachelor's degree in computer science, management information systems, or related business discipline(s).

CREDENTIALS, LICENSURE, OR CERTIFICATION, IF APPROPRIATE   Certified internal auditor (CIA) or certified information systems auditor (CISA) certification will be considered a plus.

- certification.about.com/od/certifications/p/CISA.htm

CORE COMPETENCIES AND SKILLS

- Must demonstrate leadership competencies with the ability to work effectively across all levels and functions within the business
- Strong interpersonal skills with the ability to facilitate diverse group movement toward operational efficiencies

- Extensive knowledge and experience in project management with strong analytical, problem-solving, and organizational skills
- Application development or implementation experience with systems applications products or prescription drug events is preferred
- Effective oral and written communication skills and proven presentation skills
- Proactive and results driven

COMPENSATION   The salary for a certified IS auditor can range from $65,000 to $90,000 depending on work experience, degrees, and current certification.

WORKPLACE LOCATION   Information systems auditors work in many different industries. If employed in the health care sector they would be working in the IS department of a large medical facility or corporate office.

EMPLOYMENT OUTLOOK   Employment is expected to increase 16% between the years 2010 and 2020.

FOR MORE INFORMATION
- jobsearchtech.about.com/od/historyoftechindustry/g/IT_Audit.htm
- www.isaca.org/Certification/CISA-Certified-Information-Systems-Auditor/Pages/default.aspx

66. Meaningful Use Project Coordinator

POSITION DESCRIPTION   The meaningful use project coordinator will operationalize the physician's medical group in optimizing the meaningful use initiative as defined by the CMS. The position will report to the manager of regulatory analytics and work in collaboration with clinical information systems leadership to support implementation of meaningful use requirements into ongoing clinical systems deployment efforts. In this role, there will be established timelines to ensure project deadlines are met. Activities include research, planning, design, development, implementation, and evaluation in meeting meaningful use goals as well as reporting to federal and state agencies to qualify for incentive programs.

EDUCATION AND EXPERIENCE   A bachelor's of arts or science, or undergraduate degree in health care management or a related field and 2 years of project management, systems implementation, clinical operations, or relevant experience are required. Statistical analysis experience is preferred.

CREDENTIALS, LICENSURE, OR CERTIFICATION, IF APPROPRIATE   None specified.

CORE COMPETENCIES AND SKILLS
- Knowledge of CMS EHR Incentive program requirements and other HITECH requirements.
- Previous experience with compliance, rules, and regulatory requirements preferred.
- Must have strong problem-solving, troubleshooting, and analytical skills.
- Must be able to communicate clearly and effectively and possess strong organizational and presentation skills.
- Demonstrated presentation/public speaking skills and experience required.
- Must be able to interact with providers, payers, and patients.
- Computer skills, including proficiency with Microsoft Office, Excel, PowerPoint, and Access.

COMPENSATION   The salary range is fairly wide, from $39,000 to $75,000 depending on past work experience and degrees.

WORKPLACE LOCATION   Medical group practice setting in an academic medical center.

EMPLOYMENT OUTLOOK   The HITECH Act of 2009 created expectations for medical groups and hospitals to implement EMR with the goal of achieving meaningful and demonstrable outcomes. The employment outlook is very good into the foreseeable future.

FOR MORE INFORMATION   The best place to look for a meaningful use project coordinator or similar position is the HIMSS JobMine (jobmine. himss.org/home).

67. IT Sarbanes–Oxley (SOX) Compliance Analyst

POSITION DESCRIPTION   The position requires an experienced Sarbanes–Oxley (SOX) specialist, with experience in IS, who enjoys hands-on involvement in driving the SOX Compliance Program and executing reviews and who is suitable to a fast-paced, highly demanding environment.

"The Sarbanes–Oxley Act was passed by Congress in 2002 in an effort to prevent and punish corporate corruption and to repair investor confidence. The act imposes on all publicly traded corporate organizations the requirement of mandatory accounting oversight, detailed disclosure requirements and criminal liability for noncompliance or violations of the act."[1]

Essential job functions include:

- Function as the local main point of contact and knowledge around SOX.
- Participate in all sessions dealing with access controls, change management, and quarterly user access audits.
- Perform risk assessment and identify significant processes and agree to process scope. Provide input to company-wide policies dealing with SOX and other risk management programs.
- Work with process owners and create Risk and Control Matrix for processes identified through risk assessment.
- Perform quarterly review of segregation of duties, process maps and narrative, and testing of high-risk processes.
- Lead and participate in design and operating-effectiveness testing of in-scope processes/systems.
- Identify internal control weaknesses and recommend remediation to strengthen control environment.
- Review work to ensure adherence to required documentation standards.
- Continuous follow-up with process owners and team members to ensure adherence to key deliverable and remediation timelines.
- Prepare periodic reports, track program progress, and report findings to director of SOX and HealthCare Partners (HCP) senior management.
- Provide training on internal controls to team members.
- Liaise with representatives from the internal audit and external audit firms, finance, and IS, and verify and submit evidence to auditors as needed.

---

[1] www.ehow.com/about_5082561_sarbanes-oxley-law.html#ixzz2xaO5QE8z

■ Perform special projects as assigned by the director of SOX or senior management.

EDUCATION AND EXPERIENCE   A bachelor's degree from a 4-year college and/or a professional certification requiring formal education beyond a 2-year college, or equivalent experience is required. Experience at a large health care consulting organization plus 2 or more years experience in a managed health care organization are required. One to 4 years high-level analytical, financial, and/or accounting experience is required.

CORE COMPETENCIES AND SKILLS
- Sarbanes–Oxley/audit experience.
- Strong organizational and planning skills.
  - Conversant in one or more of the following integration areas: Workflow, business process management, business activity monitoring, technology and enterprise application adapters, package-enabled re-engineering, business process redesign.
- Strong interpersonal and influencing skills and an ability to work in a team environment.
- Good communication skills (written and verbal) with all levels of the organization.
- Ability to work with minimal supervision and deliver to tight deadlines.
- Knowledge of governance, risk, and compliance framework.

COMPENSATION   This is a mid-career type of position that requires specialized experience and knowledge. The salary is evolving but is in the range of $50,000 to $75,000 depending on the size and location of the medical group. This position is also found in hospital organizations.

EMPLOYMENT OUTLOOK   The BLS estimates that the number of working health information technicians will grow 21% from 2010 to 2020. Students pursuing a bachelor's degree may find excellent job prospects as medical or health services managers as well; the number of professionals in that field is expected to increase 22% from 2010 to 2020.

FOR MORE INFORMATION
- www.mgma.com
- jobmine.himss.org
- www.ehow.com/about_5082561_sarbanes-oxley-law.html

Large medical groups:
Health Care Partners
■ www.healthcarepartners.com
Facey Medical Group
■ www.facey.com

68. Health Information Management Clinical Documentation Spec I

POSITION DESCRIPTION   This position is responsible for maintenance, analysis, and review of EMR, in order to ensure effective operation.

EDUCATION AND EXPERIENCE   An associate's degree from a RHIT-accredited program or an associate's degree in a health care–related field is preferred. Must have 4 years of health care–related experience. May have an equivalent combination of education and experience to substitute for the experience requirements.

CREDENTIALS, LICENSURE, OR CERTIFICATION, IF APPROPRIATE
■ Prefer registration as a RHIT or current licensure in a health care–related field.
■ Must pass the Medical Terminal Digit Filing test with a minimum score of 80%.
■ Must pass the Alphanumeric Data Entry test with an accuracy rate of 80%, with minimum keystrokes of 3,000.
■ Must pass the General Computer test with a minimum score of 80%.
■ Must pass the Skillcheck Medical Terminology test with a minimum score of 80%.
■ Must be able to demonstrate knowledge of EMR software applications.
■ Must have strong analytical skills and organizational skills and be detail oriented.
■ Must have a working knowledge of HIM procedures, forms, and content, and be able to comprehend and apply established policy and procedures.
■ Must successfully complete required training and meet prescribed performance standards within 90 days of employment.
■ Must be able to operate a computer and use spreadsheet, word-processing, database, and graphics software.

- Must demonstrate good decision-making skills.
- Must be detail oriented and exhibit effective organizational skills.
- Must have good written and oral communication skills with patients, visitors, and hospital staff.
- Must demonstrate knowledge regarding HIM computer software, including master patient index record tracking, deficiency analysis, release of information, and so forth.
- Must have knowledge of medico-legal and regulatory requirements.

COMPENSATION   The salary range is approximately $45,000 to $55,000 per year.

WORKPLACE LOCATION   IT department, and can be found in Medical Records and the Business Office in some organizations.

EMPLOYMENT OUTLOOK   According to the BLS, the job growth rate for medical coders is about 21% from 2010 to 2020 (www.bls.gov/ooh/Healthcare/Medical-records-and-health-information-technicians.htm).

FOR MORE INFORMATION
- jobsearch.monster.com/search/medical-coder_5?
- www.ahima.org/careers

69. Senior Data Warehouse Analyst

POSITION DESCRIPTION   The position of data warehouse and informatics analyst is found within a larger corporate medical group. The position works with business users to define and develop solutions for the company through the use of its data assets. The analyst designs, develops, and implements various reporting and analysis solutions. The position ensures improved data-based decision-making capability across the medical group.

Essential job functions:

- Designs and writes SQL scripts, stored procedures, and user-defined functions.
- Responsible for transforming, cleaning, and standardizing data and metadata so they can be loaded into a data warehouse or data mart.
- Consistently exhibits behavior and communication skills that demonstrate commitment to superior customer service, including

quality, care, and concern with each and every internal and external customer.

■ Builds data warehouse infrastructure including complex data models and strategic data sets and databases.
■ Specifies the creation of content in support of internal and external customers for data and information.
■ Interacts with company leadership as required to facilitate the development of strategic data sets for the organization.
■ Ensures the reliability and timeliness of the data warehouse systems and underlying technologies.
■ Develops solutions to streamline business processes to achieve departmental and company-wide goals more effectively and efficiently.
■ Communicates status, problems, resolutions, and so on, projects and assignments.
■ Contributes skills and knowledge to other database and reporting projects as determined by management.
■ Directs the work of other staff and serves as a mentor to junior staff.
■ Uses, protects, and discloses patients' protected health information (PHI) only in accordance with Health Insurance Portability and Accountability Act (HIPAA) standards.

EDUCATION AND EXPERIENCE   Bachelor's degree from a 4-year college and/or a professional certification requiring formal education beyond a 2-year college. A minimum of 3 years of experience with Microsoft SQL server, which includes database design and writing stored procedures using Transact SQL. Hands-on experience writing SSIS packages in MS SQL Server 2005 or 2008. Strong background in business analysis including supporting the design of new production systems or enhancements to existing systems.

CORE COMPETENCIES AND SKILLS
■ Specialization with related databases, architecture and implementation of data models and database designs, data access and table maintenance codes
■ Understanding of data warehouse methodology
■ Demonstrated achievement in building a research and analysis function

- Excellent presentation skills
- Excellent written and verbal communications skills

COMPENSATION   As a senior position in a larger medical group or large hospital organization, the salary range can be from $80,000 to perhaps $175,000 depending on the size and location.

EMPLOYMENT OUTLOOK   With EMR growth in physician practices and requirements to qualify for incentives from the government, more small practices are merging or perhaps joining larger medical groups or management services organizations (MSOs) to provide the technology and management that is too expensive for a small practitioner. These larger medical organizations have a great need for analytics and individuals who can manage the data warehouses.

FOR MORE INFORMATION   Larger medical groups such as the following generally would have positions like this one.
Facey Medical Group
- www.facey.com
HealthCare Partners
- www.healthcarepartners.com
- Jobmine.himss.org
- www.bls.gov

70. Director of Physician Practice Informatics

POSITION DESCRIPTION   A management services organization or MSO is a company that manages a large number of smaller physician offices in terms of contracting with payer, financial management, and revenue cycle management, and often human resources.

The director of physician practice informatics, under the direction of the vice president/chief operating officer, is responsible for the overall effective management of initiatives and operations related to clinical information systems (CIS), including the GE Centricity EMR system and other EMR systems managed by the organization. This leader is a member of the senior management team who provides expertise and direction of clinical informatics services to include recommendations, development, and participation in strategic long-range plans that contribute to the clinical success of the service line and financial viability of the company. Responsibilities also include providing superior service to clients and delivering innovative and compliant clinical informatics services.

The qualified candidate will have significant experience in electronic health technology. Candidates with a clinical background and/or physician practice management experience are strongly preferred. In addition to the operations related to CIS, the director evaluates and integrates other physician practice EMR clinical systems, supporting our client growth and strategic objectives for improving quality of care, patient safety, billing operations and financial performance. EMR services encompass all clients and EMR client providers of the MSO, requiring this leader to frequently engage and routinely meet with our physician leaders and EMR clients. In addition, this position involves significant collaboration with the practice management, information technology, and central business office teams. The director also participates as an active leader on compliance, clinical quality, and operations improvement teams.

Key duties and responsibilities include:

- Coordinates EMR implementation, upgrades, and maintenance activities, including clinical content development, business process re-engineering, training, and go-live implementation support.
- Develops and oversees client project teams to support the effective implementation of the EMR and to maximize benefits realization.
- Acts as the primary liaison among IT, clinical staff, and physicians to ensure that CI/EMR implementations are optimized based on clinical workflow redesign.
- Identifies, coordinates, implements, and oversees EMR interface and new module development.

EDUCATION AND EXPERIENCE Bachelor's degree in health, IT, or business administration. Master's preferred, or an equivalent combination of education and experience. A minimum of 2 years of direct experience with EMR operations; GE Centricity EMR and/or experience with multiple EMR systems is a plus.

CORE COMPETENCIES AND SKILLS
- Plan, organize, and lead collaborative cross-department meetings on CIS-related initiatives; excel in project management and in juggling competing priorities.
- Demonstrate critical thinking, initiative, and good judgment in a variety of environments.

- Possess strong interpersonal and excellent written and verbal communication skills.
- Develop and manage excellent client relations.
- Take initiative to improve, enhance, and streamline existing operations.
- Exhibit skill in preparation and presentation of reports and other materials.
- Work collaboratively with IT leadership to prioritize, stage, and monitor new interface and module development. Support and facilitate change management necessary for full testing, re-engineering, readiness, and go-live processes.
- Ensure clients have the opportunity to meet and maximize meaningful use reimbursement; develop, train, and implement meaningful use protocols and reports.

COMPENSATION As a senior-level position within a large MSO the salary range is $125,000 to $175,000.

WORKPLACE LOCATION This is a senior position within a large management services organization. MSOs are a common way for smaller physician practices to get access to new technology and have support for their office practice in terms of financial and human resource challenges. Some MSOs have more than 2,000 physicians under contract.

EMPLOYMENT OUTLOOK With EMR growth in physician practices and requirements to qualify for incentives from the government, more small practices are merging or perhaps joining MSOs to provide the technology and management that is too expensive for a small practitioner.

FOR MORE INFORMATION
- www.mgma.com
- en.wikipedia.org/wiki/Management_services_organization
- www.ehow.com/how_7890930_form-management-services-organization.html

9 ▪ HIT CAREERS IN THE MANAGED CARE AND INSURANCE SECTOR

Working in a health insurance company or managed care company is similar in many ways to working in a large non–health care organization. These companies are located in large office buildings away from the actual delivery of care. They play a critical role in the financing of health care and providing clients/patients with online services such as health education, social networking, benefit administration, and other support services. These organizations have complex information technology (IT) needs and hire individuals with skills in computer programming, systems analysis, networking architecture, data analysis, and consumer-focused services.

Chapter 4 provides websites for some of the major managed care provider organizations. The job descriptions in this chapter are typical of the type of jobs found in this sector of the health care industry. It is common for organizations like managed care companies and large hospital systems to have similar job titles and functions.

POSITION DESCRIPTIONS IN MANAGED CARE AND INSURANCE SETTINGS

71. Help-Desk Analyst

POSITION DESCRIPTION Responsible for receiving all telephone or automated requests for IT assistance, ensuring that the request or problem is accurately recorded and resoved within established time frames.

Primary duties may include, but are not limited to:

- Handles basic technical problems via the telephone and resolves first-line customer issues.
- Logs and manages calls while utilizing the correct procedures.

- Handles specialized functions including fulfillment and special projects.
- Makes appropriate and timely referrals of any requests that cannot be immediately resolved.

EDUCATION AND EXPERIENCE   Requires associate's degree or recognized trade certification; 1 or 2 years of personal computer, computer networking, telecommunications, or configuration management troubleshooting experience; or any combination of education and experience that would provide an equivalent background. Two to 3 years of customer service experience preferred.

CREDENTIALS, LICENSURE, OR CERTIFICATION, IF APPROPRIATE   None specified.

CORE COMPETENCIES AND SKILLS
- Basic to intermediate technical knowledge of:
  - Personal computer hardware and software
  - Telecommunications
  - Application software (knowledge will vary by organization)
  - Configuration management
- Excellent oral, written, and interpersonal communications skills

COMPENSATION   A help-desk analyst can earn in the range of $40,000 to $60,000, although the total salary will vary depending on the size and location of the health care organization.

WORKPLACE LOCATION   Normally this job is located within the IT department of managed care and insurance companies.

EMPLOYMENT OUTLOOK   The employment outlook for a help-desk analyst is strong. Every managed care organization in the nation is working to develop its IT infrastructure in response to demands by the federal government and the need to provide ever-higher levels of quality care. Possessing an IT background is an important requirement, but the applicant must also be familiar with the unique requirements of health care delivery.

FOR MORE INFORMATION
- www.careersatwellpoint.com/search-jobs.aspx

72. Field Support Analyst (Senior)

POSITION DESCRIPTION   Responsible for troubleshooting and repairing complex computer hardware problems utilizing advanced tools and manufacturer resources. Primary duties may include, but are not limited to:

- Meets with customers to recommend hardware that meets their needs.
- Assists other technicians with complex hardware installations and customer needs assessments.
- Works with the software bundling team on defining technical building requirements for new applications.
- Assists the software deployment team in troubleshooting instances when packages cannot be deployed as part of large-scale software deliveries.
- Provides remote-hands work for other IT groups or outsourcers.
- Troubleshoots and resolves complex computer software problems.
- Participates in single and large-scale moves and move planning meetings.
- Performs Tech Refresh installations and end user acceptance testing.
- Works with external contract labor to conduct Tech Refresh work on schedule.
- Responsible for the progression of Tech Refresh and overseeing that adequate stock is on site, salvage runs are routinely performed, and the Asset Management database is preferred.
- Participates in other lights-on projects where technical resources are needed.
- Attends regularly scheduled project meetings and may provide technical and logistical advice to a project team.
- Mentors and assists other technicians with hardware-related problems.

EDUCATION AND EXPERIENCE
- Requires associate's degree or technical school certification
- Five years of information systems experience with expert knowledge of PC hardware and operating systems software, tools, and techniques

CREDENTIALS, LICENSURE, OR CERTIFICATION, IF APPROPRIATE
- Dell hardware certification required, or any combination of education and experience that would provide an equivalent background.
- Microsoft A+, Network+, and Microsoft Certified Solutions Associate (MCSA) or Microsoft Certified Desktop Support Technician (MCDST) certifications preferred.

CORE COMPETENCIES AND SKILLS
- Advanced knowledge of networking, telecommunications, applications, and/or configuration management required
- Demonstrated proficiency in writing skills, interviewing techniques, and interpersonal skills required
- Ability to work in team environment, attention to detail, and strong organizational skills required

COMPENSATION   A field support analyst (senior) in a managed care organizations can earn in the range of $55,000 to $75,000, although the total salary will vary depending on the size and location of the health care organization.

WORKPLACE LOCATION   Normally this job is located within the IT department of a managed care or insurance company.

EMPLOYMENT OUTLOOK   The employment outlook for a field support analyst (senior) is strong but requires a background in program languages. All large managed care organizations in the nation are working to develop their IT infrastructure in response to demands by the federal government and the need to provide ever-higher levels of quality care. Possessing an IT background is an important requirement, but the applicant must also be familiar with the unique requirements of health care delivery.

FOR MORE INFORMATION
www.careersatwellpoint.com/search-jobs.aspx

73. Sales Internship
POSITION DESCRIPTION   The commercial sales intern assists in selling and retaining employee benefits for businesses having 2 to 1,000 employees. He or she helps manage a professional sales office and will

learn the sales and retention process from product design and underwriting/pricing to determine the appropriate risk to customer service and claims payment. The sales intern interacts with account executives, account managers, and sales-related departments. The intern also has the ability to assist in important project work, such as competitive analysis and workflow process improvement. While the majority of the intern's time will be dedicated to the sales department, a rotation to other important sales-related departments will give this individual a full understanding of the world-class products and services the company delivers.

Project work could be focused on, but not limited to, the following:

- Competitive intelligence: Analyzing and reviewing competitors and their pricing, and recommending strategies to compete.
- Data analysis: Reviewing demographics of current customers and clients to find trends; underwriting and pricing analysis, which requires expertise in Microsoft Excel and Access and the ability to synthesis data into actionable recommendations.
- Sales support: Supporting account executives and managers in their daily activities. This includes creating open enrollment kits, generating pertinent sales reports, capturing minutes during team meetings, proposal preparation, finalist presentation work, new group setup/implementation, renewal strategy work, open enrollment meeting presentations, workflow mapping/process improvement, and customer service issue resolution.
- Industry knowledge: Interns will be responsible for keeping up with industry trends and news both locally and nationally. It will also be important for interns to report news to sales and sales management as deemed appropriate.

EDUCATION AND EXPERIENCE
- Education/certification: Junior standing is preferred
- Minimum GPA of 3.0
- Economics, Finance, Communications, or Business or Health Administration majors
- Experience required: Microsoft Excel, Microsoft Access

CREDENTIALS, LICENSURE, OR CERTIFICATION, IF APPROPRIATE None specified.

CORE COMPETENCIES AND SKILLS

- Be able to work in a fast-paced environment, in a team environment, and on an individual basis
- Be a self-motivated, organized team player, with customer-focused attitude and attention to detail
- Possess strong analytical and problem-solving skills
- Possess strong written and oral communication skills
- Be highly proficient on the computer, with advanced use of Microsoft Excel, Microsoft Access, and social media
- Ideal candidate has understanding of both business and health insurance products
- Be currently enrolled in a program of study at an accredited college or university
- Demonstrated proficiency in writing skills, interviewing techniques, and interpersonal skills
- Ability to work in team environment, attention to detail, and strong organizational skills

COMPENSATION   A sales intern position in a managed care organization is a unique and special opportunity. Some interns are paid, and some participate as part of an educational program's curriculum requirements. Always check with your academic program as to rules and requirements for an internship.

WORKPLACE LOCATION   Normally this type of internship is located within the sales and marketing department of a managed care or insurance company.

EMPLOYMENT OUTLOOK   Students interested an internship opportunity have a variety of organizations to explore in the field of health information technology (HIT). Internships are available in managed care organizations, vendors, and provider organizations such as hospitals. The variability of requirements needs to be carefully researched. Since general qualifications are for "the current student," it is important that you coordinate the applications process with your academic program so that you can determine if the internship will meet program academic requirements.

FOR MORE INFORMATION

- www.careersatwellpoint.com/student-programs.aspx
- Chapter 4 has information on other internship opportunities.

74. MBA Consultant Internship (MBA Students)

POSITION DESCRIPTION To remain leading edge, many companies promote a highly skilled, versatile, and diverse internal management consulting team. Such a team works closely with business leaders to address pivotal business and organizational opportunities. Aiming for thought leadership and a results-driven approach, this team creates tremendous value as it leads transformation and provides unbiased and direct guidance on strategy development, effective execution, and continuous improvement.

Such a team often hosts an exciting MBA internship, which provides unique experience. As part of this summer internship, the intern will help the company address pivotal business and organizational opportunities and achieve both sustainable improvements and transformational change. The intern will establish relationships at the executive level across the organization and lead a continuous improvement initiative to enhance effectiveness and profitability.

EDUCATION AND EXPERIENCE Current student in an AACSB-accredited MBA program.

CREDENTIALS, LICENSURE, OR CERTIFICATION, IF APPROPRIATE None specified; however, proficiency in Microsoft Word and Microsoft Excel is expected.

CORE COMPETENCIES AND SKILLS The successful intern will need to demonstrate a blend of talents and skills, including:

- Strong execution skills
- Ability to provide vision and direction
- Leadership of high-priority, medium-size projects within a business unit
- Work with business partners to identify solutions to business challenges and streamline processes
- Change leadership
- Relationship management at all levels within the organization
- Engaging or leading high-performing teams
- Strong business acumen
- Excellent cost–benefit analysis skills
- Excellent communication skills
- Strong situational leadership

- Advanced decision making through data-driven analysis
- Quick and continuous learning style
- Demonstrated proficiency in writing skills, interviewing techniques, and interpersonal skills
- Ability to work in team environment, attention to detail, and strong organizational skills

COMPENSATION   An MBA consulting intern position in a managed care organizations is a unique and special opportunity. Some interns are paid and some work as part of an educational program's curriculum requirements. Always check with your academic program as to rules and requirements for an internship.

WORKPLACE LOCATION   Normally this type of internships is located within the IT department of a managed care and/or insurance company.

EMPLOYMENT OUTLOOK   Students interested in an MBA consulting internship opportunity have a variety of organizations to explore in the field of HIT. Internships are available in managed care organizations, vendors, and provider organizations such as hospitals. The variability of requirements needs to be carefully researched. Since the internship specifies a "current student," it is important that you coordinate the applications process with your academic program so that you can determine if the internship will meet program academic requirements.

FOR MORE INFORMATION
- www.careersatwellpoint.com/student-programs.aspx
- Chapter 4 has information on other internship opportunities.

75. Information Technology Internship (Computer Science or Information Systems Students)

POSITION DESCRIPTION   This is a unique opportunity to contribute and collaborate within a dynamic team-oriented environment that supports and advises the senior business operations executive management team. The intern will have the chance to grow his or her skill set within the business intelligence field and a variety of technology platforms.

An IT intern's focus will be on:

- Analyzing and documenting processes and business requirements
- Assisting developers with various programming tasks
- Validating and delivering new reporting systems to the business
- Data entry
- Preparation of workshop/presentation materials
- Web design
- Other office duties and special projects (depending on intern qualifications)

EDUCATION AND EXPERIENCE
- Must be a current student; ideally bachelor or graduate studies in computer science, information technology, or other disciplines of a technical nature.
- Experience in databases and SQL.

CREDENTIALS, LICENSURE, OR CERTIFICATION, IF APPROPRIATE None specified; however, proficiency in Microsoft Word and Microsoft Excel is expected.

CORE COMPETENCIES AND SKILLS
- Personal initiative and ability to work independently
- Knowledge of tools such as SQL Server Integration Services and reporting tools such as SQL Server Reporting Services is a plus
- Web design experience is a plus
- Demonstrated proficiency in writing skills, interviewing techniques, and interpersonal skills required
- Ability to work in team environment, attention to detail, and strong organizational skills required

COMPENSATION An IT intern position in a managed care organization is a unique and special opportunity. Some interns are paid and some participate as part of an educational program's curriculum requirements. Always check with your academic program as to rules and requirements for an internship.

WORKPLACE LOCATION Normally this type of internship is located within the IT department of a managed care or insurance company.

EMPLOYMENT OUTLOOK Students interested an internship opportunity have a variety of organizations to explore in the field of HIT. Internships are available in managed care organizations, vendors, and provider organizations such as hospitals. The variability of requirements calls for careful research. Since the internship is for a "current student," it is important that you coordinate the application process with your academic program so that you can determine if the internship will meet program academic requirements.

FOR MORE INFORMATION

- ■ www.careersatwellpoint.com/student-programs.aspx
- ■ Chapter 4 has information on other internship opportunities.

RANDALL R. BARKER
Manager, Imaging Solutions Implementation
Southern California Permanente Medical Group

Describe the sort of work that you do. I deal with the project coordination and the implementation of imaging information systems. It is my responsibility to plan for diagnostic imaging projects for Kaiser and facilitate communications for the various project teams. Once a project is near completion I work with my teams to set the date for "Go live," which means to turn on the new system and integrate it into the workflow of the imaging department.

What is a typical day like at your job? A typical day in my job is going to a lot of meetings, leading phone calls with my team, communicating through e-mails, dealing with electronic and verbal management responsibilities, and being in charge of payroll for my staff. While a typical day is filled with a variety of responsibilities, it is rewarding and I have enjoyed it for the past 12 years. The imaging part of my responsibilities can be difficult and fun at the same time.

What education or training do you have? Is it typical for your job? I am a registered radiologic technologist with the American Registry of Radiologic Technologists as well as the state of California. This is typical for a position like mine in imaging information systems, as it brings a background in clinical operations (real-life work experience in the field) to bear. I also have a BS in Health Care Administration.

What path did you take to get to the job you are in today? I received my training and license in radiologic technology while enlisted in the United States Air Force. This was a great experience and I brought that with me to Kaiser. After several years I was able to leverage my

(continued)

RANDALL R. BARKER *(continued)*

experience and eventually became a director of radiology for Kaiser Permanente. From that position I was able to move into my current position as a project manager in imaging solutions implementation.

I took a fairly long career path but each experience prepared me for my current position. Departmental management was a challenging experience and I felt that a move into digital systems implementation was a great fit for me.

Where might you go from here if you wanted to advance your career? I do not have a master's degree at present but it is a possibility for the future as I would like to advance my career by getting into other project management positions and perhaps moving to a higher position. To go further and move to higher positions in management, a master's degree is expected.

What is the most challenging part of your job? Unfortunately, the most challenging part of my job is dealing with difficult people and resistance to change. But this is a common challenge with systems implementation and is something one has to be prepared for when working in a complicated technical field like diagnostic imaging. Another big challenge is working on a significant project and where there is little or no funding available. It creates resource allocation challenges that are, again, typical in the health care environment.

What is the best part? The best part of my job is being able to give the physicians and staff tools that make their jobs easier and more efficient. When the "light bulb" goes on for users, it is great to see your efforts pay off. There is a feeling of appreciation when a project comes together. When I was an x-ray technician, I felt appreciation from a few patients as I served each of them. Now, because my work affects thousands of users and patients throughout our organization, I have even greater job satisfaction.

What advice would you give to someone contemplating a career like yours? Since my job requires specific education and training I feel that someone with those specific skills should seek experiences on

(continued)

RANDALL R. BARKER (*continued*)

the operational side of diagnostic imaging and some advanced training in project management and perhaps health administration. The
best advice is to do the best you can in whatever you do and to
always push yourself to achieve more.

76. Systems Analyst III (Senior)

POSITION DESCRIPTION This position is primarily responsible for designing, developing, and implementing new or upgraded functionality of the
organization's enterprise systems. The systems analyst III will work in
teams or alone to guide the implementation process for any of the several current or planned business or clinical systems projects. The position requires someone with excellent interpersonal and organizational
skills, as well as exceptional project management and self-management
competency. As projects wrap up, the analyst will have opportunities to
move on to other systems efforts, or to take on an elevated support role
related to management of the end product, including application support, upgrades, or ongoing development.

EDUCATION AND EXPERIENCE A bachelor's degree is required in a related
field such as computer science, information systems, or administration.

CREDENTIALS, LICENSURE, OR CERTIFICATION, IF APPROPRIATE No credential required, but can vary by organization.

CORE COMPETENCIES AND SKILLS
- Clinical layout and flow of paperwork and traffic
- Familiarity with clinical systems and how they are used to solve
  business problems in a clinical setting
- General architecture, common requirements, and
  implementation techniques related to Health Level 7 (HL7)
  interfacing
- In-depth understanding of project management, milestone
  development, and project coordination activities
- Proven analytical and creative problem-solving abilities
- Effectively prioritizing and executing tasks under pressure
- Strong customer service orientation
- Working collaboratively in a team-oriented environment

COMPENSATION   The range of salaries in this job category is from $46,000 to $60,000.

WORKPLACE LOCATION   You can find this job in a variety of health care organizations such as managed care organizations and hospitals.

ECONOMIC OUTLOOK   The U.S. Bureau of Labor Statistics predicts that the field of HIT will continue to expand at an above average rate between the present and 2020 (www.bls.gov/ooh/computer-and-information-technology/home.htm).

FOR MORE INFORMATION
- www.cra.orgwww.computer.org/portal/web/guest/home
- jobmine.himss.org

77. Information Technology Business Analyst

POSITION DESCRIPTION   IT business analyst responsibilities include systems integration based on user needs, current business practices, and medical industry requirements. The professional in this position:

- Applies IT tools to devise optimal procedures while resolving complex problems and issues.
- Analyzes departmental business needs and aligns them properly against current computer technology.
- Ensures documentation requirements are met and personnel are properly trained in appropriate software.
- Recruits and trains less experienced IT business analysts while reporting progress to senior directors.
- A successful IT manager will excel at prioritizing, organizing, and executing projects based on tight deadlines. Excellent problem-solving skills, outside-the-box thinking, interpersonal communication skills, and professionalism are essential to success.

EDUCATION AND EXPERIENCE
- Bachelor's degree from an accredited institution
  - ○ Health care administration, business administration, or information systems degree preferred
- IT/data management experience ideal

■ Proficiency in Microsoft Office, electronic medical record (EMR) software
■ Ability to code software

CREDENTIALS, LICENSURE, OR CERTIFICATION, IF APPROPRIATE
■ Complete your Certified Business Analyst Professional (CBAP) credentials through an accredited institution.
■ Project Management Professional (PMP) and Certified Associate in Project Management (CAPM) preferred.

CORE COMPETENCIES AND SKILLS
■ Coding experience necessary
■ Experience including team building, conflict resolution, group interaction, project management, and goal setting
■ Experience using EMR systems
■ Solid skills in documenting and analyzing business processes
■ Experience with multiple software applications, systems analysis/design, integration/design, or web applications/design

COMPENSATION $50,000 to $79,000 per year based on experience, qualifications, and the size and location of the organization.

WORKPLACE LOCATION Normally this job is located within the IT department of a large organization such as a managed care or insurance company.

EMPLOYMENT OUTLOOK According to the U.S. Bureau of Labor Statistics, "Employment among management analysts is expected to grow 22 percent from 2010 to 2020, faster than the average for all occupations. Demand for the services of these workers will grow as organizations continue to seek ways to improve efficiency and control costs" (www.bls.gov/ooh/computer-and-information-technology/home.htm).

FOR MORE INFORMATION
Job positions:
■ jobsearch.monster.com/search/IT-Business-Analyst_5?
Educational programs in this field:
■ www.iiba.org/Certification-Recognition/CBAP-Designation.aspx
Professional organizations in this field:
■ www.societyofbusinessanalysts.com
■ www.iiba.org

78. Information Technology Business Systems Analyst

POSITION DESCRIPTION   The IT business systems analyst (BSA) must support and develop key departmental systems across the network. These include the medical records, emergency, and behavioral health departments, and specific functions, such as

- Collect and analyze business requirements and translate them into business application systems.
- Design, develop, and implement new software solutions.
- Configure, modify, and sustain existing software solutions.
- Resolve issues and trouble tickets from customers.
- Develop and maintain reports.
- Test new applications and upgrades.
- Develop and maintain technical and procedural documentation.

The IT BSA uses a combination of knowledge of information systems and business to develop computer systems that will meet business needs. The IT BSA must be able to leverage technology and take an organization to the next level of business analysis. The IT BSA plays a key role in ensuring that the engineering organization continues to be a valued and trusted technology partner to the business. The IT BSA may also assist in identifying data quality problems and in determining options for how they will be handled. He or she will also play a role in testing and validation, and in delivering user training and communications.

EDUCATION AND EXPERIENCE   Bachelor's degree in computer or information science is preferred. Educational requirements are waived for those with equivalent combination of education and experience.

CREDENTIALS, LICENSURE, OR CERTIFICATION, IF APPROPRIATE   Advanced certificate in computer/information science.

CORE COMPETENCIES AND SKILLS   Must be a self-motivated individual who has strong interpersonal and project management skills. Personal computer experience is necessary. Other qualities include:

- Fundamental knowledge of contemporary hardware and network platforms
- Proficiency in Microsoft Access, Excel, and Word

- Minimum 3 years of experience in a BSA role
- The ability to interact professionally with a diverse group, including executives, managers, and subject experts
- Solid verbal and written communication, organization, and time management skills
- Project management experience preferred
- Creative, resourceful, and innovative at tackling complex challenges

COMPENSATION   Analysts' average salary ranges from $53,600 to $119,000 annually, depending on degrees, experience, and the size and location of the managed care organization.

WORKPLACE LOCATION   You can find this job in a variety of health care organizations such as managed care organizations and hospitals.

EMPLOYMENT OUTLOOK   Employment of computer systems analysts is expected to grow by 29% from 2006 to 2016, which is much faster than the average for all health care occupations. In addition, the 146,000 new jobs that are expected to arise over the projected decade will be substantial. Demand for these workers will increase as organizations continue to adopt and integrate increasingly sophisticated technologies. Job growth will not be as rapid as during the preceding decade, however, as the IT sector matures and as routine work is increasingly outsourced offshore to foreign countries with lower prevailing wages (www.bls.gov/ooh/computer-and-information-technology/home.htm).

FOR MORE INFORMATION
- job-outlook.careerplanner.com/Computer-Systems-Analysts.cfm
- www.onetonline.org

79. Systems Analyst Advisor

POSITION DESCRIPTION   The position is responsible for defining and managing the scope of business systems projects. Primary duties may include, but are not limited to:

- Defines functional, usability, reliability, performance, and support requirements of a system.

- Creates and performs feature testing and determines environmental needs.
- Provides the link between the technical and business views of the systems by ensuring that the technical solutions being developed will satisfy the needs of the business.
- Partners with business, architecture, and infrastructure and oversees all service levels to ensure business area satisfaction.
- Defines detailed design components with high-level architecture blueprints.
- Coordinates integration activities to ensure successful implementation.
- Ensures effective monitoring of systems.
- Defines development strategies, standards, and support tools.
- Proactively works with stakeholders to identify future systems opportunities and enhancements.

EDUCATION AND EXPERIENCE

- A Bachelor of Arts or Bachelor of Science in information systems or a related field; 8 or more years of related experience; or any combination of education and experience that would provide an equivalent background.
- Minimum of 2 years of experience working with health care data.

CREDENTIALS, LICENSURE, OR CERTIFICATION, IF APPROPRIATE None specified.

CORE COMPETENCIES AND SKILLS

- Requires a Bachelor of Arts or Bachelor of Science in computer science/information systems; 4 or more years of technical writing experience; or any combination of education and experience that would provide an equivalent background
- Demonstrated proficiency in writing skills, interviewing techniques, and interpersonal skills are required
- Ability to work in a team environment, attention to detail, and strong organizational skills are required

COMPENSATION A systems analyst or systems analyst advisor in a managed care organizations can earn in the range of $90,000 to $120,000, although the total salary will vary depending on the size and location of the health care organization.

WORKPLACE LOCATION   Normally this job is located within the IT department of a managed care or insurance company.

EMPLOYMENT OUTLOOK   The employment outlook for a systems analyst or systems analyst advisor is very strong. Every managed care organization in the nation is working to develop its IT infrastructure in response to demands by the federal government and the need to provide ever-higher levels of quality care. Possessing an IT background is an important requirement, but the applicant must also be familiar with the unique requirements of health care delivery.

FOR MORE INFORMATION
- kaiserpermanentejobs.org/default.aspx
- www.jobmine.himss.org
- www.careersatwellpoint.com/search-jobs.aspx

80. Senior Information Technology Technical Writer

POSITION DESCRIPTION   The senior technical writer is responsible for providing leadership and guidance to other technical writers. This individual organizes, develops, and documents business technical information, processes, and procedures.

Primary duties may include, but are not limited to:

- Works with a development team to evaluate documentation needs.
- Conducts interviews to gather information.
- Assists with design, development, and editing of Internet-related material.
- Gathers, writes, validates, and updates training material, end user documentation, operations manuals, and technical user guides.

EDUCATION AND EXPERIENCE   Requires a Bachelor of Arts or Bachelor of Science in computer science/information systems, 4 or more years of technical writing experience, or any combination of education and experience that would provide an equivalent background.

CREDENTIALS, LICENSURE, OR CERTIFICATION, IF APPROPRIATE   None specified.

CORE COMPETENCIES AND SKILLS
- Demonstrated proficiency in writing skills, interviewing techniques, and interpersonal skills are required
- Ability to work in a team environment, attention to detail, and strong organizational skills are required

COMPENSATION   A technical writer in a managed care organizations can earn in the range of $90,000 to $120,000, although the total salary will vary depending on the size and location of the health care organization.

WORKPLACE LOCATION   Normally this job is located within the IT department of a managed care or insurance company.

EMPLOYMENT OUTLOOK   The employment outlook for a technical writer is very strong. Every managed care organization in the nation is working to develop its IT infrastructure in response to demands by the federal government and the need to provide ever-higher levels of quality care. Possessing an IT background is an important requirement, but the applicant must also be familiar with the unique requirements of health care delivery.

FOR MORE INFORMATION
- kaiserpermanentejobs.org/default.aspx
- www.jobmine.himss.org

81. Project Manager

POSITION DESCRIPTION   Although each project manager job description will reflect the specific needs of the particular company, the project manager will generally plan, coordinate, implement, and finalize projects according to the specifications and deadlines, all while keeping the project within budget. A project manager will need to define the project's objectives, create schedules, and oversee quality control throughout the entire project. To deliver the project according to plan, the project manager will also need to attain resources and manage a team and third-party contractors or consultants. In addition, he or she will need to be able to identify, assess, and minimize risks until successful project completion.

EDUCATION AND EXPERIENCE   Bachelor's degree in a related field and/or a minimum of 4 years of equivalent work experience.

CREDENTIALS, LICENSURE, OR CERTIFICATION, IF APPROPRIATE   A minimum of 8 years of project management experience; experience tracking resources/budgets desired; experience of Lean/Scrum/Agile management methodologies desired; experience with Clarity or other electronic project management tools desired; PMP certification preferred; knowledge of or experience with health care financial business and systems desired.

CORE COMPETENCIES AND SKILLS

- Strong interpersonal skills and proven leadership skills in working with diverse and complex projects; solid collaboration, facilitation, and negotiation skills
- Detail oriented and analytical with good organization skills
- Must have the ability to prioritize multiple activities and tasks simultaneously and adapt to a rapidly changing environment; strong problem and issue resolution experience
- Possess good written and verbal communication skills and be able to communicate effectively with individuals at various levels within the organization
- Highly motivated and able to work independently with little supervision
- Microsoft Office (including Word, Excel, and PowerPoint) and Microsoft Visio, Metastorm BPM, and SharePoint experience preferred

COMPENSATION A project manager can make approximately $85,000.

WORKPLACE LOCATION Project managers can be found in a variety of organizations such as managed care organizations, hospitals, medical centers, and health technology vendors.

EMPLOYMENT OUTLOOK As we recover from the turbulent economic times, the project manager job outlook is clearly improving. According to a study published by the Anderson Economic Group, an average of 1.2 million project management positions will need to be filled each year through 2016. In a recent CNNMoney survey,[1] in the listing of the 50 best jobs in America, IT project manager was ranked at number 5.

FOR MORE INFORMATION

- www.pmi.org
- www.andersoneconomicgroup.com
- www.CNNMoney.com

---

[1] www.CNNMoney.com

82. Portfolio Manager

POSITION DESCRIPTION   Responsible for organizing a series of work into a single portfolio consisting of reports that capture project objectives, costs, timelines, accomplishments, resources, risks, and other critical factors; project delivery and budget forecasting on short-, medium-, and long-term bases. Primary duties may include, but are not limited to:

- Participates in strategic project planning and annual budgeting. Interacts closely with senior management business partners to plan and ensure project objectives are met and budget aligns with IT budget objectives.
- Provides strategic direction for aligning a specific organization's project plan of record and annual goal objectives with the annual operating budget by specifying goals, strategy, staffing, and scheduling; identifying risks, contingency plans, and budget; and achieving long-term and short-term financial objectives with the primary goal of ensuring that return-on-investment (ROI) thresholds are met.
- Coordinates portfolio and project activities of the business unit and develops relationships with the business.
- Manages execution of portfolio objectives and interacts closely with end users, business technologists, and others to prioritize business needs.
- Works with resource managers to manage the portfolio according to governance processes, budgeting, and forecasting.

EDUCATION AND EXPERIENCE
- Bachelor of Arts or Bachelor of Science degree
- Broad-based experience in planning and designing low- to medium-complexity project portfolios
- Any combination of education and experience that would provide an equivalent background
- At least 5 years professional project management experience with 3 years spent leading and directing multiple project tasks preferred

CREDENTIALS, LICENSURE, OR CERTIFICATION, IF APPROPRIATE   Multiple trade certifications or other continuing education preferred.

CORE COMPETENCIES AND SKILLS

- Accounting/financial management background preferred
- Basic understanding of vendor contractors and service level agreements preferred
- Excellent analytical skills required
- Good verbal and written communication skills required
- Ability to build and maintain solid working relationships and proven ability to negotiate with positive results
- Will be working across the IT group and will work with vendors, managers, procurement, and contracting

COMPENSATION   A portfolio manager in a managed care organizations can earn in the range of $90,000 to $120,000, although the total salary will vary depending on the size and location of the health care organization.

WORKPLACE LOCATION   Normally this job is located within the IT department of a managed care or insurance company.

EMPLOYMENT OUTLOOK   The employment outlook for a portfolio manager is very strong. Every managed care organization in the nation is working to develop its IT infrastructure in response to demands by the federal government and the need to provide ever-higher levels of quality care. Possessing an IT background is an important requirement, but the applicant must also be familiar with the unique requirements of health care delivery.

FOR MORE INFORMATION

- kaiserpermanentejobs.org/default.aspx
- www.jobmine.himss.org
- www.careersatwellpoint.com/search-jobs.aspx

ROBERT ABOULACHE
Manager, Training Environments
Kaiser Permanente's Digital Network

Describe the sort of work you do. I manage training environments that support Kaiser Permanente's digital network, which includes our EMR, medical imaging, mobile training rooms, and various web portals that distribute learning modules to our employees.

What is a typical day like at your job? Busy. There is a constant effort to keep environments, systems, and materials up-to-date. Kaiser Permanente is a very large health care provider, so meeting its many demands involves getting things done correctly. A typical day starts with reviewing my schedule, going through e-mails, attending meetings, setting direction, planning for future developments, and creating the next evolution of things. I work with all sorts of people, but the bulk of my time is spent with physicians, nurses, and technical systems administrators. Not to mention a good lunch in Pasadena and a couple of 20- to 30-minute walks to break the day up, get some fresh air, and regain perspective.

What education or training do you have? Is it typical for your job? I received my undergraduate degree in Health Education at the California State University of Northridge and my graduate degree in Clinical Holistic Health Education and Counseling from John F. Kennedy University. I have always been an early adopter of technology and thought perspectives, so making my way to this position came out of my broad understanding of informatics and health care. My educational path is not typical for my current job.

What path did you take to get to the job you are in today? I worked from an early age (first job at 13) and was always pretty entrepreneurial and not afraid to "get my hands dirty." But most directly, I started this current work while leading an integrative medicine effort at Kaiser. Through various contacts and opportunities I joined the System Solutions department because what I was offering was based

(continued)

ROBERT ABOULACHE   *(continued)*

on systemizing integrated care, making it automatic and simple to implement. The things that motivate me to stay for now in my current position are being on teams that determine best practices at the point of care within the EMR and working with providers that are visionary and programmers that are competent.

Where might you go from here if you wanted to advance your career? For now I will stay in my current position, but I am building toward greater time spent on innovation. I have been involved with various cutting-edge developments that include mHealth efforts directly related to patient care and health promotion. If I could design my perfect job, it would be doing more of that and less in the daily management of training environments, websites, and content management.

What is the most challenging part of your job? The most challenging part of my job entails making requests to modify or implement code or configurations into our environments and waiting for those requests to be implemented. The request is within my control, but waiting for engineers to approve and do the work is the most challenging part in that I have no control of their work efforts.

What is the best part? I have a high level of autonomy and trust by leadership to continue to innovate and "play" to help Kaiser Permanente develop tools and resources that renovate health care and health care delivery.

What advice would you give to someone contemplating a career like yours? Learn your craft and dare to be exceptional. And most importantly, learn to listen to others, to experts, to systems, to processes—and take the many inputs coming at you from all the various sources and stakeholders and make connections that will better the flow of information, of systems, of processes. You can change the world, but to do that, you must work together without worrying about getting credit, but instead focus on getting things done and providing real

(continued)

ROBERT ABOULACHE   *(continued)*

solutions. There is an 80/20 rule that applies: 80% of the work will be done by 20% of the people. Find and be part of the 20% getting it done; it makes life much richer and work more enjoyable. John Lennon (Beatle, musician, philosopher) said it simply: "A working-class hero is something to be." You can be remarkable (and a hero) by working with others toward the common good. There is no need to be famous or in the limelight; just do the right thing and make the right thing easy to do.

83. Developer Advisor

POSITION DESCRIPTION   Responsible for programming on specific application subsets of the company's application portfolio; participating in all phases of the development and maintenance life cycle, typically for an assigned business unit or corporate department, and utilizing various customer technology platforms. Primary duties may include, but are not limited to:

- Maintains active relationships with customers to determine business requirements and leads requirements-gathering meetings.
- Owns the change-request process and may coordinate with other teams as necessary.
- Develops and owns list of final enhancements.
- Develops and defines application scope and objectives and prepares technical and/or functional specifications from which programs will be written.
- Performs technical design reviews and code reviews.
- Ensures that the unit test is completed and meets the test plan requirements, that systems testing is completed, and that the system is implemented according to plan.
- Assesses current status and supports data information planning.
- Coordinates on-call support and ensures effective monitoring of systems.
- Maintains technical development environment.

- Mentors others and may lead multiple small- to medium-size projects.
- Facilitates group sessions to elicit complex information on requirements clarification, design sessions, code reviews, and troubleshooting issues.
- Supports vendor evaluation.

EDUCATION AND EXPERIENCE

- Requires Bachelor of Arts or Bachelor of Science degree in related field or technical institute training
- Five or more years of related experience; multiplatform experience
- Expert-level experience with business and technical applications
- Any combination of education and experience that would provide an equivalent background.

CREDENTIALS, LICENSURE, OR CERTIFICATION, IF APPROPRIATE   None specified.

CORE COMPETENCIES AND SKILLS

- Candidate should have the ability to mentor others
- Lead multiple small projects and provide troubleshooting support
- Multidatabase and/or multilanguage preferred
  - Java
  - XML
  - Quality Center or Zephyr
  - Web: asp.net
  - Web services, messaging, and API experience

COMPENSATION   A developer advisor in a managed care organization can earn in the range of $90,000 to $120,000, although the total salary will vary depending on the size and location of the health care organization.

WORKPLACE LOCATION   Normally this job is located within the IT department of a managed care or insurance company.

EMPLOYMENT OUTLOOK   The employment outlook for a developer advisor is strong, but candidate must have a background in programming languages. All large managed care organizations in the nation are working to develop their IT infrastructure in response to demands by the federal government and the need to provide ever-higher levels of quality care. Possessing an IT background is an important requirement, but the applicant must also be familiar with the unique requirements of health care delivery.

FOR MORE INFORMATION
- kaiserpermanentejobs.org/default.aspx
- www.jobmine.himss.org
- www.careersatwellpoint.com/search-jobs.aspx

84. Information Technology Business Implementation Liaison

POSITION DESCRIPTION   Solves problems, performs analyses, researches and tests functions for systems and networks. Primary duties may include, but are not limited to:

- Provides resolution of complex problems.
- Leads implementations for systems and networks; develops testing plans to ensure quality of implementation.
- Represents major upgrades and reconfigurations in change control.
- Designs and analyzes mix of vendor services meeting business requirements; maintains relationship with key vendors.
- Leads go-live initiatives to consolidate equipment or implement business relocations.
- Performs capacity analysis; recommends and implements capacity increases; supervises preventive maintenance.
- Performs the most complex operations and administration tasks.
- Builds and maintains partnering relationship with business partners, presenting agreed-upon tactical plans as well as ongoing status monitoring and communication of metrics and health of program.

EDUCATION AND EXPERIENCE
- Bachelor's degree in related field
- Any combination of education and experience that would provide an equivalent background
- Three to 6 years of experience required in a support and operations role in any of the following areas:

○ Servers
○ Networks
○ Telecommunications
○ Storage
○ Mainframe

CREDENTIALS, LICENSURE, OR CERTIFICATION, IF APPROPRIATE Multiple trade certifications and/or continuing education preferred.

CORE COMPETENCIES AND SKILLS

- Draw upon IT organization to establish core relationships and processes that will enhance ability to respond quickly and meet business objectives with the IT organization
- Escalate and manage issue resolution for the business partners
- Provide hands-on tactical IT support where and when necessary
- Continue to identify better ways to capture opportunities to enhance service to business partners
- Analyze and identify enhancement/defect issues in the processes or software programs for the business partners in a way that will increase their productivity or the quality of their jobs
- Demonstrate leadership in representing IT to the business user
- Know the IT forecast plans and assist in preparing the business for anticipated changes
- Knowledge transfer: When appropriate, train and develop other IT or business associates to improve service
- Work independently with minimal supervision, participate in projects, and be able to resolve most incidents and make configuration changes required
- Strong mentoring skills preferred

COMPENSATION An IT business escalation liaison in a managed care organization can earn in the range of $90,000 to $120,000, although the total salary will vary depending on the size and location of the health care organization.

WORKPLACE LOCATION Normally this position is located within the IT department of a managed care or insurance company.

EMPLOYMENT OUTLOOK The employment outlook for an IT business escalation liaison is strong. All large managed care organizations in the nation are working to develop their IT infrastructure in response to demands by the federal government and the need to provide ever-higher levels of quality care. Possessing an IT background is an important requirement, but the applicant must also be familiar with the unique requirements of health care delivery.

FOR MORE INFORMATION
- kaiserpermanentejobs.org/default.aspx
- www.careersatwellpoint.com/search-jobs.aspx
- jobmine.himss.org

85. Database Administrator

POSITION DESCRIPTION Building, maintaining, administering, and supporting databases are the primary job duties of database administrators. These professionals keep data secure by managing access, privileges, and information migration. Database administrators are also responsible for installing and configuring database management software, translating database design, and diagnosing database performance issues. Other job functions of database administrators include installing software upgrades, managing hardware upgrades, and maintaining computer servers. They also develop backup and recovery strategies, and monitor servers to ensure capacity is not exceeded. At times, database administrators may help devise network strategies, test systems, and develop systems standards. Evaluating new tools and technologies, analyzing user needs, and presenting findings to management are additional job duties of database administrators. They may also approve the purchase of new database products and improvements, as well as schedule, plan, and supervise their installation and testing. In many cases, database administrators will provide users with training on new database software and systems.

EDUCATION AND EXPERIENCE Most database administrators have a bachelor's degree in management information systems (MIS) or a computer-related field. Firms with large databases may prefer applicants who have a Master of Business Administration (MBA) with a concentration in information systems. An MBA typically requires 2 years of schooling after the undergraduate level.

Database administrators need an understanding of database languages, the most common of which is SQL. Most database systems use some variation of SQL, and a database administrator will need to become familiar with whichever language the firm uses.

CREDENTIALS, LICENSURE, OR CERTIFICATION, IF APPROPRIATE
- At least 6 to 10 years of experience in the field or in a related area required
- Familiarity with industry-wide practices
- Knowledge of ETL (Extract, Transform, and Load) processes using data transformation services packages
- TSQL scripting knowledge required
- Knowledge of replication and clustering preferred

CORE COMPETENCIES AND SKILLS
- Demonstrate advanced technical and programming skills
- Apply proven principles of theory and design to build and manage a database
- Implement best practices in IT management
- Determine significant features, advantages, and disadvantages of various database systems
- Leverage expert-level skills and knowledge to succeed in a database administrator career

COMPENSATION   According to Bureau of Labor Statistics findings, computer network, systems, and database administrators earned an average annual salary of $74,290. The middle 50% earned between $53,470 and $93,260. Salaries for the lowest 10% were around $40,780, while the highest 10% earned upward of $114,200. Recent bachelor's degree program graduates will typically start out at the lower end of the scale and move up in salary with experience and advanced education.

WORKPLACE LOCATION   Database administrators work in large complex organizations such as a hospital chain, or a managed care or large insurance company. They would be in the IT department.

EMPLOYMENT OUTLOOK   Employment of database administrators is projected to grow 31% from 2010 to 2020, much faster than the average for all occupations. Rapid growth in data collection by businesses, as well as an increased need for database security measures, will contribute to the growth of this occupation.

FOR MORE INFORMATION

- www.bls.gov/ooh/computer-and-information-technology/database-administrators.htm#tab-1

10 ■ HIT CAREERS IN THE PUBLIC HEALTH SECTOR

Public health is a unique sector with a wide range of job opportunities. Generally people employed in this sector have degrees and a background in public health. With the growing emphasis on population health and managing groups of people to achieve better health status, there is an intersection between medical delivery of health care and public health efforts focused on wellness and prevention. The job title "informaticist" in medical sectors denotes an emphasis on medical data to create evidence-based treatment for patients, while in the public health sector an "informaticist" focuses on data that supports prevention and wellness.

The data that are collected on the medical delivery of patient care through electronic medical records (EMR) provide a vast amount of potential information for the public health sector. There is a convergence of health information technology (HIT) in medical delivery and broader public health goals. One area that is emerging is the field of public health informaticist, which focuses on the analysis of health/medical data and on helping to form public intervention through public policies. The skill set for a public health informaticist includes epidemiology, statistics analysis, and data analytics. These skills are very useful for new accountable care organizations that need population management knowledge and skills. Several universities, including the University of California at Davis, are offering certificate programs in public health informatics.

Many public health jobs are in publicly funded hospitals and thus involve many of the same HIT positions as voluntary and proprietary hospitals. Public health agencies or county or state health departments have positions related to data analytics, population management, informatics, project management, and perhaps integration with electronic health records (EHR). The interviewee in this chapter is someone who is deep into analytics and demonstrates skills and knowledge valuable in public health settings.

POSITION DESCRIPTIONS IN THE PUBLIC HEALTH SECTOR

The following job descriptions are representative of HIT-related jobs found in the public health sector. The interview in this chapter is representative of an individual, whether in the public health or hospital sector, who works with vast amounts of data to support the care process.

86. Public Health Informatics (General Description)

Public health informatics is the application and use of informatics in areas of public health. Health informatics is a discipline at the intersection of information science, health care, and computer science that entails the design and delivery of information to improve clinical care, individual and public health care, and biomedical research. Health informatics optimizes the usability, acquisition, and processing of health-related information, using resources and tools that include people and processes, information and knowledge, algorithms and data, hardware and software.

Public health informatics includes surveillance, prevention, preparedness, and health promotion. Public health informatics works on information and technology issues from the perspective of groups of individuals. Public health is extremely broad, touching on the environment, work, living places, and more. Focuses may include the aspects of public health that enable the development and use of interoperable information systems for public health tasks such as biosurveillance, outbreak management, electronic laboratory reporting, and prevention.

The overall general description of a public health informatics worker can be found under various job titles. Some of these job titles include public health analyst, biomedical health information analyst, public health information officer, public health informatics specialist, and health analytics specialist. Typical qualifications include a bachelor's degree or higher. Areas of educational concentration include health care informatics, health economics, public health, and computer science. For a mid-level career a master's degree and an average of 5 to 7 years of experience are strongly preferred.

Based on information provided by the U.S. Bureau of Labor Statistics, a public health informatics job is categorized under the larger classification of medical and health services manager. The average reported median salary was $86,500 annually. This career field is projected to grow 22% by 2020.

- www.amia.org/applications-informatics/public-health-informatics
- sbmi.uth.edu/news/defining-bmi/public-health-informatics.htm
- www.cdc.gov/mmwr/preview/mmwrhtml/su6103a5.htm

87. Public Health Informatics Specialist

POSITION DESCRIPTION   The public health informatics specialist will perform complex analysis, research, mapping, and evaluation of health care data. Key responsibilities include working collaboratively with the business users, information technology (IT) department, and external developers to create business requirements for new reports, to generate and analyze reports, to analyze data to make recommendations for program development, and to present data in formats that are easily understood by business users and other stakeholders.

EDUCATION AND EXPERIENCE
- A bachelor's degree in a health-related field or certification in public health informatics with 8 to 10 years' experience in applied public health with responsibilities that include service within a local, state, or federal agency; or
- A master's degree in public health (MPH) with 3 to 5 years' experience in applied public health that include service within a local, state, or federal agency or medical practice; or
- A doctorate in public health (DrPH) with 2 to 3 years' experience in applied public health that include service within a local, state, or federal agency or medical practice
- Any combination of the requirements above will be considered.

CREDENTIALS, LICENSURE, OR CERTIFICATION, IF APPROPRIATE   Experience in software programming and development is desirable.

CORE COMPETENCIES AND SKILLS
- Experience with computational bioinformatics tools such as BLAST and the SMITH-WATERMAN algorithm (see website references that follow)
- Experience with genetic databases such as NCBI preferred (see website references that follow)
- Demonstrated skills and ability in performing complex business systems analysis
- Ability to communicate effectively and clearly present technical approaches and findings

235

- Experience in complex problem solving
- Experience with Business Process Analysis tools
- Knowledge and experience with Windows Office and SQL environments strongly preferred
- Advanced knowledge of data warehousing concepts strongly preferred
- Knowledge and experience in project management

COMPENSATION   The average reported median salary is between $88,580 and $110,000 annually (www.bls.gov).

WORKPLACE LOCATION   The position would be outsourced to a government agency like the Centers for Disease Control and Prevention (CDC) or in research and development.

EMPLOYMENT OUTLOOK   Public health informatics is categorized under the larger classification of medical and health services manager. This career field is projected to grow 22% by 2020.

FOR MORE INFORMATION
Job positions:
- www.cdc.gov/phifp (CDC Public Health Informatics Fellowship)
- jobmine.himss.org/jobseeker/search

Additional educational and professional information can be found at:
- www.phii.org (Public Health Informatics Institute)
- www.aphif.org (Applied Public Health Informatics Fellowship)
- en.wikipedia.org/wiki/Smith-Waterman_algorithm
- blast.ncbi.nlm.nih.gov/Blast.cgi
- www.ncbi.nlm.nih.gov

STACY COOREMAN
Health Systems Database Analyst
Vanderbilt-Ingram Cancer Center
Vanderbilt University Medical Center
Healthcare MBA Candidate, Belmont
University

Describe the sort of work you do. As part of an academic medical center, my department is held accountable for managing research-driven oncology informatics. I support personalized medicine initiatives within Vanderbilt-Ingram Cancer Center, specifically, web-based decision support tools that match tumor mutations to targeted therapies and clinical trials. The publicly available data are derived from several external sources, transposed into a consumable structure, and then annotated accordingly with disease and gene information. My current role requires me to create ad hoc reports for senior-level management and to develop tools to ensure data integrity.

What is a typical day like at your job? Each day begins with a stand-up meeting to provide project-specific updates from each team member. During these meetings we communicate milestones and discuss technical challenges that could possibly impede progress. The rest of the day involves fulfilling report requests, troubleshooting data issues, analyzing workflows, communicating with stakeholders, and attending informational meetings that are designed to contribute to the overall success of each project.

What education or training do you have? Is it typical for your job? I graduated from the University of Dayton with a business degree in management information systems, operations management, and marketing. I have participated in continuing education courses focusing on programming languages, database structures, network security, project management, interpersonal communication, data analysis, and statistics. I am also currently enrolled in a health care MBA

(continued)

STACY COOREMAN   (continued)

program to assist in transitioning to a leadership role. I do believe I have taken a traditional approach in how I personally prepared to become a database analyst and would recommend this course of action to anyone interested in health care IT.

What path did you take to get to the job you are in today? After I finished my undergraduate degree, I began my IT career as a help-desk coordinator for a mental health inpatient/outpatient facility that had implemented a proprietary software package. After 3 months of learning their system, I was promoted to an analyst role. I spent 6 years in mental health, which exposed me to a wide variety of skills ranging from user support and training, the entire software development life cycle, documentation standards, and HIPAA security. In 2010, I decided I was ready for a more challenging position at a larger facility, which has led me to my current position at Vanderbilt University Medical Center.

Where might you go from here if you wanted to advance your career? My goal is to become more involved in improving the issues that plague our health care system. Since I have a strong IT background and enjoy solving problems, I would seek to make advancements using an integrated approach of technology and strategy. Ideally, this would come from a leadership role within a hospital's administration team, or accepting a position in the consulting industry that specializes in health care improvement.

What is the most challenging part of your job? Working with large and complex data sets can be intimidating. We operate three development environments for each project to mitigate any damage to our production data. Organization and documentation are a must, but are not always a priority. Getting team members on the same page from the inception of a project to the deployment takes a lot of communication and up-front planning. You have to be able to recognize the unique personalities, strengths, and weaknesses of everyone assigned to the project.

(continued)

STACY COOREMAN *(continued)*

What is the best part? The most rewarding aspect of my job is seeing contributions I have been a part of deliver better patient care. I was recently able to observe an oncology consultation where a patient's tumor had been genetically tested. Because of the research and tools I helped develop, the patient was able to know which medications are more effective in achieving remission and which could immediately be eliminated from the treatment plan. I come to work every day knowing that what I do from a desk is helping someone live a better life.

What advice would you give to someone contemplating a career like yours? (1) Be a sponge and absorb what is happening around you. It is easy to fall into a routine by spending too much time behind a computer. The more you can sharpen your analytical skills by understanding the stories and processes behind raw data, the more successful you will be. Remember that at the end of the day, you are striving to add value for the patient. (2) Ask questions. Seek clarity if you cannot make sense of the task at hand. You will save yourself a lot of frustration and rework by not assuming what a user is really asking for. (3) Stay current. Health care and technology are both ever-changing industries. Participate in forums, conferences, and training opportunities. Read business articles and follow relevant leaders and associations on social media outlets. (4) Network. The more people you become acquainted with, the more you can collaborate and stay motivated to think outside the box.

88. Principal Information Systems Analyst (Electronic Health Records)

POSITION DESCRIPTION The principal information systems analyst is responsible for a highly specialized, integrated, complex information systems analysis to design, test, integrate, and implement one or more of the following EHR components: registration, admitting, discharge, and transfer (R/ADT); Enterprise Master Patient Index (EMPI); patient scheduling; training; clinical applications; and ancillary services applications such as lab, radiology, and pharmacy. The position provides technical leadership in IT strategic planning, business automation planning, and business process improvement.

Essential job functions include:

- Acts as a project lead or technical specialist for complex systems development projects and supervises lower-level information systems analysts and other technical staff
- Participates in the work and supervises a team of information systems analysts and other technical staff engaged in the development, implementation, or maintenance of highly complex health care systems
- Develops systems specifications through requirements gathering, research, analysis, and direct contact with business units, subject matter experts, systems users and technical staff, and hardware/software vendors for specialized and complex applications using relevant tools and techniques for systems development
- Conducts analysis and planning to revise and update the department's long-range information systems plans, business automation plans, and IT strategic plans; solves the more complex application problems
- Develops Statement of Work in accordance to systems development life cycle on hospital/clinical/financial infrastructure applications and technical enhancements, including tasks, deliverables, and pricing
- Coordinates change management documentation and ensures that approvals are managed according to departmental procedures; monitors vendor performance to ensure contract deliverables meet requirements; resolves problems, prepares reports, and reviews/approves vendor payments
- Acts as technical lead to a project manager, department management, or user management regarding one or more major health care–related systems or maintenance analysis and design efforts; represents the department at interdepartmental meetings and serves on internal IT committees and work groups when needed
- Leads technical team to service customers on new initiatives and implement EHR; collaborates with subject matter experts and vendor professional support teams; and leads the IT technical team to develop project plans, timelines, deliverables, and implementation outcomes
- Conducts systems analysis, process flows, systems interfaces, validations, testing, training, implementation, and change management; monitors conversion/migration plan development

and execution; completes systems documentation, enterprise policies, and procedures

EDUCATION AND EXPERIENCE Graduation from an accredited institution with a bachelor's degree in computer science or information technology, or a closely related field. Four years of responsible full-time, paid experience in a health care–related IT organization with knowledge and experience in health care–related systems at a medium to large public or private health care organization performing information systems analysis and design for complex systems.

CREDENTIALS, LICENSURE, OR CERTIFICATION, IF APPROPRIATE Certification from the Project Management Institute (PMI) as a Project Management Professional (PMP) is desirable.

CORE COMPETENCIES AND SKILLS
- Experience in support of EHR/EMR modules/applications
- Experience in leading one or more technical teams completing the EHR/EMR implementation support, such as Cerner Millennium System
- Experience in EMPI-related systems
- Demonstrated skills and ability in performing complex business systems analysis
- Able to communicate effectively and to clearly present technical approaches and findings
- Experience in complex problem solving
- Knowledge and experience in project management

COMPENSATION Salary in a public health organization like a county hospital ranges from $70,000 to $95,000.

WORKPLACE LOCATION This position is typical of large county government health care delivery systems that would include county hospitals, clinics, and other services. It would be located centrally in the IT department.

EMPLOYMENT OUTLOOK The principal information systems analyst (EHR) is categorized under the larger classification of medical and health services manager. This career field is projected to grow 22% by 2020.

FOR MORE INFORMATION

- jobmine.himss.org/jobseeker/search
- www.bls.gov

89. Project Manager for Electronic Health Records

POSITION DESCRIPTION   The project manager for EHR performs a wide range of specialized and complex IT systems activities in the enterprise health care environment. The manager also acts as a consultant, technical specialist, systems architect, or a project manager in a health cluster departmental IT organization.

Essential job functions include:

- Evaluates and recommends new products and technologies, provides health-related systems development or software consulting to departmental project teams and user management in a highly specialized field of health care information systems (IS) design and development
- Develops and documents enterprise systems architecture for the department
- Reviews systems proposals for conformance to standards and integration with the documented enterprise systems architecture
- Reviews proposed systems designs to ensure they are scalable, inflexible, and interoperated consistent with IT emerging technologies, state/federal, and health care IT innovation requirements
- Reviews the work of consultants and vendors to ensure that contract work meets departmental technical requirements and is compatible with enterprise architecture
- Performs highly specialized and complex IS or network analysis and design tasks; acts as consultant/specialist in IT strategic planning, business automation planning, business process improvement, or application development
- Provides leadership and overall project management for systems development projects or networks

EDUCATION AND EXPERIENCE   Bachelor's degree or higher from an accredited institution in computer science, information technology/systems, electrical engineering, or a closely related field. Four years of experience within the last 5 years at the level of principal information systems analyst or closely related job responsibility.

CREDENTIALS, LICENSURE, OR CERTIFICATION, IF APPROPRIATE Certification from PMI as a PMP is desirable.

CORE COMPETENCIES AND SKILLS
- Experience in support of EHR/EMR modules/applications
- Experience in EHR/EMR implementation
- Critical thinking and problem-solving skills
- Effective communication skills—written, oral, and presentation
- Effective team building and managing skills
- Ability to negotiate and deal with conflict management
- Be adaptable and able to deal with stress
- Proven experience in people management, change management, and strategic planning

COMPENSATION The range of compensation for an IT project manager in a public health hospital, as in other hospital settings, is between $80,000 and $110,000.

WORKPLACE LOCATION The position of IT project manager can be found in a wide variety of organizations, including vendors, hospitals, managed care, and large medical groups. This position description is modeled after a typical project manager in an IT hospital or large medical group with an EHR environment.

EMPLOYMENT OUTLOOK Project management positions are growing at an above average rate in both the vendor and health care delivery sectors. Advanced certification in project management is probably required if one wants to move to higher levels in this field.

FOR MORE INFORMATION Chapter 4 has a number of references to organizations like the Project Management Institute (www.pmi.org) that can provide more details on the project management aspects of this job description.
- jobmine.himss.org/jobseeker/search
- www.bls.gov

11 ■ HIT CAREERS IN THE EDUCATION AND TRAINING SECTOR

Careers in health information technology (HIT) education- and training-related jobs generally carry significant educational and/or work experience requirements. Chapter 3, on education programs, discussed a number of institutions that provide both degree and nondegree and certificate programs that prepare people for careers in HIT. All of those programs need faculty to deliver the curriculum. For some individuals seeking a faculty position, their educational pathway has followed a typical pattern of seeking a doctorate in a specific field, like health informatics. Others have achieved a master's degree and then pursued advanced certification and experience in a field like medical coding. Experienced HIT professionals may find a career path leading to being a faculty member training future specialists in HIT.

The faculty position descriptions that follow demonstrate the educational background and experience necessary to apply for academic faculty positions.

Another career path that is important in health care delivery organizations is that of a trainer of specific clinical or administrative applications. A person with years of experience implementing and using various information systems, or someone employed by an HIT vendor, could aspire to be a trainer for others in the use of a particular system. Within a health care facility are trainer positions that teach end users to maximize a new clinical or administrative system. Sometimes they are called "super users" or "system trainers."

The following job descriptions represent typical faculty job descriptions and also typical descriptions of trainers.

POSITION DESCRIPTIONS IN THE EDUCATION AND TRAINING SECTOR

90. Clinical Educator/Electronic Medical Record Implementation and Training Specialist

POSITION DESCRIPTION Responsible for participating in the planning, coordination, implementation, and evaluation of department educational activities. Actively teaches staff topics related to mandatory education. The clinical educator also coordinates department orientation for new hires, new hire integration, and the preceptor program. This individual also conducts various electronic medical record (EMR) activities, such as project implementation, scheduling, and delivering of EMR training to staff. The clinical educator is dedicated to assisting the entire clinical staff in the adoption of the EMR system and maximizing the utilization of system features. The clinical educator assists the department director in documentation of all department educational activities, continuing education programs, and mandatory training, and also assists the team in identifying the educational needs of all staff related the changing environment. Activities include, but are not limited to:

- Designs and delivers programs for employees to participate in professional growth and developmental programs.
- Supports the department director in the formulation of objectives, philosophy, goals, and policies and in the evaluation of the education process and programs for the department.
- Communicates changes in health care legislation, educational standards, care delivery methods, and practices related to a specific department.
- Conducts trainings in both group and one-on-one sessions.
- Participates in nursing/clinical meetings in order to improve the patient care delivery system.

EDUCATION AND EXPERIENCE Graduation from an accredited school of nursing is required, with an additional degree in technology or a related field preferred. A minimum of 5 years' experience in adult, acute care, RN-level nursing is required. Prior experience in training end users on EMR systems is also required.

CREDENTIALS, LICENSURE, OR CERTIFICATION, IF APPROPRIATE Current state licensure as a registered nurse or licensure from a state within the

Nursing Compact required. Current Basic Life Support (BLS) certification is required, and successful completion of the American Hospital Association (AHA)-approved course in Advanced Cardiac Life Support (ACLS) within 30 days of employment is required. Trainer positions also may require certification from a specific vendor such as Epic Certification or Cerner Certification.

CORE COMPETENCIES AND SKILLS

- The clinical educator must be a self-starter and willing to stay current in clinical areas through journal articles and self-study
- The clinical educator also maintains licensure and maintains cultural competency when operating within the concept of the organization's mission and vision
- The clinical educator serves as a positive role model and representative of the hospital

COMPENSATION The average salary ranges from $55,000 to $65,000. The salary can be higher depending on degrees, work experience with EMR, and prior teaching experience.

WORKPLACE LOCATION Education or training department in a hospital setting. The individual might be assigned to a specific clinical department depending on the nature of the training involved.

EMPLOYMENT OUTLOOK According to the U.S. Bureau of Labor Statistics, electronic health record (EHR) systems will continue to become more common, and technicians with computer skills will be needed to use them. The best thing to do is to obtain a certification in health information or EHR. Employment of EHR systems and health information technicians is expected to increase by 21% from 2010 to 2020.

FOR MORE INFORMATION

- www.bls.gov/ooh
- www.onetonline.org

91. Information Technology Trainer

POSITION DESCRIPTION Information technology (IT) trainers work in various sectors of the health care industry from hospitals to vendors, private companies, software houses, and private or public organizations. IT trainers are individuals who are mainly responsible for developing training programs for information and coordinating technology based on training sessions for the staff of all sorts of companies and organizations. They are the individuals who operate, configure, and maintain new technology. IT trainers are the main resource that staff members within companies and organizations go to when new software is implemented or if there is a technical problem. The successful candidate must be able to plan and prepare a lesson to education staff members on the newest systems implementation within these organizations and come up with methods, activities, and different processes for training others. The responsibilities of this job may vary depending on the department in which an individual is hired.

EDUCATION AND EXPERIENCE   An IT trainer it is required to have a bachelor's degree in computer science or computer engineering, and any other, higher degree is just an advantage for an employer.

CREDENTIALS, LICENSURE, OR CERTIFICATION, IF APPROPRIATE   Certification for professionals in HIT is required. A minimum of 2 years in computer applications training and software experience would be favored.

CORE COMPETENCIES AND SKILLS
- Need to have great communication and leadership skills
- Must obtain accurate and up-to-date knowledge within the field
- Responsible for upgrading, maintaining, and learning new and existing applications
- Must address assigned tasks comprehensively and efficiently
- Administrative skills
- Management role
- Ability to take on multiple tasks
- Ability to work effectively with management and colleagues
- Technical and troubleshooting skills
- Analytical skills
- Time-management skills
- Commitment to learning and quick adaptation to changes

COMPENSATION   According to the Bureau of Labor Statistics the average annual salary of an IT trainer ranges from $67,000 to $96,000. Depending on an individual's training and experience and the department of training she or he performs in, salary can ultimately increase.

WORKPLACE LOCATION   IT trainers either are employed in the IT department of the organization or company they work for or are employed by a technology vendor. They are the main source of reliability in a vendor's new IT investment.

EMPLOYMENT OUTLOOK   With the growth of technology, health care industries now all revolve around the different technologies that are used within these organizations and companies. As years go by the expansion of technology just keeps on increasing, and with new inventions always evolving, IT trainers will always be needed for training and guidance for health care staff members.

FOR MORE INFORMATION
- www.indeed.com/q-Information-Technology-Trainer-jobs.html
- www.aitp.org

92. Instructor, Health Information Technology Program

POSITION DESCRIPTION   This is a full-time (two terms) faculty position at a community college as a health information management educator. The successful candidate will teach courses such as Diagnosis Coding, *International Classification of Diseases, 10th Revision (ICD-10)* Overview, *ICD-10* Fundamentals, and Regulatory Coding Audits.

EDUCATION AND EXPERIENCE   Bachelor's degree from a regionally accredited institution; minimum of 2 years' documented recent experience in the qualifying field; 2 to 3 years of health information management experience in a health care setting. Two years postsecondary teaching experience in an HIT program preferred.

CREDENTIALS, LICENSURE, OR CERTIFICATION, IF APPROPRIATE   Current certification as a Registered Health Information Administrator (RHIA) or Registered Health Information Technician (RHIT).

CORE COMPETENCIES AND SKILLS
- Knowledge of current regulations and skills in medical records coding
- Practical knowledge of *ICD-10*
- Excellent communication skills: written, oral, and presentation

- Excellent interpersonal skills appropriate to an academic teaching environment
- Knowledge of teaching strategies in both online and face-to-face education environments
- Ability to stay current in the health information management profession

COMPENSATION Salary range is $35,673 to $55,650 (for two terms); the maximum salary is based on education level, full-time professional work experience, and/or full-time teaching experience. Salary will be determined when hire date is established.

WORKPLACE LOCATION This position is located in the health information management department within a community college.

EMPLOYMENT OUTLOOK The growth of EMR has led to a demand for educational programs to prepare individuals for this fast-growing profession. Instructors are in short supply and the demand will be increasing.

FOR MORE INFORMATION A good source of additional information is the American Health Information Management Association website.
- www.ahima.org

ANTHONY BLASH
Assistant Professor, Pharmacy Informatics
and Analytics
Belmont University College of Pharmacy
Medication Management Clinical Informaticist
Healthcare Corporation of America (HCA)

Describe the sort of work you do. My area of expertise and research is Pharmacy Informatics and Analytics, which lies at the intersection of pharmacy practice and technological advances in health care. The subspecialty is comprised of at least six different classifications: architect, project manager, clinical content expert, knowledge manager, builder/installer, and end user/tester. As an assistant professor at Belmont University's College of Pharmacy, I am fortunate to be able to offer a series of electives about informatics, also known as a concentration, to our pharmacy students.

As architect, my job is to face forward and identify trends that may impact the hospital, ambulatory clinic, retail establishment, or health system from a technological standpoint, then design a response either to enable us to benefit from the trend as an organization or to protect our patients from possible harm. In some cases the architect would also be responsible for attempting to secure funding and resources to implement the refinement.

As a project manager, I would use my fluency in the languages of computer science, pharmacy, and project management to plan and execute a step-by-step progression from the architect's idea to reality, preferably on time and under budget.

As a clinical content expert, I am called upon to translate clinical processes and knowledge into data that may be understood and used by nonclinical, highly technical experts and conversely reconcile highly technical system restrictions or opportunities with accepted clinical parameters.

In my role as knowledge manager I'm responsible for keeping a record of all the changes that have been implemented in the system, the anticipated impacts and outcomes, the people involved,

(continued)

ANTHONY BLASH   *(continued)*

the documents associated with the changes, and the recommended renewal date. This professional must be aware of clinical and system advances to anticipate necessary code adjustments.

The builder/installer is the systems expert, responsible for implementing new systems and making changes to existing systems. This classification is currently highly sought after in the marketplace.

As an end user/tester, I'm responsible for putting the system changes through various scenarios to ensure all the refinements are working as anticipated. The end user/tester is also responsible for identifying program glitches and reporting them back to one or all of the other classifications.

What is a typical day like at your job? Because of the lack of formally trained pharmacy informaticists in the workplace, my position at the college had gone unfilled for 2 years before I arrived. These days my job is focused on building the concentration in Pharmacy Informatics into something the marketplace recognizes and values. Students in the Pharmacy Informatics concentration at Belmont University will be prepared to successfully sit for the internationally recognized entry-level certification exam administered by the Healthcare Information and Management Systems Society (HIMSS). We are currently the only pharmacy program in the country to offer this to our graduates.

What education or training do you have? Is it typical for your job? I hold a bachelor's degree in Computer Science with a Management Information Systems concentration, a bachelor's in Pharmacy, a doctorate in Pharmacy (PharmD), and a residency in Pharmacy Informatics.

These days you will typically see a pharmacist with either a bachelor's or doctorate in Pharmacy and technical experience or a residency in Pharmacy Informatics.

What path did you take to get to the job you are in today? From my residency to an assistant professorship at a pharmacy school in the Midwest, I entered the private sector, working for two large hospital systems. From there to corporate headquarters for a health system with 19 hospitals and then back to academia at Belmont. My

(continued)

ANTHONY BLASH (continued)

practice site is at the corporate headquarters at HCA, where I assist with various informatics projects.

Where might you go from here if you wanted to advance your career? To advance my career from here I would need to accept a health care informatics advisory position within national, state, or local government. Or join the NSA. Just kidding.

What is the most challenging part of your job? There are many conversations that need to occur at the college level to prepare today's graduates for the blended health care/informatics positions they will face. My challenge is deciding which conversations are worth having during the limited amount of time I have with the students.

What is the best part? The best part of my job is helping to prepare Belmont's students for the new health care workplace, where patient safety, provider and patient satisfaction, and improved health outcomes in a computerized system require both a clinical and technical understanding.

What advice would you give to someone contemplating a career like yours? I remember back to my graduation from pharmacy school at Arnold & Marie Schwartz College of Pharmacy. The Dean, Dr. Stephen Gross, shared with us a quote that was also a favorite of the late Steve Jobs, founder of Apple Computers. From Jobs: "There's an old Wayne Gretzky quote that I love. 'I skate to where the puck is going to be, not where it has been.'" I've always tried to follow this rule, and it has served me well.

93. Education and Training Director[1]

POSITION DESCRIPTION   The education and training director functions under the direction of the senior director of information systems and provides direct supervision of the corporate training development team,

---

[1] Friedman, L. H., & Kovner, A. R. (2013). *101 careers in healthcare management.* New York, NY: Springer Publishing Company.

which is responsible for developing training materials necessary for health information systems (HIS) and technology education and support. The director is responsible for building and providing direction to the overall IT training program. The training materials and delivery media are designed to facilitate the train-the-trainer sessions and to facilitate independent interaction learning for IT system implementation and enhancements. The person in the position oversees the collaboration with content and IT system experts in developing the materials in cooperation with the care site training and support personnel. The director may oversee contract fulfillment and service levels of an outsourced training function, assign personnel to the various training tasks and direct their activities, and review and evaluate work and prepare performance reports related to training programs. The person in this position will be responsible for directing multiple concurrent projects and will provide guidance to multiple teams on issues that range from prioritizing to operational issues and conflict management that may be associated with multiple projects.

EDUCATION AND EXPERIENCE The education and training director requires a minimum of a bachelor's degree in computer science or a related area. Preferred education includes a master's degree in business administration or health administration. A minimum of 2 years of database development and design, web design, and technical assistance is required.

CORE COMPETENCIES AND SKILLS
- Outstanding interpersonal skills, including the ability to effectively communicate with persons throughout the organization
- Excellent verbal and written communication skills
- Advanced-level computer skills, including Microsoft Word, Excel, PowerPoint, Access, Visio, and Web design
- Familiarity working in a data warehouse environment
- Outstanding customer service skills
- Experience with negotiations and contract development
- Demonstrated ability to develop creative solutions to complex problems
- Ability to utilize creative and analytical problem-solving techniques in extremely varied situations
- Substantial knowledge of technology solutions in a health care provider environment

COMPENSATION Education and training directors earn in the range of $60,000 to $80,000, although the total salary will vary depending on the size and location of the health care organization.

EMPLOYMENT OUTLOOK The employment outlook for directors of HIT planning and operations is particularly strong. Every hospital in the nation is working to develop its IT infrastructure in response to demands by the federal government and the need to provide ever-higher levels of quality care. Possessing an IT background is an important requirement, but the applicant must also be familiar with the unique requirements of health care delivery.

FOR MORE INFORMATION Healthcare Information and Management Systems Society (HIMSS):
- www.himss.org

94. Tenure-Track Assistant Professor

POSITION DESCRIPTION Computer and information technology: Assistant professor to teach a variety of courses in the Bachelor of Science in information technology degree program, including courses in HIT, networking, databases, web programming, ethics, human–computer interaction, and mobile applications; advise students; maintain a program of scholarship; provide meaningful service to the computer information technology department, campus, students, community, and university.

EDUCATION AND EXPERIENCE
- Minimum qualifications: Master's degree in information technology, computing, or a related field; knowledge and skills in applied IT or computing; commitment to diversity and inclusion.
- Preferred qualifications: PhD; teaching experience; industry experience in applied information technology or computing; experience in IT project management or systems analysis; experience in an IT organization; familiarity with teaching online or hybrid courses; evidence of high-quality scholarship or service.

CREDENTIALS, LICENSURE, OR CERTIFICATION, IF APPROPRIATE No specific credential is needed to apply.

CORE COMPETENCIES AND SKILLS
- Excellent communication skills: written, oral, and presentation
- Teaching experience at the college level is desirable

- Professional association membership in related fields is desirable
- Research and demonstration of scholarly work in the field of IT is required for tenure

COMPENSATION   Salary range is $50,000 to $75,000 (for academic year). The maximum salary is based on education level, full-time professional work experience, and full-time teaching experience.

WORKPLACE LOCATION   The position is located in a university in the Department of Computer and Information Technology in the Program of Healthcare Information Technology.

EMPLOYMENT OUTLOOK   There has been a significant growth in university-based academic degree programs in the areas of HIT and health informatics. Refer to Chapter 3 on educational opportunities.

FOR MORE INFORMATION   Refer to Chapter 3 on educational programs in HIT.

INDEX